CAMBRIDGE CON(

A Concise History of Australia

Australia is the last continent to be settled by Europeans, but it also
sustains a peop'~ ~~~ ~ ~··l+··re tens of thousands of years old. For
much of th'
the old wit

on the lan
tutions an(
penal colo
nation cr
traditions

Now, wit
present-d

terms wi
repositio
date sing

STUART
before se
Universit
including
Australi(
A Histor
Commu.
Age Nor
appointe

CAMBRIDGE CONCISE HISTORIES

This is a new series of illustrated 'concise histories' of selected individual countries, intended both as university and college textbooks and as general historical introductions for general readers, travellers and members of the business community.

First titles in the series:

A Concise History of Germany
MARY FULBROOK

A Concise History of Greece
RICHARD CLOGG

A Concise History of France
ROGER PRICE

A Concise History of Britain, 1707–1975
W. A. SPECK

A Concise History of Portugal
DAVID BIRMINGHAM

A Concise History of Italy
CHRISTOPHER DUGGAN

Other titles are in preparation

A Concise History
of Australia

STUART MACINTYRE

CAMBRIDGE
UNIVERSITY PRESS

PUBLISHED BY THE PRESS SYNDICATE OF THE UNIVERSITY OF CAMBRIDGE
The Pitt Building, Trumpington Street, Cambridge, United Kingdom

CAMBRIDGE UNIVERSITY PRESS
The Edinburgh Building, Cambridge CB2 2RU, UK
40 West 20th Street, New York, NY 10011–4211, USA
477 Williamstown Road, Port Melbourne, VIC 3207, Australia
Ruiz de Alarcón 13, 28014, Madrid, Spain
Dock House, The Waterfront, Cape Town 8001, South Africa

http://www.cambridge.org

First published 1999
Reprinted 2000, 2002

Printed in Australia by Brown Prior Anderson

Typeface Sabon (Adobe) 10/13 pt. *System* QuarkXPress® [BC]

A catalogue record for this book is available from the British Library

National Library of Australia Cataloguing in Publication data
Macintyre, Stuart, 1947– .
A Concise history of Australia.
Bibliography.
Includes index.
ISBN 0 521 62359 6.
ISBN 0 521 62577 7 (pbk.).
1. Australia – History. 2. Aborigines, Australian –
History. 3. Republicanism – Australia. 4. Australia – Politics
and government. 5. Australia – Environmental conditions.
I. Title. (Series: Cambridge concise histories).
994

ISBN 0 521 62359 6 hardback
ISBN 0 521 62577 7 paperback

For my daughters

MARY and JESSIE

this is also their history

CONTENTS

ILLUSTRATIONS

ACKNOWLEDGEMENTS

A concise history is necessarily dependent on a very large body of historical scholarship. Australian historians will see the extent of my reliance on their work, and the suggestions for further reading indicate some of my principal obligations. I am indebted particularly to friends and colleagues who read and commented on drafts: Geoffrey Bolton, Verity Burgmann, Joy Damousi, Patricia Grimshaw, John Hirst, Jill Roe, John Morton, Peter Nicholson, Tim Rowse and Patrick Wolfe. Alan Frost, Renate Howe, Kim Humphreys and Lesley Johnson assisted in tracking down illustrations. I single out Jill Roe for her service to the historical profession and Geoffrey Bolton, who first put me to teaching Australian history and still teaches me. I have a broader obligation to students I have taught and postgraduates whose research I have supervised.

I am grateful to Phillipa McGuinness, the commissioning editor of Cambridge University Press in Australia, for persuading me to write the book and helping me to do so. Janet Mackenzie, with whom I began my undergraduate studies, has edited it sympathetically. Paul Watt smoothed the tasks of publication. Jonathan Ritchie and Kim Torney provided research assistance, as did Diana Bell when publication deadlines were imminent. Martine Walsh and Rosa Brezac lightened my academic duties, colleagues in the History Department of the University of Melbourne tolerated my absences, and the Australian Research Council provided a grant that paid for them. Xavier Pons drew my attention to some errors. I thank those who have given permission to reproduce copyright material, and would be pleased to hear from those I have been unable to trace.

A concise national history written for an international readership presents an opportunity and a challenge. The local reader looks for the familiar landmarks, and the local teacher expects the stock-in-trade of the subject to be assembled and labelled. The overseas reader, on the other hand, has little familiarity with these fixtures. A narrative history composed of the standard fare is unlikely to explain Australia to those who do not bring some prior knowledge to it; a roll-call of names will be of scant assistance to those who have not encountered them before. I have endeavoured to assume little, and to paint a broad-brush picture in which the detail is subordinated to the characteristic features.

That in itself is hazardous. The specialists will scrutinise the text for acknowledgement of their concerns. Those who feel strongly about particular causes will take the amount of attention accorded them as an index of sympathies. Such weighing of proportions is inevitable and I am aware that my emphases are indeed indicative of my own understanding and inclinations. My purpose, however, has been to present a narrative that explains why its component parts have a place in the national story, and how they continue to generate discussion. I have tried to set Australian history within the larger history of which it forms a part, and to draw out comparisons with other parts of the world. These intentions are meant to serve the overseas reader who might have seen an Australian film or glimpsed the natural history of this country on television but finds it infrequently reported in current affairs. In writing it I have in mind the visitor who encounters the landscape and local usages but finds their connecting logic difficult to decipher. I hope that it serves to connect what they see and hear with a more systematic account of how it came to be.

The book is aimed also at a younger generation of Australians who are poorly served by a school curriculum in which history has become a residual. I have dedicated it to my two daughters, born in England, raised in Australia, who have too often had their father play the pedagogue and all along have been instructing him in their interests and concerns.

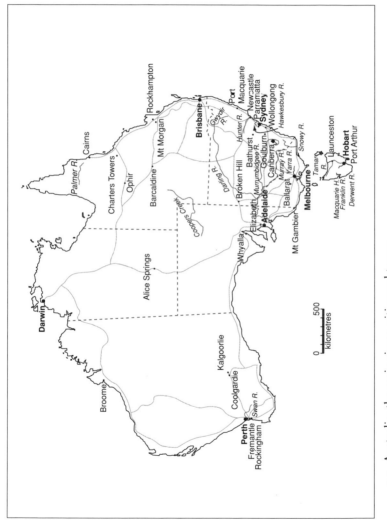

1.1 Australia: the main rivers, cities and towns

I

Beginnings

How and when did Australia begin? One version of the country's origins – a version taught to generations of schoolchildren and set down in literature and art, memorials and anniversaries – would have it that Australian history commenced at the end of the eighteenth century. After several centuries of European voyaging in the South Seas, the English naval lieutenant James Cook sailed the eastern coast in 1770, named it New South Wales and claimed possession in the name of his monarch. Within twenty years the British government despatched an expedition to settle New South Wales. On 26 January 1788 its commander, Arthur Phillip, assumed government over the eastern half of the country. The thousand officers, troops, civilian officials and felons who landed at Sydney from the eleven vessels of the First Fleet formed a bridgehead for later immigrants, bond and free, who spread out over the continent, explored and settled, possessed and subdued it.

This is a story of a sleeping land brought to life by purposeful endeavour. The chroniclers of the First Fleet recorded the advent of civilisation as the newcomers unloaded their stores, cleared a space on the wooded slopes of Sydney Cove and erected their first habitations. The sound of an axe on wood, English steel on antipodean eucalypt, broke the silence of a primeval wilderness. The scientific passion of Cook, and the diligent foresight of Phillip, redeemed this strange and distant redoubt of nature from earlier neglect.

The newcomers brought with them those potent agents of European civilisation: the objective rationality of the Enlightenment and the corresponding belief in human capacity, the moral certainty and stern duty of evangelical Christianity, and the acquisitive itch of the market. Those ways of thinking and acting made possible the establishment of European dominion over the rest of the world. That accomplishment in turn shaped the understanding of economics, resources, navigation, trade, botany, zoology, anthropology – and history. The science of the past was by no means the least important weapon in the intellectual arsenal of the imperial powers. A new awareness of geography and chronology, of space and time as objectively fixed and measurable, encouraged an understanding of history as a branch of knowledge independent of the standpoint of the observer, while at the same time it disclosed an insistent, global momentum of improvement and progress that legitimated the supersession of the old by the new. Seen thus, the history of Australia formed a late chapter in British, European and world history.

This version of Australia's beginning emphasised its strangeness and archaic novelty. The flora and fauna, even the human inhabitants, confounded the existing taxonomies; they were both old and new. The monotremes and marsupials, warm-blooded animals that reproduced by egg or carried their offspring in a pouch, seemed to be primitive forerunners of the placental mammal, and at the same time a bizarre inversion of nature. Hence the puzzlement of the early New South Wales judge and rhymester, Barron Field:

> Kangaroo, Kangaroo!
> Thou Spirit of Australia!
> That redeems from utter failure,
> From perfect desolation,
> And warrants the creation
> Of this fifth part of the Earth
> Which would seem an after-birth . . .

In this version of Australian history, the novelty of the place – it was New Holland before it became New South Wales – was softened by attaching its destiny to imperial origins. Colonial history took the British and European achievement as its point of departure. Behind the rude improvisation on the furthest frontier of settlement at the extremity of the British Empire was the inheritance of institutions, customs and expectations. A naval officer who in 1803 watched a team of convicts yoked to a cart that was sunk up to axles in the unpromising sandhills of a southern bay comforted himself with the vision of 'a second Rome, rising from a coalition of Banditti ... superlative in arms and arts'.

This settlement was abandoned, and the officer returned eventually to England, but others stayed and reworked his anticipation. These subsequent visionaries thought of Australia not as mere imitation but as striking out anew, as a New World that could redeem the failures of the Old. For so many who came after the First Fleet, this vast island-continent offered the chance to leave behind the evils of poverty, class, privilege and make a fresh start. With the transition in the middle of the nineteenth century from penal colony to free and self-governing dominions, the emphasis shifted from colonial imitation to national experimentation. With the gold rush, land settlement and urban growth, minds turned from dependency to self-sufficiency, and from a history that worked out the imperial legacy to one of self-discovery.

During the nineteenth century and well into the twentieth, the sentiment of colonial nationalism served the desire to mark Australia off from Britain and Europe. Then, as the last imperial ties were severed, even that way of distinguishing the child from the parent lost meaning. In its place arose the idea of Australia as a destination for allcomers from every part of the world, which served the multicultural attitudes that formed in closing decades of the twentieth century and further undermined the foundational significance of 1788. The blurring of origins turned Australian history into a story of journeyings and arrivals, shared by all and endlessly repeated. But such smudging was too convenient. It failed to satisfy the need for emotional attachment and it left unappeased the pricking of conscience. The desire for a binding national past that would connect the people to the land was frustrated by the feeling of rootlessness, of novelty without depth. The longing for an indigenous culture, for belonging, was denied by the original usurpation. A history of colonisation yielded to a realisation of invasion.

By the end of the twentieth century it was no longer possible to maintain the fiction of Australia as *terra nullius*, a land that until its settlement in 1788 lacked human habitation, law, government or history. An alternative beginning was apparent. Australia – or, rather, the earlier landmass of Sahul, a larger island-continent that extended northwards into Papua New Guinea and embraced the present island of Tasmania – was the site of a civilisation of unique longevity. It was peopled at least 40,000 years ago. The growing recognition of this vastly enlarged Australian history spoke to late-twentieth-century sensibility. It revealed social organisation, ecological practices, languages, art forms and spiritual beliefs of great antiquity and richness. By embracing the Aboriginal past, non-Aboriginal Australians attached themselves to their country.

They did so, however, not simply out of a desire for reconciliation and harmony but because they were confronted by the Aboriginal presence. The rediscovery of this longer history and the revival of indigenous organisation and culture occurred together, the one process feeding into the other and yet each possessing its own dynamic. For the Aboriginal and Torres Strait Islander peoples, the European invasion was a traumatic event with lasting consequences for their mode of life, health, welfare and very identity. But theirs was also a story of survival – the survival of their customs and practices and of the stories and songs through which they were maintained. While the sharing of their culture drew attention to their survival and entitlements, they were reluctant to surrender control of it.

For non-Aboriginal scholars, even the most sympathetic, it thus became necessary to find new terms on which their studies could be conducted. Anthropologists were no longer able to assume they could take up residence among a local community, observe its ways, record its testimony and speak on its behalf. Ethnologists could no longer define tribes or distinguish between degrees of Aboriginal sanguinity. Archaeologists could no longer excavate sites without regard to Aboriginal sensitivities; indeed, they had to surrender collections of artefacts and human remains. Even as researchers pushed back the earliest known date of the Aboriginal presence in Australia, they were forced to accommodate these constraints. The second version of Australian history, the one that begins not at AD 1788 but at least 40,000 and possibly 60,000 or more years before the present, is at once more controversial, more rapidly changing and more compelling.

It is controversial not simply because of issues of cultural ownership, but because of the intellectual challenge it poses: even if it is permissible to appropriate other cultures, is it possible to comprehend them? The older history noticed Aborigines only as a tragic and disturbing presence, victims of the iron law of progress. The Latin term *Ab origines* means, literally, those who were here from the beginning: its persistence, despite attempts to find other, more specific designations such as are used for aboriginal peoples in other parts of the world, attests to their abiding presence. The remnants of this Aboriginal way of life were recorded, collated, and fitted into the jigsaw-puzzle of prehistory that revealed a hierarchy of civilisations advancing in complexity, sophistication and capacity. Their oral traditions were of interest for the light they shed on this prehistory, for in the absence of written records, chronology and political authority, the Aborigines had no history of their own. Denied both effective individuality and agency in the history that began in 1788, they were no more than objects of history.

It is precisely this idea of history that is now cast into doubt. The idea of history as the unfolding of a necessary past no longer satisfies the imagination. The idea of Australian history as a story of national self-fulfilment succumbs to arguments over other attachments and memberships. The idea that this country has followed the path of the West in a journey that led from ancient Greece and Rome to Christian Europe, the Renaissance and Enlightenment with liberty, democracy and prosperity as its end-point, is challenged by alternative routes and destinations. The idea of an objective and universal record of the past exactly as it happened yields to the myriad interpretations of a disposable past. The idea of the historian as an impersonal, unselfconscious narrator is replaced by an appreciation of the historian who is present in the story. Time and memory are reworked in the history that is now found to have commenced so much earlier. Traditional knowledge jostles with new discoveries to redefine beginnings.

The island-continent of Australia, so the scientists tell us, formed as the great supercontinent of Pangea broke up in the remote past. First Laurasia in the north separated from Gondwana in the south.

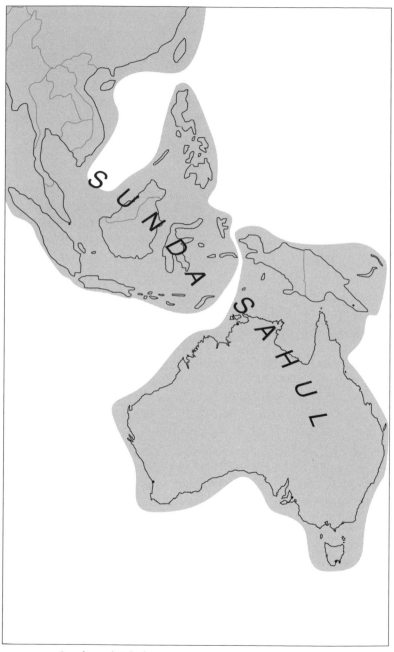

1.2 Sunda and Sahul

Then what would become India, Africa, South America and New Zealand broke free from Gondwana and drifted north, and later still – perhaps 50 million years ago – Australia and New Guinea did the same until finally they stopped short of the island-chain that extends from Indochina down to Timor. Although the oceans rose and fell with periods of warmth and cold, this vast land-raft was always surrounded by water. The deep channel that today separates South-East Asia from the north-west coast of Australia narrowed at times to as little as 100 kilometres but it has never closed. It always separated Sahul, the continental shelf that encompassed Australia, Tasmania and New Guinea, from Sunda, the archipelago that took in Malaya, Sumatra, Borneo and Java. It came to be known as the Wallace Line, after the nineteenth-century scientist who showed that it was a permanent zoological divide that demarcated the Eurasian species from those of Australia and New Guinea.

Australia was thus isolated. It was also remarkably geologically stable. There was little of the buckling and folding of the earth's crust that elsewhere produced high mountain ranges or deep rifts. Together with the relative absence of glaciation and the infrequency of volcanic activity, this left an older, flatter landmass, rich in mineral deposits but shallow in soil covering. Weathering and erosion leached the soil of nutrients. The remarkable diversity of plants and animals that evolved and flourished in this environment had to adapt to major climatic changes. Rainforests expanded and contracted, inland lakes filled and emptied, carnivores were less durable than herbivores.

When the last ice age ended some 10,000 years ago, and the present shoreline formed, Australia extended 3700 kilometres from the northern tropics to the southern latitudes, and 4400 kilometres from east to west. Much was arid plain, and much of the rain that fell on the line of mountains running down the eastern seaboard flowed into the Pacific Ocean. More than any other landmass, this one was marked by the infrequency and unreliability of rain. Scientists have recently identified the El Niño Oscillation Index to measure a climatic phenomenon that occurs when the trade winds that blow from the east across the Pacific Ocean fail. With that failure, warm water accumulates off the South American coast and brings fierce storms to the Americas; conversely, the colder water on this side of the Pacific reduces evaporation and cloud formation, and thus causes prolonged drought in eastern Australia. The El Niño cycle lasts from two to eight years, and climatologists can detect it in records going back to the early nineteenth century. It is probable that it has operated for much longer, and shaped the evolution of the Australian environment.

The natural historians who marvel at the rich diversity of this singular environment find in it an ingenious anthropomorphism. The plants best suited to such circumstances sent down deep roots to search for moisture, used narrow leaves and tough bark to minimise evaporation and loss of vital fluid, and scattered seeds capable of regeneration after lying for long periods on the dry earth. They were frugal in their eking out of nutrients and prodigal in their reproduction. Some of them, such as the stands of eucalypts which spread a blue haze under the hot sun, actively enlisted the assistance of the conditions by strewing the ground with incendiary material that would burn off competitors and stimulate their own regeneration. In the pyrohistory of Australia, the vast and sleeping continent is reconfigured as an arena in which the gum trees kindled a fiery vortex.

Such fires would have been ignited periodically by lightning strikes or other natural causes, but by this time there was another incendiary agent – humans. The acquisition of control over fire by *Homo sapiens* provided protection, heat, light and power: the domestic hearth became site and symbol of human society. It might well have been the sight of columns of smoke rising on the northwestern shore of Sahul that attracted people on island extremities of Sunda to cross the intervening sea. We do not know when this passage occurred, why or even how. It was probably achieved by bamboo rafts, as the result of population pressure and at a time when the Timor Sea was low. The most recent lowpoint, 100 metres below present sealevel, was about 18,000 years ago; but the evidence of prior occupation is clear. The same lowpoint occurred about 140,000 years ago, probably too early. In between these two approximate dates, the sea receded to some 60 metres less than today about 70,000 years ago and did not regain its present level until the last ice age ended in the last 10,000 years.

The archaeological evidence for human presence in Australia remains frustratingly close to the limits of reliable dating. Arrival at least 40,000 years ago is now generally accepted; there are strong arguments for 60,000 years, and a still longer presence cannot be ruled out. Furthermore, a mounting body of evidence suggests a rapid occupation of Australia, with human habitation extending from the lush tropics of the north to the icy rigours of the south, the rich coastal waterlands and the harsh interior. Whenever the first footprint fell on Australian soil, it marked a new achievement by *Homo sapiens* – maritime migration out of the African-European-Asian landmass into a new land.

The truth is, of course, that my own people, the Riratjungi, are descended from the great Djankawa who came from the island of Baralku, far across the sea. Our spirits return to Baralku when we die. Djankawa came in his canoe with his two sisters, following the morning star which guided them to the shores of Yelangbara on the eastern coast of Arnhem Land. They walked far across the country following the rain clouds. When they wanted water they plunged their digging stick into the ground and fresh water followed. From them we learn the names of all the creatures on the land and they taught us all our Law.

The Djankawa story told by Wandjuk Marika is only one of many Aboriginal stories. Others tell of different origins, of ancestors coming from the land or from the sky, and of the mutability of humans with other life forms. This story is of origins that begin with a journey, of the signs that led the ancestors to their destination, and of the bounty of the land that sustained them. Such creation stories are to be found for other peoples, as with the books of Genesis and Exodus in the Old Testament, but they bear lightly on the consciousness of those who still read them today. Ancestral events, as recorded in stories, songs and rituals, have a particular significance in Aboriginal lives, for they express a particularly close relationship to the land. The events that occurred during the Dreamtime or the Dreaming – both English terms are used as inexact translations of that used by the Arrernte people of Central Australia, *altyerre* – created the hills and creeks, plants and animals, and imprinted their spirit on the place.

The preservation and practice of this knowledge thus affirms the custodianship of the land. Here is how a Northern Territory man, Paddy Japaljarri Stewart, explains its importance:

My father's grandfather taught me the first, and after a while my father taught me the same way as his father told jukurrpa [Dreaming], and then my father is telling the same story about what his father told him, and now he's teaching me how to live on the same kind of jukurrpa and follow the way what my grandfather did, and then what my father did, and then I'm going to teach my grandchildren the same way as my father taught me.

When my father was alive this is what he taught me. He had taught me traditional ways like traditional designs in body or head of kangaroo Dreaming (that's what we call marlu Dreaming) and eagle Dreaming. He taught me how to sing song for the big ceremonies. People who are related to us in a close family, they have to have the same sort of jukurrpa Dreaming, and to sing songs in the same way as we do our actions like dancing, and paintings on our body or shields or things, and this is what my father taught me. My Dreaming is the kangaroo Dreaming, the eagle Dreaming and budgerigar Dreaming, so I have three kinds of Dreaming in my jukurrpa and I have to hang onto it. This is what my father taught me, and this is what I have to teach my sons, and my son has to teach his sons the same way as my father taught me, and that's the way it will go on from grandparents to sons, and follow that jukurrpa. No-one knows when it will end.

Paddy Japaljarri Stewart recorded this testimony, by tape-recorder, in his own language in 1991. He evokes the continuity of Dreaming from grandfather and father to son and grandson, down the generations and across the passage of time; yet the insistence on the obligation to preserve and transmit his three jukurrpas attests to the corrosive possibilities of secular change. He goes on to aver that the maintenance of the Dreaming has to be 'really strict', so that his family will not 'lose it like a paper, or throw it away or give it away to other families'. The overlay of new technology on customary knowledge heightens the contrast between a binding tradition and a fragile, disposable past. The history that is recorded on paper, like other documents such as land titles, can be lost or surrendered to others. The history that is lived and renewed within the ties of the family remains your own.

The Aboriginal people who occupied Sahul encountered radically different conditions from those they left in Sunda. The absence of predators – for there were few carnivorous competitors here – gave them an enormous initial advantage. They spread over an extra-ordinary range of ecologies – tropical northern forests, Tasmanian glaciated highlands, the dry interior – and had to adjust to major climatic changes. Over hundreds of generations they adapted to these different, changing environments, and in turn they learned how to manipulate them to augment the food supply. As hunter-gatherers, they lived off the land with a precise and intimate know-ledge of its resources and seasonal patterns. They organised socially in extended families, with specific rights and specific responsibilities for specific country, and rules to regulate their interaction with others.

Hunter-gatherer is both a technical term and something more. It refers to a mode of material life; it signifies a stage in human history. Forty thousand years ago, when Australia was populated by hunter-gatherers, every human society in every part of the world prac-tised hunter-gathering. Subsequently, agriculture replaced hunter-gathering in Europe, much of Asia, Africa, and the Americas. Agri-culture enabled greater productivity, sustained higher population densities, gave rise to towns and the amenities of urban life. As it became possible to produce more than a subsistence, wealth could be accumulated and allow a division of labour. Such specialisation fostered technological improvement, commerce and industry; it supported armies, rulers and bureaucrats who could control large political units with a corresponding extension of capacity. When British and other European investigators first encountered the Australian Aborigines, they fitted them into a ladder of human progress on which the hunter-gatherer society occupied the lowest rung. The nineteenth-century historian James Bonwick, who wrote extensively of Aboriginal history, emphasised the Arcadian virtue of their way of life but always assumed that they were doomed to yield to European ways. For him, as for most of his contemporaries, the indigenous people represented a primitive antiquity that lacked the capacity to change: 'they knew no past, they wanted no future'.

More recent interpretations suggest otherwise. Prehistorians (though the persistence of this term indicates that the new sensibility is incomplete) are struck by the remarkable longevity and adapt-ability of hunter-gatherer societies. Demographers suggest that they maintained a highly successful equilibrium of population and

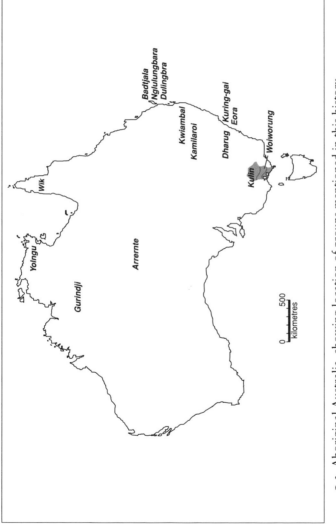

1.3 Aboriginal Australia, showing location of groups mentioned in this history. (D. R. Horton (ed.), The Encyclopaedia of Aboriginal Australia, Canberra: Australian Institute of Aboriginal and Torres Strait Islander Studies and Auslig 1994. This map indicates only the general location of larger groupings of people which may include smaller groups such as clans, dialects or individual languages in a group. Boundaries are not intended to be exact. The views expressed in this publication are those of the author and not those of AIATSIS. For more information about the groups of people in a particular region contact the relevant land councils. This map is not suitable for use in native title and other land claims.)

resources. Economists have found that they produced surpluses, traded, made technological advances, all with far less effort than agriculturalists. Linguists are struck by the diversity and sophistication of their languages. Anthropologists discern complex religions that guided such people's lives and movements, encoded ecological wisdom, assured genetic variety and maintained social cohesion. With their egalitarian social and political structure, far-flung trading networks and above all their rich spiritual and cultural life, the Australian Aborigines were described by the celebrated French anthropologist Claude Lévi-Strauss as 'intellectual aristocrats'.

These reappraisals overturn the rigid hierarchy of historical progress through sequential stages, from primitive to modern, and enable us to appreciate the sophistication of a civilisation of greater longevity than any other in world history. Yet there remains the challenge to explain the apparent incapacity of the Aboriginal Australians to withstand the invasion of 1788. For all its advantages, and its ability to withstand challenges over more than forty millennia, the indigenous population could not maintain sovereignty when confronted by British settlers. It was by no means alone in this incapacity, of course: other hunter-gatherer societies, as well as agricultural ones and even those with more extensive commercial institutions, succumbed to European conquest in the seventeenth, eighteenth and nineteenth centuries. The Australian experience points up the particular vulnerability of an isolated civilisation to external aggression.

The Aborigines were not wholly cut off from external contact. The native dog, the dingo, reached Australia some 4000 years ago; it was the first and only domesticated animal. Traders from South-East Asia were visiting the northern coast before European settlement, bringing pottery, cloth and metal tools. Such external influences were far less significant, however, than internal processes of change wrought by the Aborigines themselves. Their arrival had almost certainly hastened the extinction of earlier megafauna. Their use of fire to burn off undergrowth and encourage new pasture for the remaining marsupials, as well as their systematic harvesting of staple plants, had altered the landscape. Their technological innovation accelerated with the development of new tools, the digging stick and the spatula, fishing net and canoe, boomerang and

woomera, net and spear, hafted axe and specialised stone implements. The construction of weirs and channels to trap eels supported populations of several hundred in semi-permanent housing.
The evidence of this inventiveness is confirmed by the absence of
many such items from the island of Tasmania, which was separated
from the mainland some 10,000 years ago, while the disappearance
of Aboriginal communities on the smaller Flinders and Kangaroo
islands attests to the fragility of remote settlements. The intensification of the hunter-gatherer economy probably supported larger
numbers – we do not know the population history, but recent
estimates suggest perhaps three-quarters of a million people lived
here in 1788.

The way of life held the population at a level determined by
the food that was available at the times of greatest scarcity, but it
was far from a constant struggle for subsistence. The hunting of
game, fishing, snaring, and harvesting of foodstuffs were part of an
elaborate system of environmental management; and this essential
activity was undertaken along with other activities to provide
shelter and clothing, renew equipment, conduct trade and communication, maintain law and order, and practise ceremony and
ritual. The Aboriginal way of life is seen as affording a large amount
of leisure time for cultural and artistic pursuits, but such a distinction between work and leisure separates domains of life that
were conjoined. Equally, artistic expression entered into the most
central forms of material practice, and Aboriginal religion encompassed all aspects of life. It is this organic character of belief and
social practice that attracts so many present-day admirers of a
Dreamtime wisdom: a cosmology that prescribed the necessary
knowledge of a people and saturated their every action with
spiritual significance.

Did the deep respect for tradition stifle more radical transformations that might have allowed the Aboriginal people to resist
the invasion of 1788? The passage of time and temporal change, so
central in Western thought, do not have that status in Aboriginal
ontology. If the land is primary and place immutable, then history
cannot have the same determinate role. For the Europeans who
took possession of the land, history exercised a powerful forward momentum of constant change and improvement. For the

Aborigines, the pattern of events was rhythmical as well as linear. The Dreamtime was not a time but a set of abiding events. In a society made up of small groups whose members set their feet carefully in the footsteps of those who had gone before, change could only be incremental. *As distinguished from?*

It would certainly appear that their economy and forms of organisation set limits on the capacity to concentrate resources or mount a concerted resistance. The basic unit was the extended family, linked by intermarriage, belief and language into larger territorial groups. Europeans described such groups as tribes, but that term has now fallen into disfavour and the preferred designation is people – thus the Eora people of present-day Sydney, or the Wajuk people of present-day Perth. These peoples in turn interacted with neighbouring peoples through trade, alliance and antagonism: there were some 250 distinct language groups but most Aborigines would have been multilingual. They came together in enlarged numbers from time to time for ceremonial occasions that were constrained in size and duration by the availability of food. Crops and herds would have relaxed those constraints and allowed greater density of settlement, larger concentrations of wealth and power; but Aborigines did not domesticate animals, apart from the dingo, and they did not practise agriculture.

The failure to do so was not for want of precedent. The movement of humans into Sahul occurred when Australia was continuous with New Guinea, and the two countries were still joined by a neck of land near Cape York up to 8000 years ago. By that time pigs were kept and gardens cleared to grow taro in the Highlands of New Guinea. The Aborigines of the Cape York region continued to hunt for their meat and gather their plant food. The preference – it can only have been a choice between alternatives because the Cape York Aborigines possessed such New Guinean items as drums, bamboo pipes, and outrigger canoes – might be explained by differences of soil and regional climate. For the rest of Australia, the environment probably made the necessary investment in agricultural production and storage uneconomic. Unless the El Niño phenomenon is a recent one, the periodic lack of rainfall over the eastern two-thirds of the continent made dependence on crops too risky. The Aborigines were mobile fire-stick farmers rather than sedentary slash-and-burn agriculturalists; they tended their plants as they visited them, fed their animals on open grassland rather than by hand, and killed their meat on the range instead of in the pen. They tracked the erratic sources of their livelihood with simplified rather than elaborate shelters, and a portable tool-kit that met their needs. This was an ingenious and closely calibrated response to a unique environmental challenge.

2

Newcomers, c. 1600–1792

The stories of the Dreaming tell of beginnings that are both specific and general. They narrate particular events that occurred in particular places, but those events are not fixed chronologically since they span the past and the present to carry an enduring meaning. Archaeologists and prehistorians seek a different sort of precision, yet their hypotheses and conjectures can provide only broad approximations for the first human habitation in Australia. By contrast, the story of the second settlement is known in minute particularity. It consisted of 1066 people who had sailed in eleven vessels to New South Wales from the southern English naval town of Portsmouth, via Tenerife, Rio de Janeiro and Cape Town, on a marathon voyage of just over eight months; thirty-one died during the voyage. The survivors reached the north shore of Botany Bay on 18 January 1788, but landed 12 kilometres to the north in a cove of Port Jackson eight days later. On a space cleared in the wooded slope that is now central Sydney, the British flag was hoisted as the commander, Captain Arthur Phillip, took formal possession of the new colony.

We have his account of the voyage and settlement, as well as other published accounts, and the official instructions, despatches, logs, journals, diaries and letters of those who accompanied him. We know the names of every person, their status and duties, the stores they brought with them and the livestock, plants and seeds, even the books, they brought ashore to establish the colony. We can plot the actions of the colonists with an amplitude of detail beyond almost all other similar ventures, for this was a late episode in European expansion and the most powerful of all the European states brought an accumulated organisational capacity to it. Furthermore, the settlement at New South Wales was the bridgehead for British occupation of the whole of Australia, the landing at Sydney Cove the formative moment of a new nation that would afterwards re-enact its origins in the celebration of 26 January as Australia Day.

Yet in the marking of the anniversary, as well as the unending stream of writing on the foundation of European Australia, there is constant disputation. On the centenary of British settlement in 1888, radical nationalists attacked the official celebrations for sanitising the past of the convicts who made up the majority of Phillip's party. Fifty years later Aboriginal critics boycotted the re-enactment of the landing and declared 26 January a Day of Protest and Mourning. During the bicentenary in 1988 the official organisers arranged a passage up Sydney Harbour of ships from around the world in preference to the unofficial flotilla that retraced the voyage from Portsmouth; but this reach for commercial inclusiveness rather than divisive exactitude did not assuage the Aboriginal protesters who flung a copy of a new bicentennial history into the waters of Sydney Cove. Even the public authority responsible for organising the commemoration of Australia Day has canvassed alternatives to 26 January more acceptable to late-twentieth-century sensibilities.

As with public ritual, so with the scholarly interpretation of British settlement: its initiation, purpose, efficacy and consequences are all debated more vigorously now than ever before. Was it part of a larger imperial design or an improvisation? Was Australia meant to be a dumping-ground for convicts or a strategic and mercantile base? Did it begin with an 'indescribable hopelessness and confusion', as the country's most eminent historian put it, or was it a place of order and redemption? Was it an invasion or peaceful occupation, despoliation or improvement, a place of exile or hope, estrangement or attachment? The accumulation of research brings more exact knowledge of the formative events, while the passage of time weakens our connection with them and allows a multiplicity of meaning to be found in them. With the end of the age of

European empire and revival of the indigenous presence, the story of the second settlement of Australia is no clearer than the first.

The expansion of Europe began with internal conquest. The imposition from early in the second millennium of the Christian era of monarchical government and market economy on barbarian and infidel peoples in its border regions prepared the ground for movements north into the Baltic, east over the Urals, west into the Atlantic, and south down the African coast and across to East Asia. These excursions gathered pace from the fifteenth century onwards but initially involved only limited numbers. Acquisition by trade and conquest was the object, and European adventurers absorbed the knowledge (compass and gunpowder), techniques (crossbow and printing press) and products (potato and tomato) of other civilisations. In Asia, where the adventurous hunter-gatherers encountered literate societies with highly developed economies, they established garrisons and trading centres for the acquisition of spices, coffee, tea and textiles. In the Americas they reaped windfall gains of bullion, and in the Caribbean they worked sugar and tobacco plantations with slave labour shipped from Africa. Only in North America and the temperate regions of South America did they settle in significant numbers: as late as 1800 just 4 per cent of the European population lived abroad.

There were non-European empires, that of Manchus in China, the Moghuls in India, the Ottomans and Safavids, Aztecs and Incas, but none of them withstood the growth of European power. They were built on large, contiguous territories with a coherent unity; the European ones were far-flung networks thrown across oceans, more mobile and enterprising. Spain, Portugal, Holland, France and Britain – the principal maritime states on the Atlantic coast of the European peninsula – jostled and competed with each other, spurring further growth and innovation. Yet the same rivalry imposed a growing cost. Britain and France, which emerged during the eighteenth century as the two leading European powers, taxed their strength as they fought repeatedly on sea and land. From the Seven Years War (1756–63) Britain emerged victorious with control of North America and India. In the following round of hostilities,

France took several of the West Indian islands and Britain lost most of North America to its own colonists in the War of American Independence (1774–83). By then France was on the verge of revolution, and Britain strained under the remorseless demands for revenue and lives needed to sustain its imperial garrison state.

Britain's loss of its American colonies at the end of the eighteenth century signalled a new phase of empire. Britain turned of necessity away from the Atlantic to the East, and settlement of Australia was part of its expansion in Asia and the Pacific. The same reverse also encouraged a reconsideration of how the empire should be conducted. After the conclusion of the Napoleonic Wars in 1815, there was a shift from the expensive military effort needed to protect trade monopolies, with its accompanying burden of domestic taxation, towards self-sustaining economic development and free trade. The transition was less marked in India, where the cost of expanding the empire was transferred from the British taxpayer to the local peasant, than in settler colonies such as Canada, Australia, New Zealand and South Africa.

These colonies of settlement, like the former British colonies in the United States and the Iberian colonies in Argentina and Uruguay, mark out a distinctive zone of European expansion. There was little effort in them to maintain the existing order, to enter into commercial relations with their inhabitants or recruit them as labour; instead, these lands were cleared and settled as fresh fields of European endeavour. Their temperate climates were sufficiently similar to support European livestock, pasture and crops; their local biota were less diverse and less resistant to the weeds and pests the Europeans brought with them; their indigenous inhabitants were decimated by imported diseases. Before the nineteenth century the settler colonies played a minor economic role in the European imperial system; thereafter, as large-scale industrialisation created a mass market for the primary products of their virgin soil, they became the wealthiest and most rapidly growing regions outside Europe.

An account of the colonial settlement of Australia that relies on the logic of economic and ecological imperialism leaves too much unexplained. The implication that the Australian Aborigines simply disappeared with the advent of European pathogens is as unsatisfactory as the suggestion that the Maori provided no effective resistance to the pakeha in New Zealand. It required a substantial European effort to subdue the indigenous peoples of the regions of settlement, and no less an effort to justify their expropriation. Notions of providence and destiny dignified images of the native based on innate cultural difference and racial inferiority. The British came to the Pacific with their sense of superiority as the inheritors of Western civility and bearers of Christian revelation enhanced by the further advantages of scientific knowledge, industrial progress and liberty. The last of these might seem an unlikely claim for a colony that began with convicts, but was no less influential for that. A Briton's freedom was based on obedience to the Crown under a system of constitutional government that safeguarded the subject's rights. The example of the American colonies and the republican doctrines proclaimed there as well as in France served as a salutary reminder of the consequences of violating such rights.

The settler societies spawned by Europe were thus extensions and new beginnings. They applied and adapted technologies with prodigious results, cultivated principles as well as plants, and sent them back to where they had come from with enhanced potency. Yet even in the United States, and the former Spanish and Portuguese colonies of Central and South America that threw off their tutelage to forge the distinctive features of the democratic nation-state, the settler-citizens remained tied to their origins. The new republics defined themselves as white brotherhoods. However much they emphasised their difference from their metropolitan cousins, whatever their conscious and unconscious adaptation to local ways, they remained estranged from the indigenous peoples. The nation that arose on the grasslands of Australia, like those on the North American plain and the Argentine pampas, was a creole society insistent on its place in the European diaspora.

The British were laggards in the Pacific. The Spanish, Portuguese and Dutch preceded them into the archipelago that extends down its western fringe. Spain alone held the eastern extremity from the Strait of Magellan up to California. Between these two sides of the

2.1 Australia and the region

Pacific basin stretched 15,000 kilometres of water dotted with thousands of volcanic or coral islands, few of sufficient size or wealth to attract European attention. They had already been navigated and settled in a series of movements that began with the human occupation of Sahul more than 40,000 years earlier and culminated at the beginning of the last millennium with the occupation of Easter Island in the east and New Zealand in the south. These people of the sea practised agriculture, kept domestic animals and sustained a mosaic of polities. In 1567 the Spanish despatched an expedition in search of gold to the Solomon Islands, but that ended in massacre and counter-massacre. In 1595 and 1605 they repeated the venture in the Solomons and Vanuatu, which Pedro de Quiros named La Australia del Espiritu Santo, with the same result; his colleague Torres sailed west through the strait that separates Australia from New Guinea.

Meanwhile the Portuguese had pushed south from India as far as Timor, possibly to the Australian coast. After them came the Dutch, who in the seventeenth century established a trading empire in the East Indies. The route from Holland to Batavia took their ships round the Cape of Good Hope and then east with the prevailing winds across the Indian Ocean before they turned north for Java. Given the difficulty in establishing longitude, many of their vessels encountered the western coast of Australia, sometimes with fatal consequences – the location, study and retrieval of the contents of Dutch wrecks makes Western Australia a centre of marine archaeology. By the middle of the seventeenth century the Dutch had mapped the western half of Australia, which they called New Holland, and traced some fragments of coast further east. In 1606 William Jansz sailed east through the Torres Strait and unwittingly along the north-east corner of Australia. In 1642 Abel Tasman led an expedition that charted the southern part of the island now named after him and the east side of New Zealand.

Whether these shores were part of a single landmass remained unclear. It was apparent only that the great south land was separate from the Antarctic, and that it straddled the Indian and Pacific oceans. This location continues to create uncertainty. Since 1788 the great mass of the Australian population has always lived on the eastern seaboard, facing the Pacific, and its islands have drawn them as traders and missionaries, administrators and adventurers. Australians commonly regard themselves, along with the New Zealanders, as part of Oceania, and they have liked to think they enjoy a special relation with the most powerful of all English-speaking countries on the other side of that ocean. Yet for those who live in Western Australia, Indonesia is the most proximate neighbour, the historical links with India, South Africa and even Mauritius more significant. As the balance of regional power has shifted, so Australians increasingly claim they are part of Asia and regard their earlier presence in the Pacific as a romantic interlude in tropical islands far removed from the business hub of the Asian tigers.

The difference is not simply one of economic advantage. The Pacific signifies peace, a far-flung constellation of island people living in harmony with nature, where the colonial imagination could find a soft primitivism of noble savages predisposed to friendship and hospitality. Asia, on the other hand, presented a dense tangle of peoples with polities, cultures and traditions even more deeply embedded than those of Europe. As the late-developing nation-states on the Atlantic seaboard imposed control over the older civilisations of the Eurasian continent, they hardened a distinction between the West and the East. The lands to the east of the Mediterranean became known as the Orient, the place from where the sun rose. The Orient came to stand for a whole way of life that was inferior to that of the West: indolent, irrational, despotic and decayed. Such typification of the alien other, which the critic Edward Said characterises as Orientalism, had a peculiar meaning in colonial Australia where geography contradicted history. Fascination and fear mingled in the colonists' apprehension of the zone that lay between them and the metropole. As a British dependency, Australia adopted the terminology that referred to the Near, Middle and Far East until, under threat of Japanese invasion in 1940, its prime minister suddenly recognised that 'What Great Britain calls the Far East is to us the near north.'

For early European navigators, Australia was *Terra Australis Incognita*, the south land beyond the limits of the known world. It was a place of mythical beasts and fabulous wealth in the imagination of those who had long anticipated it, a blank space

2.1 A sketch of Aborigines in canoes made in 1770,
possibly by Joseph Banks. His use of art as an aid to
scientific knowledge is suggested by the careful attention
to boat construction and the method of spearing fish.
(British Library)

where their fantasy could run free. Early mapmakers inscribed an
indeterminate continent and decorated it with lush vegetation and
barbarous splendour. Yet just as the Spanish expedition to the
Solomons found 'no specimens of spices, nor of gold and silver, nor
of merchandise, nor of any other source of profit, and all the people
were naked savages', so Tasman reported 'nothing profitable' in the
island he named Van Diemen's Land (which is now Tasmania), 'only
poor, naked people walking along beaches; without rice or many
fruits, very poor and bad-tempered'. Once its commercial prospects
were discounted, the great south land served merely as a place of
invention. In *Gulliver's Travels* (1726) Jonathan Swift located his
imaginary Lilliput in South Australia, and in a final chapter he
satirised the conventional account of New World settlement:

A crew of pirates are driven by a storm they know not whither; at length a
boy discovers land from the topmast, they go on shore to rob and plunder;
they see an harmless people, are entertained with kindness, they give the
country a new name, they take formal possession of it for the King, they set
up a rotten plank or a stone for a memorial, they murder two or three

dozen of the natives, they bring away a couple more by force for a sample, return home, and get their pardon. Hence commences a new dominion acquired with a title by *divine right.*

It was a strangely prescient prediction of the foundation of New South Wales.

French and British interest in the Pacific revived from the middle of the eighteenth century with a renewed sense of possibilities. The two countries sent a series of ships whose names – *Le Géographe, Le Naturaliste, Endeavour, Discovery, Investigator* – suggest their purpose. The expeditions were despatched by the respective governments in conjunction with the savants of the French Academy and the scientists of the Royal Society. They tested new navigational aids and advanced cartography to new standards. They carried natural historians, astronomers, landscape painters, botanical draftsmen; they measured, described, collected and classified flora and fauna, seeking always plants that might be propagated and utilised. They sought out the islanders and endeavoured to learn their ways. These were men of reason hungry for knowledge rather than bullion.

The most celebrated of them is James Cook, a merchant seaman who joined the Royal Navy and led three expeditions to the Pacific. On the first (1768–71) he sailed to Tahiti to observe the transit of the planet Venus across the sun, then headed west to make a detailed circumnavigation of the two islands of New Zealand and trace the east coast of Australia into the Torres Strait. With only one ship, a converted collier renamed the *Endeavour*, and that just 30 metres in length, he charted more than 8000 kilometres of coastline and established the limits of the Australian island-continent. On the second (1772–74) he went further south than anyone before him and tested a new chronometer to fix longitude at sea by lunar tables. On the third (1777–79) he was killed by islanders of Hawaii. Cook became a model for a subsequent generation of maritime explorers. He was a hero for his time – a practical visionary, resourceful and courageous, a man who restrained his hot temper, eschewed conjecture for accurate observation, fused curiosity and moral certainty – and for some time after he was hailed as the founder as well as the discoverer of Australia. A posthumous engraving shows him ascending to the clouds after his death with a sextant in his hand.

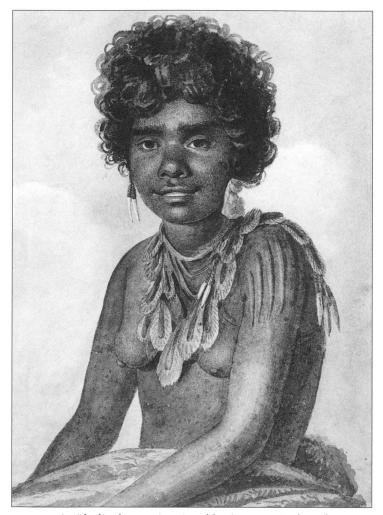

2.2 An idealised portrait painted by Augustus Earle and entitled *A Woman of New South Wales*. The classical beauty of the form and features contrasts with the derogatory caricature of Aborigines exposed to European vice by the same artist, which appears in the following chapter (p. 46). (National Library of Australia)

He had with him on the first voyage Joseph Banks, a young gentleman-scientist who would become director of Kew Gardens in London and make it the central collecting and distributing point

2.3   Cook is borne aloft as the hero-victim of European
discovery in the Pacific, with Universal Fame on one side and
Britannia on the other. (Alexander Turnbull Library,
Wellington, New Zealand)

in a botanical imperium, as well as the president of the Royal
Society, member of the Privy Council and patron of the colony of
New South Wales. There was also Daniel Solander, a pupil of the
Swedish botanist Linnaeus, whose system of classification provided
a framework for interpreting the hundreds of specimens gathered
during the voyage. Cook's instructions were that after observing the

transit of Venus he was to sail south from Tahiti, where 'there is reason to imagine that a Continent or Land of great extent may be found'; should it not be found, he was to proceed west and navigate New Zealand. He did both those things, the first fruitlessly, the second superlatively, and then decided to continue west. On 19 April 1770 the *Endeavour* sighted land at the entrance of Bass Strait on the south-eastern corner of the Australian mainland. As the ship coasted northwards, the country struck Banks as bare as a 'lean cow' with 'scraggy hip bones' poking through the rough timber covering. On 28 April the *Endeavour* entered a large bay fringed, according to Cook, by 'as fine meadow as ever was seen', and Banks and Solander were kept busy for a week collecting plant, bird and animal species hitherto unknown to European science. They named it Botany Bay. For four more months the company travelled north, surviving accident in the Great Barrier Reef, and recording their repeated landfalls with inscriptions cut on trees. Finally, at Possession Island off the northernmost tip of Cape York, Cook laid claim to the entire eastern coast under the name of New South Wales.

The idea that Cook discovered Australia strikes many today as false as the British claim to sovereignty over it. How can you find something which is already known? His voyage to New Zealand was preceded by that of Polynesian mariners some thousand years earlier, his Australian landfall came 40,000 years after the original human presence there. Cook's description of the Aborigines, frequently quoted, attests to the European Enlightenment apprehension of the noble savage:

From what I have said of the Natives of New Holland, they may appear to some to be the most wretched people upon Earth, but in reality they are far more happier than we Europeans; being wholy unacquainted not only with the superfluous but the necessary Conveniences so much sought after in Europe, they are happy in not knowing the use of them. They live in a Tranquillity which is not disturb'd by the Inequality of Condition; the Earth and sea of their own accord furnishes them with all things necessary for life.

Those Aborigines whom Cook encountered certainly seemed uninterested in European conveniences. They spurned the trinkets he offered, resisted his overtures and fired the bush where he landed: 'all they seem'd to want is for us to be gone'. Cook's presence in the

Pacific as an explorer and an appropriator, his endeavour to transcend cultural difference with a mix of conciliation and force, ended with his death on a Hawaiian beach. He figures in international debates among anthropologists in a postcolonial age as a crucial test case of the limits of one culture to comprehend another. In white Australian histories Cook is a fading hero, in Aboriginal oral narratives he is a powerful and disruptive intruder. He did not so much discover Australia as make it accessible to European travel, available for British settlement.

The decision to settle was taken by the British government fifteen years after Cook and Banks returned with their reports of New South Wales. By this time Britain had lost its North American colonies and was no longer able to transport convicts there as it had done for most of the eighteenth century. A plan to establish a new penal colony was prepared. Initially it was to be in Africa but, when no suitable site was found there, Botany Bay was chosen in the 'Heads of a Plan' submitted to the cabinet by Lord Sydney – the minister for the Home Office with responsibility for colonial affairs – and adopted in 1786.

The reasons for this choice are keenly debated. Some would have it that the purpose was to get rid of a dangerous social problem, and the further away the better. Others contend that Botany Bay had strategic advantages. Situated on the blind side of the Dutch East Indies, it could provide a naval base for British expansion into the Asia-Pacific region. After the loss of Nantucket in the United States, it would allow a resumption of southern whaling. Most of all, they claim, it offered two precious commodities, timber and flax. Both were in keen demand by the navy for masts, sailcloth, ropes and cordage, and Cook's second voyage had reported that both grew in abundance on Norfolk Island, which lay 1700 kilometres east of Botany Bay. The dispute over the motives for settlement is necessarily difficult to resolve because the official documentary record is so circumstantial. The 'Heads of a Plan' provides support for both parties when it justifies the scheme as 'effectually disposing of convicts, and rendering their transportation reciprocally beneficial to themselves and the State'. The British official who probably prepared the plan coupled the availability of flax and timber with 'the removal of a dreadful Banditti from this country'. Those who argue that Australia was settled as a dumping-ground for convicts see in these inauspicious origins the necessity of a new beginning. Those who hold to the geopolitical design seek a more affirmative continuity with imperial foresight.

The new colony was a product of maritime exploration, trade and penology. While the cost of imperial expansion weighed heavily on the British economy, the commercial benefits were shared unevenly. New wealth and new ways of increasing it, the spread of commerce and cupidity into all corners of human relationships, strained the bonds of social station and mutual obligation, with a corresponding increase in crime. The government, which remained a makeshift combination of property-owning legislators, tiny administrative departments and local squires, responded by extending the criminal code to make even the most minor transgression a capital offence. Between the insufficient deterrent of summary punishment by fine or infliction of pain and the intolerable recourse to wholesale execution there was the intermediate penalty of extended imprisonment, but the ramshackle system of local prisons could not accommodate the swollen numbers of convicts. Hence the earlier recourse to transportation to the American colonies, where the convicts could be set to work by the sale of their labour to local entrepreneurs. Those who came before the assizes and were spared the gallows would now provide the basis of a new settlement.

To found a colony with convicts was a more ambitious undertaking. Since there was no-one to buy convict labour, they were expected to become a self-sufficient community of peasant proprietors. Of the 759 who were selected, the men outnumbered the women by three to one. Because they would have to be controlled, four companies of marines were sent with them. Because there was no government, it would be a military colony but the rule of law would prevail, courts would be established and customary rights would be maintained. Its governor, Arthur Phillip, was a naval captain but he held a civil commission.

The First Fleet, consisting of two warships, six transports and three storeships, carried seeds and seedlings, ploughs and harnesses, horses, cattle, sheep, hogs, goats and poultry, and food for two years. An initial inspection of Botany Bay revealed that it was sandy, swampy and unsuitable for settlement; Cook and Banks had seen it in late autumn but Phillip arrived in high summer when the green cover was bleached to reveal its poverty. To the north Port Jackson offered a superb harbour, a large stretch of sheltered water opening into smaller coves and surmounted by timbered slopes in a majestic amphitheatre; Sydney Cove had a fresh water supply. Even here, however, the land was poor and the first-sown vegetables quickly withered and died. Axes lost their edge on the gnarled and twisted trunks of the blackbutt and redgum, shovels broke on the sandstone beneath the shallow soil, stock strayed or died or was eaten. The marines refused to supervise the convicts, most of whom did not take up smallholdings but worked on public farms for rations. The women, who were encouraged to take partners, were fortunate if they found a reliable companion. Meanwhile the party that had been despatched to Norfolk Island found the native flax could not be processed and the pine was hollow.

In October 1788 Phillip sent a ship to the Cape of Good Hope for additional supplies and reduced the ration; it returned in May 1789 with the provisions, but a large supply ship sent from Britain failed to arrive. The rations were reduced and reduced again, until by April 1790 the weekly distribution consisted of a kilogram of crumbling salt pork, a kilogram of rice alive with weevil, and a kilogram of old flour the exiles boiled up with local greens. These were the hungry years when men and women fought over food and listless torpor overtook even the most vigorous. The fact that the rations were distributed equally, with no privileges for rank, alleviated resentment. Even so, the colonial surgeon wrote of 'a country and place so forbidding and so hateful as only to merit execration and curses'.

The arrival of the Second Fleet in mid-1790, with fresh supplies – though fully one-quarter of its prisoners had died on the voyage and those who survived were incapable of work – and then a third fleet in the following year, eased the crisis. The cultivation of fertile soil at Parramatta on the upper reach of Sydney Harbour guaranteed survival. By the end of 1792, when Phillip returned to England, there were 600 hectares under crop, and thriving vegetable and fruit gardens. There was fish in the harbour, pasture on the Cumberland

Plain. Once the newcomers adapted to the scorching summer heat – the temperature reached 44 degrees centigrade in December 1788 – the climate was benign. Bodies and minds attuned to higher latitudes, hard winters and damp, green fecundity were coming to terms with the heady smells of hot, dry scrub and the sparse canopy that filtered a dazzling brightness. The commanding officer of the New South Wales regiment that was sent in 1792 discovered 'to my great astonishment, instead of the rock I expected to see, I find myself surrounded with gardens that flourish and produce fruit of every description'.

Phillip had held the colony together through the early years of desolation and ensured its survival. He took back with him in December 1792 kangaroos, dingoes, plants, specimens, drawings and two Aboriginal men, Bennelong and Yemmerrawannie. His greatest failure was in relations with the Aboriginal people of the region. He had been instructed to 'open an intercourse with the natives, and to conciliate their affections, enjoining all our subjects to live in amity and kindness with them'. He had endeavoured to comply, offering gifts as a token of goodwill and punishing any of his party who molested the inhabitants. Even when he was himself speared, in 1790, he forbade reprisals. Frustrated in his attempts to establish closer relations, he captured several Aboriginal men. The first, Arabanoo, died of the smallpox epidemic that swept the Aboriginal people of the region within a year of the European arrival. Another, Bennelong, escaped but returned to Sydney Cove following Phillip's injury to restore relations. Only when his huntsman, John Macintyre, was speared did the governor resort to indiscriminate vengeance: he ordered troops to bring back six Aboriginal heads.

That military expedition failed and Phillip returned to his fruitless endeavour to keep the peace. Not all encounters were violent. Aborigines helped the newcomers with their fishing, and exchanged their tools or weapons for hatchets, mirrors or clothing. Europeans cared for those Aborigines who sought treatment for smallpox. Such transactions occurred across a gulf of language and perception that was painfully apparent when those on one side seized the possessions or violated the customs of those on the other. European firearms and European disease gave the invaders a lethal advantage,

and the 3000 or so inhabitants of the land around Port Jackson
came to shun the huddle of buildings on Sydney Cove as well as the
foraging parties that spread out from them. 'Our intercourse with
them was neither frequent nor cordial', wrote an officer of the
marines. He thought at first that the spearing and clubbing of strag-
glers was caused by 'a spirit of malignant levity', but subsequent
experience led him to 'conclude that the unprovoked outrages
committed upon them by unprincipled individuals among us caused
the evils we had experienced'. Another perceived that as long as the
Aborigines 'entertained the idea of our having dispossessed them of
their residences, they must always consider us as enemies'.

The British authorities took possession of New South Wales
according to the doctrine, derived from international law, that it
was *terra nullius*, land belonging to nobody. A territory might be
acquired by conquest, consent or original occupation. In the first
two cases, the acquisition of sovereignty did not extinguish the
property rights of its inhabitants, but in the third case there were no
such rights since the inhabitants were deemed to be in a state of
nature without government, law or property. Cook had sailed in
1768 to search for the great south land with instructions 'with the
consent of the natives to take possession ... or if you find the
country uninhabited take possession for His Majesty by setting up
proper marks and inscriptions, as first discoverers and possessors'.
From their observations along the east coast in 1770, he and Banks
judged that the Aborigines were few in number, mere nomadic
inhabitants rather than proprietors. Accordingly they inscribed their
graffiti on the trees and proclaimed British possession; and for the
same reason the British government regarded New South Wales as
a better site for colonial settlement than New Zealand because it
required no treaty or act of purchase from the inhabitants.

Phillip and his officers were therefore surprised by the number of
Aborigines round the settlement. They quickly came to appreciate
that these people had social organisation, settled localities, customary law and property rights. The whole claim of sovereignty
and ownership on the basis of *terra nullius* was manifestly based on
a misreading of Australian circumstances, not that this prevented
Phillip from hoisting the Union Jack in 1788 and expropriating the
owners of Sydney Cove. Not until the High Court gave its Mabo

judgement in 1992 was there a legal recognition that Aborigines had owned and possessed their traditional lands. A similar recognition of prior or continuing sovereignty has yet to occur.

We do not have the direct testimony of those Aborigines who dealt with the first European newcomers, and cannot recapture how they understood their usurpation. We know from contemporary descriptions that Arabanoo, Bennelong and others were horrified by such barbarous excesses as flogging, terrified by demonstrations of musket fire, amused by European manners and forms of hierarchy. We can only guess at their reaction to violation of sacred sites, destruction of habitat, their ravagement by disease, and the growing realisation that the intruders meant to stay. Their society was characterised by a shared and binding tradition. Familial and communal restraints imposed order, mutuality and continuity. They were confronted by a new social order in which the autonomy of the individual prevailed and a form of political organisation based on impersonal regularity. Its freedom of choice and capacity for concerted action brought innovation and augmented capacity. Its self-centredness and moral discord generated social conflict, criminality and exile. Such an encounter could only be traumatic.

3

Coercion, 1793–1821

A prison situated 20,000 kilometres from the courts that sentenced its inmates was necessarily expensive. Since it was now clear that the cost would not be defrayed by the production of naval supplies, it became all the more important that this distant outpost achieve at least some measure of self-sufficiency. To labour in chains was to hobble productivity, so the colony of New South Wales would be conducted as an open-air prison. To serve time without hope of eventual freedom was to shackle the human spirit in sullen despair, so the penal settlement would have to be something more.

Beyond a recognition of these exigencies, the British government gave only limited direction to its new territory. In 1789 France was convulsed by a revolution from which emerged a radical republic that proclaimed the principles of liberty, fraternity and equality as its national goal and international mission. In 1793 Britain joined a European alliance to put down this revolutionary threat. After a temporary peace in 1802 the former republican general, Napoleon Bonaparte, now Emperor, vanquished all his continental opponents and Britain was left as the sole obstacle to French supremacy. Until the final defeat of Napoleon at Waterloo in 1815, the war on sea and land strained British capacity to the utmost. With the pressing demand for manpower, the number of transported convicts fell: after 4500 in the first four years, fewer than 2000 followed from 1793 to 1800, and barely 4000 in the succeeding decade. John Hunter, a naval captain who had served in the First Fleet and preceded Phillip back to England, did not return to succeed him as

governor until late in 1795, leaving military officers to administer
the colony. Hunter was succeeded in 1800 by Philip Gidley King,
another naval man who had previously been lieutenant-governor of
Norfolk Island, and King in 1806 by William Bligh, who had served
under Cook.

As these appointments suggest, the war gave greater strategic
significance to British control of the Pacific. After Matthew Flinders
encountered a French expedition on the south coast of Australia
during his circumnavigation of Australia in 1802, King sent a
party from Sydney to occupy Van Diemen's Land (the name given
to Tasmania by its Dutch navigator). Another fleet of marines
and convicts sailed from London to settle Port Phillip Bay on the
south-east of the mainland in 1803; finding the site unsuitable, it
withdrew to Van Diemen's Land and joined the earlier party at
Hobart on the Derwent estuary. Yet another contingent founded an
additional base at Launceston on the Tamar estuary to the north
of the island in 1804. In the same year King re-established a penal
settlement at Newcastle, at the mouth of the Hunter River, 100
kilometres north of Sydney.

The early years in Van Diemen's Land were as hungry as those on
the mainland. Crops failed, convicts stole or absconded to the bush.
The lieutenant-governor, David Collins, had seen it all before at
Sydney Cove. He worked as unremittingly as Phillip (whom he had
served as secretary) to maintain discipline, but in 1807 he himself
was robbed. The island colony survived on game and fish until
arable land could be sown and harvested. It earned an income by
whaling and sealing.

During these years the British huddled close to the ocean. The
settlements at Sydney, Hobart and Launceston were all chosen
for their maritime location as well as for the promise of their
hinterlands. Phillip's glowing description of Sydney Harbour –
'a thousand sail of the line may ride in the most perfect security'
– emphasised the importance of this factor. The rapid creation
of port facilities as well as the attention given to completing a
survey of the Australian coast suggested not an occupation of the
Australian continent but rather an investiture of the South-West
Pacific with new stations for Britain's expanding presence east
of India.

In their early activities the colonists also faced outwards and only after turned inwards. As early as 1792 the newly arrived officers of the New South Wales Corps arranged for a ship to bring trading merchandise from Cape Town; in the same year the first American trading vessel arrived at Sydney. Whales were already hunted in the Pacific for their oil, and the transport vessels chartered for the First Fleet were whalers that could search the neighbouring seas as soon as they dropped their human cargo. Soon seals were slaughtered in Bass Strait and their pelts exported to China – sealing and whaling would contribute more to the colonial economy than land produce until the 1830s. Merchants brought pork from Tahiti, potatoes from New Zealand, rum from Bengal. They collected and re-exported sandalwood from Fiji, pearl-shell and *bêche-de-mer* from the Melanesian islands. The tang of tar and salt air, the cry of seabirds, preceded the smell of the gumleaf and the magpie's ragged carol.

The officers of the colony had a head start in trade, though they were soon joined by enterprising ex-convicts and ambitious younger men lured from mercantile operations in other parts of the British Empire by fresh opportunity. Their advantage in landed enterprise was probably greater and certainly more durable. From 1793 those responsible for the defence and administration of the colony were eligible for grants of land, and whereas the soldiers as well as the ex-convicts received smallholdings of up to 20 hectares, there was no such limit on their superiors. Furthermore, the military and civil officials were able to draw on convict labour to work their farms. Finally, they had a ready market in the government commissariat, which bought agricultural produce for the issue of public rations. Through their dual role as public officers and private entrepreneurs, a dual economy quickly emerged: a public sector which included the government farm and its convict workers, along with others labouring on construction projects and the provision of services; a private sector of traders and farmers who benefited from the public largesse. Both sectors were mutually dependent on the British government, for the land which it took from Aboriginal owners and gave them, for the labour it provided through transportation of convicts, and for capital injected into the colony by the Crown's expenditure on the commissariat.

The British government's direction of this extraordinary arrangement was episodic and inconsistent. From time to time it instructed the governor to augment the public farm and economise on purchases from private producers; yet governors who were expected by London to reduce outlays were understandably tempted by the opportunity to take their convicts off the rations by assigning them to the very officials on whom they relied for advice on the allocation of labour and land. The effect was to privatise the public sector, an arrangement which usually fosters cronyism and here created a clique of wealthy colleagues. By 1801 John Macarthur, the paymaster of the New South Wales Corps, had accumulated more than 1000 hectares and 1000 sheep.

Macarthur and his wife lived near Parramatta at Elizabeth Farm, named after her, where they grew wheat and kept an orchard. 'It is now spring', she wrote to an English friend in September 1798, 'and the eye is delighted with the most beautiful variegated landscape – almonds, apricots, pear and apple trees are in full bloom.' There were 1500 settlers by 1800 at Parramatta and the lightly timbered surrounding country, which Elizabeth Macarthur likened to an 'English park'. Most of it was better suited to grazing sheep and cattle than growing crops, and the large landowners on the Cumberland Plain quickly gravitated to pastoralism in preference to agriculture. Cereal production developed along the rich river flats of the Hawkesbury, which flowed north through the plain and on which a further 1000 colonists had settled by 1800. They were mostly ex-convicts on blocks of 20 hectares or less, who tilled the soil by hand, grew wheat and maize, perhaps ran poultry or a few pigs, lived in wattle-and-daub huts on earthen floors, and cooked their evening meals in the smoky gloom over a fire beneath a sod and bark chimney. Lacking capital, they were locked into small-scale farming and always vulnerable to the merchants' control of prices and credit. There was a high turnover of such farmers.

The pattern of settlement on the Hawkesbury placed soldiers as well as former convicts on the land. This was a well-established imperial device, used by the Romans and the Chinese long before the British adopted it to maintain security on turbulent frontiers. Raids on Hawkesbury settlers began almost immediately as the Dharug people sought to harvest the new crops that had been

3.1 In 1808 the officers of the New South Wales Corps overthrew the governor, William Bligh. This cartoon, alleging that soldiers found Bligh hiding under his bed at Government House, was displayed in Sydney by the victorious junta. (Mitchell Library)

planted in their old yam beds. Conflict over scarce resources quickly escalated into violence, and as early as 1795 a military expedition was sent from Sydney to kill the natives and hang them from gibbets – the earlier injunction to amity and kindness was now but a distant memory. By 1800 the war on the Hawkesbury had inflicted twenty-six white and many more Aboriginal casualties. Meanwhile Pemulwuy, the Eora man who had speared John Macintyre in 1790, mounted a sustained resistance to the colonial invasion, including an attack on Parramatta, until in 1802 he was shot down and his head placed in a barrel of spirits to be sent to Joseph Banks in England.

There is no entry for Pemulwuy in the *Australian Dictionary of Biography*. During the 1960s, when the editors of that authoritative reference work were preparing the volume in which he would have appeared, the Aborigines were regarded as no more than a minor impediment to the colonial occupation, and appeared at best as a tragic footnote in Australian history. Since then he has been elevated to the status of a hero: a novel celebrating Pemulwuy as the Rainbow Warrior appeared in 1987 and even an Aboriginal school in inner Sydney was named after him in 1991. He now figures as the first great resistance leader who sought to repel the British invasion, inaugurating a continuous struggle for Aboriginal survival. That resistance to the incursion was undoubtedly common, and the subsequent denial of it in colonial history only attests to the fear it engendered at the time, but it was not the only response. Aborigines also imparted their knowledge of the land; they exchanged food and materials for British goods; and they adapted to the presence of the newcomer on the pastoral frontier. But a more sustained economic relationship would have required them to abandon their own way of life and the invader to accept their property rights over resources or to incorporate them into the labour process. Neither side was prepared to make such an accommodation.

One recurrent cause of conflict was sexual relations. From the beginning there was a gross imbalance in the proportion of male and female settlers, roughly four to one until after 1820. The promoters of the new colony had perceived this imbalance as a force for disorder, and instructed Phillip that his men might take partners from the women of the Pacific islands. During the voyage of the First Fleet, Phillip and the officers had great difficulty in separating the female convicts from the men, and his encouragement on arrival of partnerships was meant to encourage the civilising influence of the family. The governor also had a particular fear of male homosexuality, and believed that sodomy should be punished with the utmost severity: 'I would wish to confine the criminal till an opportunity offered of delivering him to the natives of New Zealand, and let them eat him.' Since these schemes of Pacific concubinage and punishment were stillborn, the problem of lust and promiscuity weighed heavily on those responsible for the penal colony.

Phillip also thought that in time the Aboriginal men might 'permit their women to marry and live' with the convicts. As soon as the coloniser's eye turned to Aboriginal women, it perceived them as chattels. The officers' accounts of first encounters round Sydney were framed in the genteel language of civilised men confronted by women living in a state of nature, 'wood nymphs' and 'sooty sirens' innocent in their naked immodesty. The carefully composed writings of these educated Englishmen emphasised the complete subordination of native women to their male companions, and recoiled in moral disapproval from incidents when Aboriginal men offered women to them. Sexual exchange between soldiers, convicts and Aboriginal women was common: the spread of venereal disease marked its occurrence. Yet lasting relationships were infrequent and misunderstandings of the nature of the transaction typically a cause of friction. Desire and affection were too often outweighed by shame and contempt for intermarriage to form a junction between the two peoples.

By the turn of the century the rudiments of a permanent presence were evident. The 5000 British residents of New South Wales were divided equally between Sydney and the hinterland (with a further thousand on Norfolk Island), indicating the balance of mercantile and agricultural activity. The colony was approaching self-sufficiency in food, and the rapid growth of local enterprise supported a standard of living at least comparable with that of the parent country. This successful transplantation, achieved far more quickly than earlier colonial foundations in North America, was already straining the penal principles that had governed its foundation. In keeping with the purpose of a place of exile, Phillip had prohibited the building of all but the smallest boats, yet by 1800 there was a busy shipyard on the western side of Sydney Cove. The colony had been established as a place of punishment that would deter crime but its very success seemed to reward the wrongdoer: hence the jibe of the English clergyman, Sydney Smith, that 'the ancient avocation of picking pockets will certainly not become more discredited from the knowledge that it may eventually lead to the possession of a farm of a thousand acres on the River Hawkesbury'.

Moreover, the conditions that governed the convicts' lives apparently confirmed them in their incorrigibility. Samuel Marsden, the censurious colonial chaplain, complained to Governor Hunter in 1798 that 'riot and dissipation, and licentiousness and immorality ... pervaded every part of this settlement'; Hunter himself reported that 'a more wicked, abandoned and irreligious set of people have never been brought together in any part of the world'. For Jeremy Bentham, the penal reformer who was pressing the British government to adopt his scheme of building a new kind of prison in England, one designed so that the inmates could be brought to penitence by constant supervision, the scheme of transportation was deficient in both economy and moral effectiveness.

All these judgements were informed by values and assumptions that entered into every observation about the convicts and that still pervade the arguments of even the most insistently objective historians. Those sympathetic to the convicts draw heavily on popular ballads and broadsides as well as the protests of contemporary humanitarians to present them as victims of a harsh penal code and brutal regimen; in his vast panoramic evocation of *The Fatal Shore* (1987) Robert Hughes portrays early Australia as a place of banishment, exile, privation and death – as a Gulag. Those cliometricians who seek to establish the character of the convicts from penal records find them to be criminals. Those economic historians who are more interested in the convicts as a workforce reconfigure the same records and find the same people to possess skills that they put to good use. Feminist historians of the 1970s took the masculine preoccupation with the immorality of the female convicts as indicative of an oppressive patriarchy, yet subsequent champions of female achievement reconstructed their life stories to show them as exemplary mothers. Each of these schools of interpretation seeks to release the convicts from the shackles of prejudice, yet every attempt is caught inextricably in the tangle of language and imagery used to describe them.

The convicts who arrived in the early years were mostly English; one-fifth were Irish and there was a sprinkling of Scots. Most had been convicted of a property offence, and brought only a few meagre possessions. Among them were Henry and Susannah Kable, both in their twenties, who had met in Norwich Gaol and brought their baby with them on the First Fleet. The parcel of clothes bought for them by public subscription disappeared during the voyage, and in the first civil action in the colony they were awarded compensation. The Kables were unusually successful – Henry became a constable and later a successful merchant – but this case established a crucial precedent. These transportees were not felons 'dead in law' as the eminent eighteenth-century jurist Blackstone put it, but subjects of the Crown with legal rights.

In these foundation years, also, the essential conditions of their treatment were established. Those on public labour and public rations worked until the early afternoon, when they were free to work on their own account to pay for their lodgings, since the government did not provide them with accommodation, and to buy drink or tobacco or other solaces. Those who were assigned to a master received food and lodging from him, and again often a further income – the records of storekeepers reveal convict purchases extending to elegant clothes. In both cases discipline was enforced by the lash; floggings of up to 500 strokes could be administered but only on the order of a magistrate. For the recalcitrant there were further sanctions including removal to the special penal settlement established at Newcastle in 1804. Supplementing these deterrents there was the carrot of a 'ticket-of-leave' that entitled the convict to work on his own account, which was an innovation of Governor King. Those female convicts who did not have partners or were not assigned to domestic service performed lighter labour; though some were flogged in the early years, their usual punishment was confinement.

Upon the expiry of a sentence or by early pardon, the convict was emancipated. By 1800 two-thirds of the New South Wales colonists were free, but most of these were former convicts and that status was not easily expunged. Even those who did not bear scars on their backs still carried an indelible stigma in the eyes of the respectable. The division between the 'exclusives' and the 'emancipists' – those who came free and those who were transported – bedevilled all aspects of public life in a confined, intimate society and persisted into the next generation and beyond until the numbers and attitudes of the 'native born' finally prevailed.

The responses of convicts evade easy judgement. Those historians who seek to 'normalise' the convict experience stress the comparative advantages of fresh opportunity, superior climate and diet, demographic vigour, and the paradoxical restoration of rights with fresh force in a regimen where rules had to substitute for rank and custom. There is much in these claims: some convicts accumulated substantial wealth, most ate better, their children were more fortunate, and they had a keener sense of their entitlements than the agricultural labourers or urban poor of the United Kingdom. Yet how can the tyranny of the lash be weighed in these calculations? How might the desolation of separation from loved ones, the lack of recourse from arbitrary decision and the sheer hopelessness of fate be tallied? From the earliest years some convicts simply bolted into the bush or ventured onto the ocean in frail craft. George Bass, the surgeon and sailor who in 1797 first navigated the strait (named after him) that separated Van Diemen's Land from the mainland, found five escapees marooned on an island there and set them back on the shore to walk the 700 kilometres to Sydney. The remains of some absconders were recovered, while others lived for long periods with Aborigines. In 1791 a party of twenty-one convicts set off north from Parramatta and, when a settler asked where they were going, answered 'to China'.

The officers who related this ridiculous enterprise interpreted the convicts' answer as evidence of their childish ignorance, as perhaps those who gave it intended. Gaoler and gaoled communicated across a gulf of mutual antagonism: against the formally declared and forcibly imposed authority from the one side, the felons had their own private communication, the 'flash' language of old lags, and associated methods of withholding themselves even as they outwardly obeyed. Patterns of compliance and resistance drew on the official regulations, rights set down in British law and also on the less tangible but sometimes more compelling notions of entitlement embedded in popular custom. Convicts used their knowledge of the rules to appeal against excessive treatment or insufficient rations. They engaged in collective protest by withdrawing their labour, damaging property, shows of dumb insolence or theatrical protest, as with the group of female convicts who turned about to pull up skirts and smack their buttocks before a governor.

There was some safety in numbers, but in 1804 the most numerous and overt challenge to penal rule brought savage retribution. Irish convicts sentenced for their part in the rebellion there in 1798 rose up on a government farm at Castle Hill and led 300 men first to Parramatta and then to seek support from the farmers of the Hawkesbury. The rebels were overtaken by troops and their uprising put down. A score or so were butchered on the spot, eight hanged and more flogged in an effort to obtain information.

A second uprising followed four years later, which became known as the Rum Rebellion. It shed no blood and was conducted by the officers of the New South Wales Corps, who overthrew the governor, William Bligh. He had been sent in 1806 to impose order and brought with him a considerable reputation as a naval disciplinarian who a quarter-century earlier had provoked the celebrated

3.2 The first known portrait in oils of an Aboriginal was exhibited by Augustus Earle in 1826. It shows Bungaree, a man of the Kuring-gai people, whom the early governors valued as a mediator; Macquarie had presented him with a breastplate as 'King of the Blacks'. The artist poses Bungaree in the grand manner with the fort at Sydney Harbour in the background. A subsequent lithograph divested him of his dignity by including an Aboriginal woman with pipe and alcohol in a squalid Sydney street. (National Library of Australia)

mutiny of the crew of the *Bounty* and then directed eighteen men in an open boat half-way across the Pacific to salvation. Upon his arrival in Sydney, Bligh quickly antagonised the regimental officers with his high-handed manner and reissued an order that forbade the barter of spirits for food or wages. This trade had begun in 1792 when a group of officers, headed by John Macarthur, bought a consignment of rum. It was commonly used as a means of payment and often blamed for ruining emancipist farmers. Governors Hunter and King had tried to curb the trade in spirits; and King had sent back to London one of its instigators, Macarthur, for wounding a superior officer in a duel. Macarthur deftly resigned his commission, persuaded influential British patrons of the potential of the wool samples he took back with him, and returned with an order that he be granted a further 2000 hectares. Once Bligh fell out with him, impounded his trading schooner and put him on trial, Macarthur persuaded his former colleagues to seize power. Bligh was placed under house arrest until he sailed for Hobart in 1809; the commanding officer assumed the title of lieutenant-governor, and Macarthur styled himself 'Secretary to the Colony'. The members of the junta helped themselves to additional land and labour.

London could scarcely ignore this challenge to its duly constituted rule, and despatched a military man, Lachlan Macquarie, with his own regiment to replace the discredited New South Wales Corps. Even before the conclusion of the Napoleonic Wars in 1815 resulted in a wave of new transportees, he effected a substantial consolidation of the colony – as was often the case in the British Empire, it was the local crisis that was the trigger of expansion. Macquarie was a planner and a builder. He established a bank and introduced a currency. He laid out Sydney afresh and embarked on a major programme of public works: roads, bridges, a lighthouse on the South Head, a new barracks for the soldiers and also for the male and female convicts, a hospital (financed by a licence to import spirits) of sufficient substance that part of it still serves as a house of parliament. He planned in straight lines and built in Georgian symmetry.

Three years after his arrival the Europeans found a route across the mountain range that ran down the eastern seaboard and hemmed them in. While from the coast it appeared as a dark blue line

on the horizon of the Cumberland Plain, this fretted plateau presented a maze of towering escarpments that defied earlier efforts to
find a passage. After the conquest of the Blue Mountains in 1813
released the colony from the limits of the Cumberland Plain,
Macquarie had a highway constructed to the new town of Bathurst
on the other side, which served the spread of settlement into rich
grazing country. The tiny settlements of Hobart and Launceston
simultaneously thrust north and south into a corridor of fertile
land that was well suited to both agriculture and pastoralism, and
well served by waterways. From 1816 to 1820 there was a rapid
increase in the arrival of convicts, more than 11,000 in New
South Wales, 2000 in Van Diemen's Land. The population of the
mainland colony reached 26,000 by 1820, that of the island
offshoot 6000.

Macquarie, a Highland bonnet laird turned professional soldier,
was a benevolent despot who regarded New South Wales as a place
for 'the reformation, as well as the punishment, of the convicts'.
This required an improved discipline (hence the construction of the
convict barracks) but also the chance to make amends, for 'when
once a man is free, his former state should no longer be remem-
bered, or allowed to act against him'. The governor used freely his
prerogative to pardon convicts for good conduct; he continued to
provide them with grants of land on the expiry of their sentences,
and he favoured their agriculture over the pastoral interests of the
large landowners. He was especially indulgent towards educated
and successful emancipists such as the surgeon William Redfern, the
architect Francis Greenway, the merchant Simeon Lord and the poet
laureate Michael Robinson. The appointment of such men to
official positions and entertainment of them at the governor's table
scandalised the exclusives, as did Macquarie's discouragement of
the free settlers drawn after 1815 by the increasing prosperity
of the colony: 'Is there no way for a man to get to New South Wales
but by stealing?' asked a British treasury official in 1820. Nor was
Macquarie daunted by the constitutional impropriety of his appointment of ex-convict attorneys to the new supreme court, despite
the opposition of the judge who presided over it. 'This country
should be made the home and a happy home to every emancipated
convict who deserves it', he insisted.

Discipline and reformation required public morality and personal restraint. Macquarie prohibited nude bathing and unseemly behaviour in pubs and brothels. He refused to sanction cohabitation with convict women, and the increased opportunities he allowed reformed males locked women more tightly into marriage and domesticity. He enforced the Sabbath. This active enlistment of Christianity in the colonial project marked a break with the past, for even though Phillip, Hunter and King had paraded unwilling congregations of convicts to listen to sermons on civil obedience, the early governors did so not out of piety (leading officials in both Sydney and Hobart lived openly with convict mistresses) but rather because the Church of England was an arm of the state. A Spanish priest who visited the colony in the early years was startled by the perfunctory character of its worship. 'The first thought of colonists and of Government in our colonies is to plant the cross and erect sacred edifices of religion.' The foundation years in New South Wales fostered a military chaplaincy style of religion that was perfunctory in its forms and had little to do with personal faith.

That emerged with new forms of ministry. In 1798 eleven missionaries arrived from Tahiti, rebuffed in their attempt to convert the Polynesians. They were members of the London Missionary Society, founded three years earlier by the Nonconformist denominations to minister to the heathens. The advent of Methodist and Congregationalist preachers brought a less formal and hierarchical religion with a stronger emphasis on individual conversion and salvation. Whereas Samuel Marsden, the leading Anglican minister, thundered from the magistrate's bench as well as from the pulpit against the depravity of the felons, these Nonconformists sought to reclaim the sinner to godliness. There was also an acceptance of the right of Catholics to practise their devotions. As early as 1803 King allowed an Irish convict to exercise his clerical functions, though that privilege was withdrawn in the following year when the priest was suspected of using the mass to plan the Castle Hill rising. In 1820 two new priests came voluntarily from Ireland with official permission to fulfil their compatriots' religious obligations.

Marsden was himself a proselytiser. Through the Anglican Church Missionary Society he hoped to convert the Pacific islanders and

personally led a mission to the North Island of New Zealand in
1814. The Maoris, as a 'very superior race of men', might be
weaned from their savage vices and brought to Christianity through
an appreciation of the advantages of civilisation which would be
apparent if they were instructed in agriculture and commerce. Trade
and the gospel made unreliable partners in Marsden's settlement
at the Bay of Plenty, but he saw little chance of the Aborigines
adopting such practices and did not participate in the training farm
Macquarie established for them in the same year or the Native
Institution that was founded to educate their children and conducted by a Congregational missionary.

'It seems only to require the fostering hand of time, gentle means
and conciliatory manners to bring these poor unenlightened people
into an important degree of civilisation', the governor assured the
minister for the colonies. He instituted an annual gathering or
'Congress' of Aborigines at Parramatta. It began in 1814 with a
distribution of roast beef, plum pudding, tobacco, clothing and
blankets as symbols of his gift of Christian civilisation, and also
with the presentation of breastplates to Aboriginal men in an effort
to provide them with a recognisable structure of authority. These
attempts to incorporate the Aborigines came as the pressure of
colonial expansion brought renewed conflict. By 1816 Macquarie
resorted to a punitive expedition that took fourteen lives. While he
was still 'determined to persevere in my original plan of endeavour-
ing to domesticate and civilise these wild rude people', it was
apparent that this could only be done by removing and remaking
them. The Aboriginal women who attended the Congress of 1816
cried when a dozen children from the Native Institution, clad in
neat suits and dresses, processed with Mrs Macquarie and the
missionary's wife. Those tears have flowed well into the present
century.

By this time the governor's own problems were falling in upon
him. He had brought regularity and direction to the conduct of the
colony. He had insisted that it should be a place of reclamation as
well as punishment, and balanced the demands of exclusives with
the needs of the emancipists. Pastoralists still received land and
labour, for Macquarie assigned the majority of transportees, but
they were not allowed to monopolise opportunity, so that the

3.3 An early sketch of Aboriginal warriors was made by a draftsman on Cook's 1770 expedition. The two Gwiyagal men appear as classical heroes, resolutely defiant of the intruder. (National Library of Australia)

nine-tenths of the population who had begun as or were descended from convicts held roughly half the wealth. But the numbers that disembarked after 1815 swamped the assignment system. With more convicts on the governor's hands, expenditure mounted. Macquarie's local critics, who alleged that he favoured the fallen over the free and enterprising, joined officials in London who condemned the cost of his public works. In 1819 London despatched

J. T. Bigge, the chief justice of the colony of Trinidad, to conduct an inquiry into New South Wales. Before Bigge presented the first of his reports in 1822, Macquarie resigned.

In 1803 Matthew Flinders reached Sydney after charting the Australian coast for the British Admiralty. Since his ship, the *Investigator*, was unfit for further service, he embarked for England in a schooner, but it too proved unserviceable on the voyage across the Indian Ocean and he called at French Mauritius for assistance. By this time France was again at war with Britain, and the governor of Mauritius detained him until 1810. It was not until 1814 that Flinders's account of *Voyage to Terra Australis* appeared, and a further three years before Macquarie's eye lighted on a passage in it: 'Had I permitted myself any innovation upon the original name, it would have been to convert it into AUSTRALIA; as being more agreeable to the ear.' At the end of the year Macquarie suggested that the name should be adopted for the whole of the island-continent in preference to the common designation of New Holland, which strictly applied to only half of it. On 26 January in the following year he honoured the thirtieth anniversary of the colony's foundation with a public holiday and celebratory ball. Anniversary Day became an annual festival, the *Australian* the name of the insistently independent newspaper founded in 1824.

The British had occupied only a small part of the south-east of Australia. In Van Diemen's Land they congregated on the central plain; in New South Wales they extended north and south along the coast, west into the transalpine slopes. Sealers and other adventurers ventured further but the mainland settlement was contained in a 150-kilometre arc from Sydney. While by this time the invaders probably outnumbered the Aborigines of Van Diemen's Land, in New South Wales they still constituted a minority of perhaps no more than one-third. There were many Aboriginal peoples in central and western New South Wales, and many more to the north and west of the continent, who had still not encountered the white man, seen his livestock and crops, or heard the sound of his musket. Yet they were marked by the advent of the intruder as surely as the smallpox scars borne by those who survived the spread of the diseases the colonists brought with them. The settlement thus far constituted a bridgehead for the far more rapid expansion that would follow, its telltale signs of denuded sealing grounds, missing stands of timber and soil already impoverished by overcropping an augury of the devastation still to come.

A settler empire, according to an American geographer, meant 'the permanent rooting of Europeans in conquered soil', a transplantation of technology, institutions and mental habits such that 'settler colonies took on a life of their own to a degree quite unparalleled by any other type of imperial holding'. The process of plantation was clearly apparent in Australia, but so too was the accompanying process of settler colonists attaching themselves to the new place. The life that was emerging blended what was brought with what was found. 'It is certainly a new world, a new creation. Every plant, every shell, tree, fish and animal, bird, insect different from the old', wrote Thomas Palmer, a Unitarian minister and radical transported from Scotland for sedition. His experience was also different. He was free from the usual restraint, allowed to engage in trade and shipbuilding, and even to send back his criticisms of Governor Hunter. Everything was topsy-turvy, and even the attempts to faithfully reproduce familiar institutions brought hybrid results. A vigorous and often rancorous society had emerged in which captivity meant freedom, and the gentleman chafed while the outcast enjoyed the governor's favour. Then, with the arrival of Commissioner Bigge, the empire struck back.

4

Emancipation, 1822–1850

Within a month of landing at Sydney, John Bigge was in dispute with Lachlan Macquarie over the appointment of the emancipist surgeon, William Redfern, to the magistracy. Over the next fifteen months of his inquiry the commissioner reached conclusions about the future of the Australian colonies sharply at odds with those of the governor. Perhaps those differences were inevitable. The two men were divided by background, training, temperament and expectations of empire. Macquarie, the career soldier and fervent paternalist, always viewed New South Wales as a 'penitentiary or asylum on a grand scale'. It was destined to grow from a penal to a free society and 'must one day or other be one of the greatest and most flourishing colonies belonging to the British Empire', but that would depend upon the rehabilitation of its convicts under his tutelage. Bigge, a cool and systematic younger man, brought a lawyer's judgement and a tendency to judge local circumstances by English standards.

The two men belonged to different generations, represented different eras. Macquarie, in his late fifties, spanned the collapse of clan society in the Scottish Hebrides and the remaking of his nation as north Britons in the service of the empire. He combined the eighteenth-century values of reason and sentiment with the habit of command, and the regularity he sought was one tempered by paternalism and patronage. Now, after his forty years of military service, the empire was at peace. The defeat of Napoleon left Britain free from external threat, and the enormous effort of war could be diverted into commerce and industry. Through a series of political and administrative reforms the imperial garrison state reduced its fiscal burden, increased its efficiency, and reformed oligarchical rule into a more broadly representative government. The engrossment of wealth by restrictive regulation and exclusive trading gave way by degrees to an open market in which all could participate. *Laissez faire*, let things be, became by the middle of the nineteenth century the guiding maxim of British policy.

As the logic of the market took hold, it entered into every aspect of individual and collective life. A social order based on rank and station, in which relationships were personal and particular, yielded to the idea of society as an aggregation of autonomous, self-directed individuals, everyone seeking to maximise their own satisfaction or utility. Utilitarians propounded a simple behavioural algorithm: given appropriate institutional stimuli, the impulse of the human actor to pursue pleasure and avoid pain would be channelled into behaviour conducive to the general benefit. Bigge, as a public official committed to the rule of law and still in his mid-thirties when the wartime emergency ended, was an early agent of the corresponding transformation of government policy. In penology, as in political economy and most branches of social policy, the doctrine of utilitarianism took hold to reconstruct the subject as an object of bureaucratic administration. The criminal must be deterred. Bigge was accordingly to inquire into the prospects of New South Wales both as a gaol and a colony, but above all the instructions of the minister for the colonies emphasised that transportation should be 'an object of real terror'.

His three reports, presented in 1822 and 1823, suggested how this might be done. Deterrence called for greater severity in the punishment of convicts through greater regularity. They should not be given special indulgences or allowed to earn money in free time to spend on town pleasures, but instead be assigned to rural labour under strict supervision. They should not receive land grants on expiry of their sentences but continue to work for a living. They should not be admitted to positions of public responsibility but rather remain in a subordinate status. Bigge's recommendations on the penal system simultaneously defined the future development of the colony. It would rest on free settlers who would possess the land, employ the convicts and grow wool – John Macarthur had caught his ear. It would require a system of government suitable for free subjects of the Crown: a legislature to curb the governor's arbitrary powers and a judiciary to safeguard the rule of law.

With the implementation of these recommendations the colonial presence in Australia was transformed. Pastoralism flourished and the greatly increased numbers it attracted burst the limits of settlement. Explorers and surveyors opened up the interior, and new settlements were planted on the southern and western coasts. Relations between Aborigines and settlers on the vastly extended frontier deteriorated into endemic violence. Stricter supervision of the greatly increased numbers of convicts exacerbated conflict between the emancipists and the exclusives. The restraints on rule by decree opened up a three-cornered contest for power between these two groups and the governor. Australia was incorporated into an empire of trade, technology, manners and culture, while at the same time its own distinctive forms became clearer.

The internal exploration of the country proceeded rapidly after the crossing of the Blue Mountains in 1813. A series of expeditions from 1817 onwards used Bathurst as a base from which to follow the inland river system that drained from the western plains of New South Wales into the Murray, and by 1830 traced that river to its outlet on the south coast. Northern ventures pushed through the high country of New England onto the Darling Downs in 1827 and well into western Queensland in 1832. A journey south to the future site of Melbourne was made in 1824, in 1836 the grasslands of western Victoria were traversed, and in 1840 a route through the Snowy Mountains into Gippsland was found. By this time the topography and resources of the south-east had been ascertained.

The explorers are central figures in the colonial version of Australian history. Celebrities in their own time, they were commemorated afterwards with statues and cairns, celebrated in school textbooks – even today, schoolchildren trace the paths of their journeys onto templates of an empty continent. They figured as exemplary heroes of imperial masculinity: visionary individuals who penetrated into trackless wilderness, survived attacks by savage and

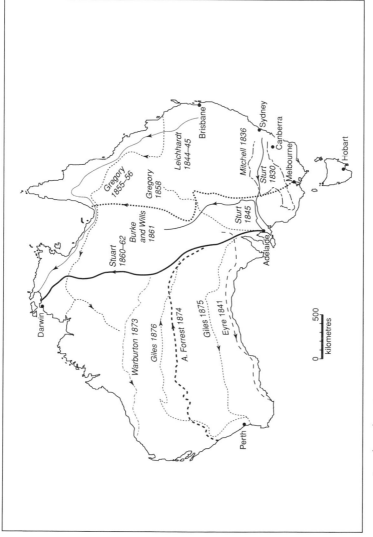

4.1 Land exploration

treacherous natives, endured hunger and thirst in their endeavour to know the land. Recent writing has undermined this heroic status. The epic version of exploration history left out the role played by sealers and drovers, travellers and outcasts who often preceded the explorer. When John Wedge, the assistant surveyor of Van Diemen's Land, made his journey of discovery into the mountainous south-west in 1826, he discovered the hideout of a bushranger. When Thomas Mitchell, the chief surveyor of New South Wales, reached the Victorian coast in 1836, he found a collection of whalers' huts and nearby a family farm. The celebrants of exploration also minimised the role played by Aboriginal guides. Mitchell employed three of them and, while he exulted in 'a land so inviting and still without inhabitants', scarcely a day passed without him recording in his diary an encounter with the owners of that land. Once the Aboriginal presence is recognised, the idea that the explorers were engaged in a process of discovery yields to the realisation that they were superimposing their own form of knowledge for their own purposes.

The explorers are thus wrested from the imperial and masculine embrace only to fall under the merciless gaze of cultural studies. Recent writers working in this mode con the records of the explorers for their textual effects, their inscription of features and names and meaning onto landscape, and their evasions of exploration as an act of conquest. Postcolonial critics suggest how the explorers used literary techniques to make the country picturesque and panoramic, cartographic precision to render it known and available. They point to the narrative strategies whereby the explorers dealt with the threat of the alien other. These critics' ingenuity is sometimes illuminating. They enable us to see that the land was not lying dormant, waiting to be found; it was brought into being by the very acts of travelling, apprehending and naming. The same ingenuity is sometimes redundant. We hardly need to deconstruct the writings of Thomas Mitchell to appreciate his exploration was a conquest, for it is overt in his journals. Hence his report of an affray on the Murray River in 1836, where the Aborigines 'betook themselves to the river, my men pursuing them and shooting as many as they could ... Thus, in a very short time, the usual silence of the desert prevailed on the banks of the Murray, and we pursued our journey unmolested.'

Major Mitchell was a military man, a Scottish career soldier who brought the survey techniques he had learned on the Spanish battlefields of the Napoleonic Wars. Some of the epic feats of land exploration in the nineteenth century were performed by Britishers born too late to win martial glory, for whom conquest of unknown territory was proof of manhood in imperial service – a tradition that continued right up to the eve of the First World War with Robert Scott's dash to the South Pole in 1912. In Australia it culminated with an equally vainglorious journey to the north coast led by an Anglo-Irish gentleman in 1860, but by then the locals were achieving greater success. They travelled more lightly in the outback, had fewer preconceptions, adapted equipment to local conditions. When force-fed to school students, the explorers blur into a bearded bore; freed from the palimpsest of cultural studies, their mixture of motives and methods is better appreciated.

The pastoral occupation proceeded apace. During the 1820s stockholders moved out of the Cumberland Plain (which was now surrounded by nineteen new counties of New South Wales that extended more than 250 kilometres from Sydney), over the Blue Mountains and along the inland creeks and rivers. In the 1830s they breached the boundaries of the nineteen counties, and rapidly occupied the grasslands south of the Murray, which became known as the Port Phillip District. In Van Diemen's Land the lines of settlement north and south of the estuarine bases met in 1832 and quickly broadened. Sheep numbers on the mainland increased from 100,000 in 1820 to one million in 1830, and from 180,000 to one million in the island colony. Production of other livestock, especially cattle, and cultivation of cereals also increased rapidly but in the next two decades sheep surpassed all instruments of the European economy. They were the shocktroops of land seizure. New South Wales flocks numbered four million in 1840 and thirteen million in 1850. By then there were some two thousand graziers operating on a crescent that stretched more than 2000 kilometres from Brisbane down to Melbourne and across to Adelaide.

Australian sheep produced wool for British manufacturers to spin and weave. The mechanisation of textile production began the industrial revolution that made Britain into the workshop of the world. While Lancashire's cotton industry was the more spectacular, the mill towns of Yorkshire turned out ever-increasing quantities of woollen cloth, garments, blankets and carpets that consumed ever-increasing volumes of fine wool. Between 1810 and 1850 British imports of fleece increased tenfold. Spain and then Germany catered to this growing demand but, as Australian producers improved the quality of their wool with the introduction of the merino breed, they captured an increasing share of the British market – one-tenth in 1830, a quarter in 1840, half in 1850. By then sales of Australian wool amounted to over £2 million per annum, more than 90 per cent of all exports. Here was the staple that sustained Australian prosperity and growth for a century.

It was produced in circumstances that allowed newcomers to enjoy rapid success: plentiful land at minimal cost, a benign climate that required no handfeeding in winter, a high-value product that would keep on the long voyage to market and could absorb transport costs. Such opportunities attracted army and naval officers discharged after the Napoleonic Wars, and younger sons of gentry families in England and Scotland who sought their own estates. An entrant required some initial capital to buy stock; he then hired labour and drove his animals to the edge of settlement; laid claim to an area that might extend 10 kilometres or more; arranged his flocks under the care of shepherds who pastured them by day and penned them by night; put rams to the ewes to build up numbers; clipped the fleece, washed and pressed, and despatched it for sale.

There were fortunes to be made in this first, heady phase of the pastoral industry, but it was a young man's calling and not one for the faint-hearted. Drought, fire or disease might ruin the most resolute. A downturn in British demand at the end of the 1830s caused prices to tumble, and millions of sheep had to be boiled down for tallow. The insecurity of conditions, as well as the absence of land title, kept the pastoralist's eye fixed on speedy returns so that, beyond improvement of stock lines, there was little effort to increase efficiency or conserve resources. Stock quickly ate out native grasses. The cloven hoof hardened the soil and inhibited regrowth. Patches of bare earth round the stockyards, eroded gullies and polluted watercourses marked the presence of the pastoral invader.

So did the signs of human loss, the ruined habitats and desolate former gathering places of the Aboriginal inhabitants, the skulls and bones left unburied on the sites of massacres, and the names that became associated with some of them. There was Slaughterhouse Creek, on the Gwydir River of northern New South Wales, where perhaps sixty or seventy were 'shot like crows in the trees' in 1838, Rufus River on the lower Murray where the water ran red in 1841, and other such places that recorded past atrocities with chilling frankness: Mount Dispersion, Convincing Ground, Fighting Hills, Murdering Island, Skull Camp. The poet Charles Harpur was equally frank:

> A tribe entire, with many a shriek
>> Was pent, and held at bay,
> Till there, like sheep, in one clear leap
>> Their slaughtered bodies lay.

White settlers sometimes suppressed the memory of such disturbing events and sometimes preserved it in local lore, so that in a pub conversation in rural New South Wales 170 years later an old hand could relate how the firstcomers had 'rounded all the blackfellas up at the top of the gorge, and shot at them till they all jumped off'.

Aboriginal versions of these encounters have an extra dimension. Their stories are both specific and cumulative, telling of particular events at particular places and of their larger meaning. 'Why did the blackfellows attack the whites?' the South Australian commissioner of police asked Aboriginal survivors after the Rufus River affray. 'Because they came in blackman's country', he was told. So far from obliterating the indigenous presence, the white onslaught produced an enlarged awareness of a pattern of conquest that began with the first British landfall. 'You Captain Cook, you kill my people', expostulated a Northern Territory stockman in the 1970s.

The violence was on such a scale that white colonists spoke during the 1820s and 1830s of a 'Black War'. That designation was quickly abandoned, and has resurfaced only in the past twenty-five years as the Aboriginal presence in Australian history has been more fully restored. In 1979 the historian Geoffrey Blainey suggested that the Australian War Memorial should incorporate a recognition of Aboriginal–European warfare. In 1981 the pre-eminent white historian of frontier contact, Henry Reynolds, argued that the names of the fallen Aborigines be placed on our memorials and cenotaphs 'and even in the pantheon of national heroes'. The desire to instal

Aborigines into a more inclusive national mythology meets continuing resistance. White supremacists oppose it utterly. White traditionalists are reluctant to accept the disturbing implications of conquest as an essential component of the Australian story, and condemn the 'black-armband' historians for insisting on such dissonant themes.

There are also historians sympathetic to the Aboriginal cause who query the emphasis on frontier violence and destruction, suggesting that the martial interpretation fails to understand Aboriginal actions in their own terms. The pastoral incursion was undoubtedly traumatic. Indigenous populations shrank dramatically (one national estimate suggests from 600,000 to less than 300,000 between 1821 and 1850), but disease, malnutrition and infertility were the principal causes: perhaps only one death in ten was caused directly by white violence. Aboriginal survivors responded to this disaster with a variety of strategies, and accommodation was one of them. During the 1830s and 1840s they incorporated themselves into the pastoral workforce as stockworkers, shepherds, shearers, domestic servants and sexual partners. There was loss, but also persistence.

The idea of a Black War undoubtedly attests to the extent of Aboriginal resistance. In Van Diemen's Land, where in a single month of 1828 there were twenty-two inquests into settlers killed by Aborigines in the outlying district of Oatlands, the governor declared a state of martial law. After parties of bounty hunters failed to quell the threat, he ordered 3000 men to form a cordon across the island and drive the Aborigines southwards to the coast. This Black Line, 200 kilometres in length, captured just one man and one boy, and even while it was moving down the island during 1830, four more settlers were killed and thirty houses plundered. Martial law was declared also in mainland regions where Aborigines inflicted sufficient casualties and caused enough damage to check the white advance: in the late 1830s pastoralists abandoned nearly 100 kilometres of land along the Murrumbidgee River. Yet these successes could only delay the white advance. In contrast to the Iroquois of northern America or the Zulu of southern Africa, the Aboriginal warriors did not fashion a confederation capable of concerted hostilities but rather presented a more localised resistance. This was not a single, unified Black War but an extended series of engagements.

Sometimes the invaders fought with regular troops. More than 500 soldiers were employed in Van Diemen's Land as part of the futile Black Line exercise in 1830 and afterwards for punitive purposes. The governor of the infant colony in Western Australia led a detachment of the local regiment into the Battle of Pinjarra of 1834, when perhaps thirty of the Nyoongah were shot, and military garrisons were deployed in the other new settlement in South Australia as late as 1841. Alternatively, the governors deployed mounted police, and later native mounted police. The mobility and firepower of such paramilitary forces were difficult to withstand, and with the enlistment of Aborigines the British followed the common imperial device of using conquered peoples to overrun the remaining independent societies. Under the command of Major James Nunn, the mounted police of New South Wales conducted a 'pacification' expedition during 1838 that inflicted more than a hundred casualties on the Kamilaroi people of the northern plains.

Yet these set-piece encounters again give a misleading impression of the conflict. When trained men fell on assemblies of Aborigines in open country, the firearm prevailed over the spear, especially after the repeater rifle replaced the musket. The Aboriginal warriors had no fortifications, and made little use of their enemies' military technology. In contrast to the Maori, who tied up 20,000 British troops in New Zealand for twenty years, they could not sustain a formal warfare of massed battle. They quickly learned to avoid such encounters, and typically used their advantages of mobility and superior bushcraft to conduct guerilla resistance. Destruction of livestock and surprise attacks on pastoral outstations exacerbated the fear and insecurity of white settlers 'waiting, waiting, waiting for the creeping, stealthy, treacherous blacks'.

The result was a particularly brutal form of repression conducted by the settlers themselves. The most notorious instance occurred in 1838 near the Gwydir River at Myall Creek in northern New South Wales, when a group of stockmen riding in pursuit of Aborigines wanted for spearing cattle came instead upon a party of Kwiambal people, mostly women and children, who had taken shelter with a hutkeeper. There was goodwill between the men of the station and the Kwiambals, who cut bark, helped with the cattle and were allowed to keep up their hunting of game; several of the Aboriginal women had formed relationships with the white men. There was

4.1 Guns against spears – mounted troopers do battle with
Aboriginal warriors across a creek. This portrayal of a
violent encounter on the pastoral frontier suggests that the
invaders will prevail, though the adversaries are more evenly
matched than they would be after repeater firearms replaced
the musket. (Charles Mundy, *Our Antipodes*, London:
Richard Bentley, 1852)

foreboding and irresolution from the station hands when the white
vigilantes took the Aborigines into the bush and butchered the
entire party. There was bombast from the murderers when they
returned alone, and then furtive guilt as they returned to try to
destroy the remains of their victims. We know about the Myall
Creek massacre because the station overseer reported it at a time
when the governor had been put on notice by the British government that such atrocities were not to be condoned. He brought
those responsible to trial and, when a Sydney jury found them not
guilty, ordered a retrial.

Seven of the murderers were eventually convicted and executed,
an outcome that astounded most colonists. The official response
to the Myall Creek massacre was quite exceptional, both in the
decision to prosecute and in the availability of white witnesses prepared to give evidence against them. Since Aborigines could not
swear on oath that they would tell the truth, they were unable to
testify against those who did them injury. The ostensible even-
handedness of British justice – proclaimed by Lieutenant-Governor

4.2 George Arthur, the lieutenant-governor of Van Diemen's Land, issued this pictorial proclamation in the same year that he declared martial law. The upper panels promote inter-racial amity, the lower ones indicate the penalties for violence. Arthur himself appears in official dress as the embodiment of authority and justice. (Tasmanian Museum and Art Gallery)

Arthur of Van Diemen's Land in a poster that depicted first a black spearing and then a white shooting, each treated as crimes and each punished – rested on a fundamental inequality. In both panels it was the white man who prescribed the rules and meted out the punishment. The Aboriginal rejoinder to such one-sided justice was delivered in the year that Arthur conducted his Black Line: 'Go away, you white buggers! What business have you here?'

Earlier encounters between Aborigines and colonists had established the fundamental incompatibility of two ways of life. The Aborigines had tried through negotiation and exchange to incorporate the Europeans into their ways, but the Europeans had little desire to assimilate into Aboriginal society. Even so, the restricted nature of colonial settlement up to the 1820s left open the possibility of some form of coexistence. The rapid extension of the pastoral frontier removed that possibility since it resulted in a succession of sudden, traumatic encounters. There was still room for both peoples, for the Europeans spread along open grasslands, leaving the more heavily timbered higher slopes, and some initial accommodation based on mutual exchange of goods and services did occur. But Aborigines were loath to accept the occupation of their hunting ranges and despoliation of their waterways, while pastoralists commonly responded to stock losses with unilateral action aimed at nothing less than extermination of the original inhabitants. The colonial authorities, having set this lethal chain-reaction in motion, were unable to prevent the spread of killing.

There were some whites who recoiled before the enormity of their compatriots' actions, who perceived that such inhuman conduct compounded the unjust expropriation, and who warned that 'the spot of blood is upon us'. The formation by evangelical Christians in London of the British and Foreign Aborigines' Protection Society in 1836 encouraged local humanitarians to establish their own branch of the society in Sydney in 1838. The society also pursued the cause in the British parliament and a select committee of the House of Commons found in 1837 that the colonisation of South Africa, Australia and northern America had brought disastrous consequences for the native people: 'a plain and sacred right', an 'incontrovertible right to their own soil', had been disregarded. The British government was already concerned by reports of massacres and martial law against the natives of the Australian colonies. 'To regard them as aliens with whom a war can exist', the minister for the colonies wrote to the governor of New South Wales in 1837, 'is to deny that protection to which they derive the highest possible claim from the sovereignty that has been assumed over the whole of their ancient possessions.' He insisted that the Aborigines be protected.

None of the schemes of protection was successful. In Van Diemen's Land Lieutenant-Governor Arthur had already commissioned a local tradesman, George Robinson, to round up the remaining Aborigines. Robinson's 'friendly mission' employed Aboriginal companions to succeed where the Black Line had failed. Between 1830 and 1834 he conciliated and captured the last defiant Aborigines

4.3 In 1829 Lieutenant-Governor Arthur commissioned George Robinson to make contact with the remaining Aborigines of Van Diemen's Land and persuade them to settle on a reserve. Benjamin Duterrau's 1840 painting, *The Conciliation*, shows a man of peace and compassion. Despite his promises to the Aborigines of Tasmania, Robinson arranged for them to be deported to Flinders Island. (Tasmanian Museum and Art Gallery)

and placed them on Flinders Island, in Bass Strait, where their numbers declined until the survivors were returned to a reserve near Hobart in 1847. Similar reserves or mission stations were established on the mainland during the 1820s and 1830s, usually by Christian missionary societies with government support. Some wellwishers, including the judge who presided over the trial of the Myall Creek murderers and who had earlier experience at the Cape Colony, wanted larger reserves on which the natives might be settled and protected from the perils of white civilisation. Settlement was a word of many meanings. The Aborigines were to be settled so that colonial settlement could proceed unhindered: indeed, one of the Myall Creek culprits announced that he and his mates had 'settled' the 'blacks'. The governors of New South Wales, however, preferred incorporation to segregation and appointed white protectors to accompany Aborigines in their wanderings and help settle them. George Robinson became the chief protector of Aborigines in the Port Phillip District, sometimes able to curb the worst abuses, powerless to prevent the continuing encroachment on their lands.

There was another possible course of action. In 1835 a group of entrepreneurs from Van Diemen's Land led by John Batman crossed Bass Strait to take up land in the Port Phillip District. In return for a payment of blankets, tomahawks, knives, scissors, looking-glasses, handkerchiefs, shirts and flour, and an undertaking to pay a yearly rent, they claimed to have received 200,000 hectares from the Kulin people. This unofficial and contrived agreement fell a long way short of the treaties negotiated by British colonists with indigenous people in New Zealand (it was more like the 'trinket treaties' arranged in the American West), but did suggest some acknowledgement of Aboriginal ownership. The minister for the colonies dismissed the arrangement on the grounds that 'such a concession would subvert the foundation on which all property rights in New South Wales at present rest'. Yet in the same year the Colonial Office insisted that the new colony proposed for South Australia must respect the 'rights of the present proprietors of the soil' and its commissioners stipulated that the land should be bought and a portion of the purchase price paid to the Aborigines.

The South Australian settlers ignored these conditions. Within five years the Aboriginal people on the outskirts of the new settlements at Melbourne and Adelaide were reduced to beggary. In Sydney their numbers dwindled and by the 1840s most were camped near the heads at Botany Bay. An old man there, 'Mahroot', told an English visitor of the changes he had witnessed: 'Well Mitter ... all black-fellow gone! all this my country! pretty place Botany! Little pickaninny, I run about here. Plenty black-fellow then, corrobbory; great fight; all canoe about. Only me left now, Mitter – Poor gin mine tumble down, all gone!'

White town-dwellers complained of the riotous dissipation and drunken squalor of these Aboriginal residents. White artists caricatured them as semi-naked figures who sprawled over public spaces with tobacco, alcohol, mangey dogs and neglected children, shameless in their vices and incapable of responding to the virtues of civilisation. Such representations of Aboriginal depravity established the victims as responsible for their fate, but there were

4.4 An 1839 depiction of Aborigines in Sydney, degraded by alcohol. The male figure still wears a breastplate, but his ragged clothing and dissolute appearance declare that the earlier effort to incorporate Aborigines into the colonial order had failed. (Mitchell Library)

alternative and far more disturbing images of the wild and untamed native. Captivity narratives circulated of white men who fell into the hands of Aborigines and returned to a state of nature, or of white women who survived their ordeals in the wild. The most celebrated of these was Eliza Fraser, who survived a shipwreck in 1836 and for fifty-two days lived with the Nglulungbara, Badtjala and Dulingbra peoples on an island off the coast of central Queensland. Her 'Deliverance from the Savages', as the title of one of many contemporary publications put it, dwelt on the killing of her husband and male companions, and the sexual degradation of an unprotected white woman. Fraser herself appeared as a sideshow attraction in London's Hyde Park, telling her tale of barbarous treatment, and the episode has formed the basis for a novel by Patrick White, paintings by Sidney Nolan, and several films.

By such means the land was taken, settled and possessed. To make it productive and profitable there were the convicts. A total of 55,000 convicts landed in New South Wales between 1821 and 1840, and 60,000 in Van Diemen's Land where transportation continued for a further decade. The great majority were assigned to masters, and most served out their time in rural labour. There was keen demand for them because a pastoral station needed large numbers of shepherds, stockmen and hutkeepers, and bond labour could be made to endure the isolation and insecurity that deterred free labour. Convicts, who cost no more than their keep, underwrote the rapid growth and high yields of the pastoral economy.

Assignment was now accompanied by a far tighter regulation. Convicts were no longer allowed free time at the end of the day, or permitted to receive 'indulgences'. As Bigge had recommended, there were fewer pardons and no more land grants to convicts on the expiry of their sentences. Officials exercised a closer control over the treatment of assigned convicts and the magistrates before whom they were brought for infraction of the rules. Lieutenant-Governor Arthur in Van Diemen's Land went furthest in his construction during the 1820s and 1830s of an elaborate system of supervision documented in 'Black Books' that set out a full record of every felon's behaviour 'from the day of their landing until the period of their emancipation or death'. His regimen was less brutal than that of his predecessors, though one convict in six was still flogged annually, but perhaps more chilling in its bureaucratic regularity. As the convict system was made more regular and its caprices smoothed out, so the opportunities to circumvent its rigours were closed. That made it less, not more normal.

Those who broke the rules were subjected to further punishment, now carefully graduated in severity: first, flogging or confinement, then consignment to public works or the chain gang, and finally secondary transportation to one of the special penal settlements set well away from civilisation. These settlements multiplied rapidly: Port Macquarie, up the coast from Newcastle, in 1821, and Moreton Bay, further north, in 1824; Macquarie Harbour on the west coast of Van Diemen's Land in 1822 and Port Arthur on the south-east corner of the island from 1832. Norfolk Island was also used for the same purpose from 1825. They were chosen for their isolation, and the natural beauty of the locations only emphasised the horrors attached to their reputations. Macquarie Harbour was approached through a narrow and treacherous entrance, Hell's Gates, and its inmates had to cut down the giant eucalypts from the rainswept hills and haul them to the water's edge. Port Arthur, where the stonework still stands in the lush green surrounds of the Tasman Peninsula as a major tourist attraction, has served as a prison, asylum, boys' prison and, most recently, the site of a gun massacre. Moreton Bay, where eventually the city of Brisbane arose, had a death-rate of one in ten, and its commander was killed in 1830 by Aborigines at the instigation, it was claimed, of the convicts he mistreated. Norfolk Island's new commander in 1846, John Price, began by hanging a dozen mutineers and was accused by his own chaplain of 'ferocious severity' that included chaining men to a wall in spead-eagle position with an iron bit in the mouth. Some years after Price left Norfolk Island to become inspector-general of prisons at Melbourne, a group of men fell on him and beat him to death.

The infamies of Norfolk Island and other penal settlements undoubtedly achieved their deterrent purpose in Britain. Earlier complaints that exile to Botany Bay resulted not in penitence but pleasure were replaced by the 1830s with an image of New South

Wales and Van Diemen's Land as sites of close confinement and desperate extremity. This reputation, however, strengthened the hand of another group of critics. These were the evangelical Christians who campaigned for the abolition of transportation. They publicised the scandals that emerged from the penal settlements to clinch their argument that the convict system was immoral and unnatural. Along with the campaigns against slavery and oppression of native peoples in other parts of the empire, and exploitation of the weak and vulnerable in their own country, the anti-transportation movement created a humanitarian conscience that was more sensitive to pain, more vigilant in moral surveillance. It also fostered the pejorative British attitudes towards the Australian colonies that affronted the colonists, and possibly contributed to a lingering condescension: well into the twentieth century a prickly Australian could be accused of 'rattling his chains'.

Within Australia there was a reluctance to acknowledge the convict stain. The gothic horrors of Macquarie Harbour, Port Arthur and Norfolk Island lodged subsequently in the popular imagination through the writing of Marcus Clarke (who based a character in the novel *His Natural Life* [1874] on Price), William Astley (who wrote of the same events during the 1890s in *Tales of the Convict System and Tales of the Isle of Death*), and more recently in Robert Hughes's epic *The Fatal Shore*. Against such dark and brooding imagery contend the revisionist historians, who point out that most convicts never experienced secondary punishment. Their emphasis on the utility of the convict worker and the normality of the convict experience within a comparative framework of global movements of labour in the nineteenth century is now in turn challenged by cultural historians fascinated by the otherness of the convicts. They have little interest in evocation of atmosphere or calculation of outcomes. They direct our attention not to the weals on the convict's back or the poison in the old lag's soul but his tattooed arm and her shaven head. They are concerned with self-fashioning.

Seen from such a perspective, the tattoos with which so many convicts decorated themselves served both as a form of identification and an inversion of that device's usual purpose. Whereas gaolers scrutinised the bodies of convicts for marks or scars as part of the official surveillance of the carceral subject, the tattoo embedded a text beneath the skin as a statement of the wearer's choice. The shaving of female convicts' heads, similarly, was introduced in the 1820s as a punishment for incorrigibles that robbed them of their femininity and unsexed them. While the practice drew violent protest, and some women wore wigs to disguise the loss of hair, the cropped skull also served to mark out a separate, transgressive and defiant identity.

Women, who constituted one-sixth of all the transportees, have particular salience in these reworkings of convict history because they emerge in them as actors in their own right. Earlier historians assessed the female convicts according to their performance of particular social functions, usually posed in moral or economic terms. Were these women 'damned whores' or virtuous mothers? Robust human capital or a wasted resource? Given the dual subordination of convict women, to the state and to men, such questions could hardly resolve the contradictions of their condition. The female transportees brought valuable qualities – they were younger, more literate and more skilled than the comparable female population of the British Isles – but had a minor role in the pastoral industry and were usually employed in indoor labour. They played a vital demographic role – they were more fertile than those whom they left behind – but the assignment system made it difficult for them to marry.

Mary Sawyer, a female convict in Van Diemen's Land, applied to marry a free man in 1831. Her record showed a series of misdemeanours – she was insolent, she had absconded, she had been 'tipsy' – and she was refused permission to marry until she had been 'twelve months in service free from offence'. Two years later Sawyer was back in detention. Since the authorities were reluctant to send females to the penal colonies, there was a heavy reliance on special 'female factories' built at Parramatta, Hobart and then other centres. These served as places of secondary punishment but also as refuges for the unemployed and the pregnant, and provided the women with a space to assert their own rough culture. By the 1830s the factories and their idle, unruly inhabitants stood for some observers as the visible symbols of a disordered society.

The convict system cast a long shadow over societies that were ostensibly moving towards civic normality. In keeping with Bigge's recommendation that the Australian colonies should be places of free settlement, the British government constrained the governor with a legislative council to authorise his measures and an independent court to ensure that they were not repugnant to English law. The first legislative council was a primitive affair of just seven appointed members, and Macquarie's immediate successors were slow to grasp that they no longer possessed an absolute authority. In 1826 Governor Ralph Darling altered the sentence of the court against two soldiers who had stolen to obtain a discharge, and ordered that they be worked in chains. The death of one of them brought condemnation of the governor's actions by the press, which he in turn attempted to suppress with a law that the chief justice disallowed. Several years later Darling had one of the editors imprisoned with new legislation, which the Colonial Office disallowed. Other restrictions included the exclusion of former convicts from jury service, a slight that provoked the emancipist poet, Michael Robinson, to propose a toast at the anniversary day dinner on 26 January 1825: 'The land, boys, we live in'.

By this time a line of cleavage was apparent between those who wished to preserve political authority and social esteem for the wealthy free settlers and those who sought broader, more inclusive arrangements. The division was no longer simply one between exclusive and emancipist, for a new generation of those born in the colony had come of age – hence the common designation of 'currency lads and lasses' (in reference to locally minted money) as opposed to the 'sterling' or 'pure merinos' (since they flaunted their unsullied pedigrees and pastoral wealth). The most prominent of the currency lads was William Charles Wentworth, the son of a convict mother and highwayman father who had agreed to come out as a colonial surgeon instead of as a convict, and prospered under Macquarie as a trader, police commissioner, and landowner. His son was educated in England and returned in 1824 with a keen resentment of the exclusives after rebuff in a suit for the daughter of John Macarthur. Darling described him as a 'vulgar, ill-bred fellow'; he denounced Darling as a martinet.

Through the newspaper he helped establish, the *Australian*, Wentworth agitated for an extension of freedom, an unfettered press, a more inclusive jury system, a more representative legislature. These objectives were gradually won against the lingering restrictions in a society where so many strangers were suspect – a Bushranging Act introduced in 1830 gave such extraordinary powers of arrest that even the chief justice was apprehended while walking near the Blue Mountains. A partly elected legislature, which was conceded in 1842, had to await the cessation of transportation, for reasons the minister for the colonies made clear: 'As I contemplate the introduction of free institutions into New South Wales, I am anxious to rid that colony of its penal character.'

More than this, the popular movement that gathered force in the 1830s asserted the equal rights of all colonists, regardless of origin or wealth. It sought to break down the disparities and distortions that pastoralism generated in combination with transportation, and to replace a social hierarchy in which a rich oligopoly controlled land and labour with a more open and inclusive society that would allow all to share in the bounty of the land. Its members styled themselves Australians or natives, and that term signified an attachment to place – the freedom they sought was for the colonisers, not the colonised – but their movement also drew on the growing numbers of new arrivals. From 1831 the British government used revenue from sale of land to subsidise the passage of a new class of 'free' migrants seeking a fresh start. They arrived in New South Wales in increasing numbers, 8000 in the 1820s, 30,000 in the 1830s, and chafed at the restrictions they encountered.

The new land laws replaced grants with sale by auction and generated sufficient revenue to finance a major programme of assisted migration. It altered the balance of population movements among the settler societies: whereas in 1831 98 per cent of emigrants from the British Isles crossed the Atlantic to the United States or Canada, in 1839 a quarter of them chose Australia. A further 80,000 free settlers landed in New South Wales during the 1840s. Sale of land also weakened the arbitrary character of colonial rule, for it replaced the grace and favour system of land grants with the impersonal operation of an open market.

4.5 Emigration as a remedy for poverty. In this English celebration of the colonies, the sullen discontent of the poor during the 'hungry forties' is contrasted with familial plenty across the seas. The references to Chartism, socialism and legal repression emphasise the contented harmony of colonial life. (*Punch*, 1848)

The engrossment of land continued, however, because the pastoralists moved beyond the official limits of settlement to occupy their runs by simply squatting on them – that term of disparagement originally applied to former convicts who gleaned a living on 'waste land' but soon came to designate a privileged class, the 'squattocracy'. The governors tried to control the squatters with licence fees and, in 1844, an obligation to purchase, but this threat to their privileges was set aside by the British government when in 1847 it gave them fourteen-year leases. By this time they had legitimated their illegal occupancy and turned possession into property. The hapless governor who had proposed the 1844 measure remarked that 'As well might it be attempted to confine the Arabs of the Desert … as to confine the Graziers or Wool-growers of New South Wales within any bounds.'

Nor was assisted migration as sharp a break with the past as was hoped. Under a bounty system, agents in Britain were paid for every migrant they sent to Australia. One source for the human cargo was the workhouses, where those on poor relief were confined. This process of 'shovelling out paupers' produced an immigrant cohort that was hardly different in background and circumstances from the convicts – it is no exaggeration to regard them as quasi-transportees – but the difference in legal status was crucial, and in any case such pauper migrants were outnumbered by those who came voluntarily. By the late 1830s the pressures for the abandonment of penal transportation were thus becoming irresistible. A parliamentary committee in London gathered evidence of the iniquity of the convict system, and the government suspended transportation to New South Wales in 1840. An attempt to revive it in 1849 brought indignant colonial protest and final abandonment.

That left Van Diemen's Land as the destination for criminal exiles. The island colony (it was separated from New South Wales in 1825) had in any case a higher proportion of transportees and a smaller proportion of free settlers: three-quarters of the population in 1840 consisted of convicts, ex-convicts and their children. The gap between the exclusive and the felon was wider, more poisonous in its effects. The eagle-eyed Governor Arthur kept a far closer control than his mainland counterparts, extending to a law in 1835 that imposed special penalties on convicts, ticket-of-leave men and even expirees. Bushrangers were a far more serious problem than in New South Wales because, as rebels against an oppressive regime, they drew on information and assistance from the ex-convict stockmen and hutkeepers.

The pastoral gentry built country seats of impressive grandeur and planted the amenities and institutions of English landed society, as if to ward off the raw novelty of life on a distant island where the brooding hills and sombre forests pressed in upon them. The finest of all colonial artists, John Glover, built his house on the north-east plain on a property of 3000 hectares. He painted it in 1835 with orderly rows of imported flowers and shrubs in the foreground, the eerie native growth behind. His farm scenes of Arcadian tranquillity reconstructed a familiar English world in Tasmania. Yet the veneer of civilisation was thin, and the rapid increase in convict numbers during the 1840s – more than 25,000 were added to a population of less than 60,000 – increased the demand to remove the criminal incubus and start anew. With its abandonment of transportation in 1853, Van Diemen's Land became Tasmania.

4.6 John Glover was a successful English artist who settled in Australia in 1831. His painting *A View of the Artist's House and Garden in Mill Plains, Van Diemen's Land* domesticates the landscape with European plants. (Art Gallery of South Australia)

One reason for the stagnation of Tasmania during the 1840s was that so many of its enterprising residents crossed Bass Strait for the Port Phillip District. While the British government rejected the land grab that John Batman and his colleagues negotiated with the Aborigines in 1835, it was powerless to prevent pastoralists from moving there. Within a year there were 200 illegal occupants, and the district was thrown open to settlement. A stream of overlanders who followed Thomas Mitchell's route from New South Wales quickly joined the overstraiters spread over the rich grasslands. By 1841 the district contained 20,000 people and a million sheep. Land in the principal settlement of Melbourne at the head of Port Phillip Bay was already attracting speculative English investment. The rectangular grid design of the new town, laid out in 1837, marked a break with the older settlements of Sydney and Hobart. They were dominated by their garrisons and barracks, an improvised and irregular streetscape marking out the administrative, commercial and residential quarters, with the well-to-do commanding the higher spurs and the lower orders huddled close to the water's edge. Melbourne, by contrast, was a triumph of utilitarian regularity, a series of straight lines imposed on the ground that allowed investors to buy from the plan.

Two other new settlements used commerce as the basis of colonisation. The first of them, the Swan River Colony, began with an eye to the threat of French occupancy: in 1826 the governor of New South Wales sent a party to King George's Sound on the far south-west to forestall that possibility and a naval captain, James Stirling, to explore the principal river further up the coast. The decision in 1829 to annex the western third of Australia and create a colony on the Swan River favoured a group of well-connected promoters who were assigned land in return for their contribution of capital and labour. They created a port settlement, Fremantle, and a township, Perth, but their hopes of agricultural bounty were soon dashed. By 1832, out of 400,000 hectares that had been alienated just 40 were under cultivation. The failure of the original expectations stemmed partly from the poor soil and dry climate, but most of all from shortage of labour: the 2000 who arrived in the foundation years scarcely increased for a further decade. In 1842 an Anglican clergyman visited one of the colony's original promoters.

His cousin, Robert Peel, had been a minister in the government that authorised the colony and was now the prime minister. Yet Thomas Peel, the proprietor of more than 100,000 hectares, was living in 'a miserable hut' with his son, mother-in-law and a black servant. 'Everything about him shows the broken-down gentleman – clay floors and handsome plate – curtains for doors and piano forte – windows without glass and costly china.'

Such a fate had been predicted by a perceptive, if erratic critic, Edward Gibbon Wakefield, when the Swan River Colony was proposed. Writing in 1829 from Newgate prison (where he was imprisoned for eloping with a young heiress) a work that he passed off as a *Letter from Sydney*, Wakefield observed that cheap land made labour expensive because the wage-earner could too easily become a proprietor. His own scheme of 'systematic colonisation' would set a higher price on land to finance migration and ensure that the migrants remained labourers – like Bigge, he sought to replicate the British class structure, only he would replace the convict depot with the labour exchange. Land, labour and capital could be combined in proper proportions by providing that settlement was confined and concentrated. 'Concentration would produce what never did and never can exist without it – Civilization.' An accomplished mesmerist, Wakefield appealed to both utilitarians and political economists with his idea of harnessing self-interest and social improvement in model communities created by private initiative with a self-regulating division of labour, generous provision of parks, churches and schools, and the greatest measure of freedom. Systematic colonisation was implemented in six separate New Zealand settlements. It was first attempted in South Australia.

The Province of South Australia, established in 1836, distributed power between the Crown and a board of colonisation commissioners responsible for survey and sale of land, and selection and transport of its migrant labour force. While the principal settlement, Adelaide, and its surrounds were carefully laid out by William Light, the surveyor-general, the arrangement soon succumbed to land speculation and South Australia reverted to the status of an ordinary Crown colony in 1842. It recovered, nevertheless, with fertile wheatlands surrounding the indented coast, and rich copper deposits. By 1850 the white population had passed 60,000. The

colony fulfilled its founder's expectations in other ways: it was a
free colony, untainted by convicts, and with a measure of self-
government; it was familial, with a closer balance of male and
female than any other Australian settlement; and it offered religious
freedom, with the Nonconformist denominations imparting an
improving respectability to its public life.

With the British occupation of the central portion of Australia,
the whole of the continent was formally taken up. The increase in
colonial population – 30,000 in 1820, 60,000 in 1830, 160,000 in
1840, 400,000 in 1850 – reveals a quickening tempo, as does the
spread of settlement after 1820 beyond the original narrow enclaves
in the south-east. Even so, the plantations in the south and the west
were confined to high-rainfall zones close to the coast, while the
Queensland outpost only got under way after the Moreton Bay
penal colony was abandoned in 1842 and the district thrown open
to settlement; the white population in 1850 was just 8000. Attempts
to establish new colonies further north invariably failed and the
white population above the Tropic of Capricorn was negligible.
After sixty years of endeavour, two-thirds of the white population
still lived within the south-eastern corner of the mainland, no more
than 200 kilometres from the Pacific Ocean. Whether by foresight
or self-fulfilling prophecy, the same proportion has held ever since.

Already 40 per cent of the population lived in towns. The preference for contiguity was a pronounced feature of the older penal
settlements and even stronger in the new, voluntary ones. The
graziers of New South Wales might roam like the Arabs of the
desert, but the less favoured clung to the comforts of the oasis. For
all the attempts of the governors after the Bigge report to send
convicts up-country, they drifted back to more congenial surrounds,
such as the Rocks area of inner Sydney with its rough conviviality
and networks of support. Isolation in the bush had its own measure
of freedom, and generated its own fraternity of mateship, but
isolation reduced choice and increased exposure. Life in the Rocks
was rowdy and violent, most children were born out of wedlock,
and there was a constant turnover of residents, but this very fluidity
shielded the inhabitants from surveillance and control. In the free
colonies a different logic produced a similar result. There was no
desire for anonymity here but rather a hunger for sociability that

would soften the emotional rigours of separation and ease lone-
liness. Adelaide, Melbourne and Perth quickly created a fabric of
voluntary associations, civic, religious and recreational, to incorporate their residents into community life.

In the penal colonies such institutions were more likely to be
imposed from above. For as long as the convict system lasted these
colonies had to be administered because they could not be trusted to
govern themselves, and those who were subjected to such control
were less inclined to submit themselves willingly to its operation. In
the absence of representative assemblies, people turned for protection from over-zealous officialdom to the courts, so that political
debate was displaced into arguments over legal rights. The custodians tried persistently to civilise these colonies and plant the
institutions that would redeem their inhabitants, yet every one of
the civilising devices they employed was distorted by the coercive
purpose to which it was put.

The family was one such device. In 1841 Caroline Chisholm, the
wife of an army officer, established a female immigrants' home in
Sydney to rescue single women from the mortal sin to which they
were so perilously exposed. She accompanied them into rural areas
and placed them in domestic employment under suitable masters
in the hope that matrimony would follow. To end the 'monstrous
disparity' between the sexes and rescue the colonies from 'the
demoralising state of bachelorism' was her aim, so that 'civilisation
and religion will advance, until the spire of the churches will guide
the stranger from hamlet to hamlet, and the shepherds' huts become
homes for happy men and virtuous women'. In this scheme of
'family colonisation' the women were to serve the men as wives and
mothers in order to reclaim them to Christian virtue; or, as she put
it, they were pressed into service as 'God's police'.

Religious worship was in turn promoted in New South Wales
with grants to the principal Christian denominations, but they were
scarcely a force for social cohesion. The local hierarchy of the
Church of England was reluctant to accept its loss of privileged
status; the English Benedictine who was sent as Catholic vicar-
general in 1832 wrestled with the Irish temper of his charges;
and John Dunmore Lang, the leading Presbyterian minister, was
an implacable foe of both the episcopal denominations. Anglican,

Catholic and Presbyterian alike complained of the neglect of the
Sabbath, the profanity and immorality, and shared with the smaller
Nonconformist evangelical denominations a preoccupation with
sin. Alongside the ballads and broadsides that proclaimed defiance
of conventional morality –

> Land of Lags and Kangaroo,
>   Of possums and the scarce Emu,
> The Farmer's pride but the Prisoner's Hell,
>   Land of Sodom – Fare-thee-well!

– there were some contrite convict statements. Typically composed
in narrative form as moral tracts, these confessional works described the wretched degradation of penal life, told of the blessed
moment when the sinner became conscious of God's grace, then
recorded the good works and purposeful endeavour that brought
sobriety, industry and happiness after the convert put aside vicious
habits and associates. Such homilies only emphasised the heathen
character of the mass of the felonry.

The colonists drew also on the arts of civilisation. In prose and
verse, art and architecture, they marked the course of progress,
order and prosperity. Landscape painting contrasted the primitive
savage with the industrious swain, the sublime beauty of nature
with the divided fields and picturesque country house. Didactic and
epic odes celebrated the successful transformation of wilderness
into commercial harmony:

> Now, mark, where o'er the populated Plain
> Blythe Labour moves, and calls her sturdy Train;
> While, nurs'd by clement skies, and genial Gales,
> Abundant Harvests cloathe the fruitful Vales.

The imagery was neoclassical, casting back to the ancient civilisations to affirm the course of empire and suggesting how through
successful imitation the colonists were participating in universal
laws of human history to fulfil their destiny. Hence Wentworth's
'Australasia', submitted for a poetry prize while he was a student in
Cambridge in 1823:

> May this, thy last-born infant, – then arise,
> To glad thy heart, and greet thy parent eyes;
> And Australasia float, with flag unfurl'd,
> A new Britannia in another world.

The neoclassical sought to affirm and renew a received model of social order that was organic and hierarchical. Through restraint and regularity it endeavoured to dignify the harsh circumstances of involuntary exile and brutal conquest, to elevate colonial life and instruct the colonists in the arts and sciences of civilisation. As the coercive phase of the penal foundations gave way to emancipation and free settlement, the neoclassical model yielded to the utilitarian project of moral enlightenment. The emphasis here was on schemes of secular as well as spiritual improvement, temperance, rational recreation, cultivation of the mind and the body. It found expression in the pastoral romance of the bush, where the merry squatter achieved freedom and fulfilment in a way of life that was no longer imitative but distinctive and new.

The very names that the settlers placed on the land suggest a similar emergence of new from old. The principal settlements were named after members of the British government (Sydney, Hobart, Melbourne, Brisbane, Bathurst, Goulburn) or birthplace (Perth) or royal birthplace (Launceston) or consort (Adelaide). Harbours and ports were more likely to honour local figures (Port Macquarie, Darling Harbour, Port Phillip, Fremantle). Familiar names were transferred to some localities (the Domain, Glebe), some were simply descriptive (the Rocks, the Cowpastures, the Cascades, the Swan River) and some evocative (Encounter Bay) or associational (Newcastle). There were few Aboriginal names in the early years of settlement (Parramatta, Woolloomooloo, though Phillip named Manly after one) but they were more common by the 1830s (Myall Creek). By then the obsequious habit was in decline. Rather than seek favour with official patrons in London, the locals proclaimed their places of origin. Hence the regional clusters of English, Scottish, Irish, Welsh and, from the 1840s, German place-names.

These ethnic identities found their way into work and worship. The maintenance of networks, the searching out of compatriots and the reproduction of customs were a natural response to the anonymities of resettlement. None of the national groupings, however, formed a permanent enclave. All of them were porous, allowing for movement, interaction and intermarriage. The display of Cornishness, for example, was more the advertisement of particular qualities and attributes well suited to work in the copper mines of South Australia than of any irredentist impulse. The ersatz Scottishness that compounded Burns suppers and Highland games was a secondary identity for those who chose to practise it.

The same impulse was apparent in the commercial centres of the new colonies, where land was bought and sold, and the owner built as he chose. The symmetrical balance of Georgian and Regency design used, with local adaptations, in Sydney and Hobart, succumbed in Melbourne and Adelaide to a multiplicity of styles – medieval Gothic, renaissance revival and the round-arched Italianate – which proclaimed the new measure of civic freedom and autonomous identity. Between 1822 and 1850 the Australian colonies relaxed coercion by the state for reliance on the market and its associated forms of voluntary behaviour. The transition was accompanied by violent expropriation, and the convict experience left its own legacy of bitter memories. Yet the outcome was a settler society characterised by demographic vigour, high rates of literacy, general familiarity with commodities, productive innovation, and impressive adaptation to the challenge of uprooting and starting anew. What began as a place of exile had become a location of choice.

5

In thrall to progress, 1851–1888

At the end of 1850 Edward Hargraves returned to Sydney from a year on the other side of the Pacific. He was one of the 'forty-niners' who had converged on California in search of gold. Although unsuccessful in that quest, Hargraves was struck by the similarity between the gold country there and the transalpine slopes of his homeland. In the summer of 1851 he crossed the Blue Mountains to Bathurst and washed a deposit of sand and gravel from a water-hole to disclose a grain of gold in a tin dish. 'This is a memorable day in the history of New South Wales', he told his companion. 'I shall be a baronet, you will be knighted, and my old horse will be stuffed, put into a glass-case, and sent to the British Museum.' Hargraves named his place of discovery Ophir and set off back to Sydney to claim a reward from the governor.

Hargraves was not the last Australian miner to engage in self-promotion or seek public recognition and reward. He was not even the first colonist to find gold: shepherds had picked up nuggets from rocky outcrops, and a clerical geologist collected many such specimens. In 1844 the scientist showed one to Governor Gipps and claimed that he was advised to 'Put it away, Mr Clarke, or we shall all have our throats cut.' This again was one of the tall tales spun from the precious metal. The colonial authorities were certainly worried that buried treasure would excite the passions of the criminal class and distract men from honest labour. Faced with the fact of a local rush, however – and within four months of Hargraves's trumpeting his success, one thousand prospectors were camped on Ophir – they accepted it and devised an appropriate response. There would be commissioners to regulate the diggings and collect licence fees, which entitled the holder to work a small claim. The same pragmatic policy was extended to the Port Phillip District (which in July 1851 was separated from New South Wales and renamed the colony of Victoria) when the rush spread there three months later.

The deposits of gold in south-east Australia were formed by rivers and creeks that flowed down the Great Dividing Range and left large concentrations of the heavy sediment in gullies as they slowed where the gradient flattened. Much of this gold was close to the surface and could be dug with pick and shovel, washed in pans and simple rocking cradles. Together with the licence system, the alluvial nature of the goldfields allowed large numbers to share in the wealth. There were 20,000 on the Victorian diggings by the end of 1851 and their population peaked at 150,000 in 1858. The diggers worked in small groups, for the surface area of a claim was often no larger than a boxing ring, and moved on as soon as they had exhausted the ground below.

During the 1850s Victoria contributed more than one-third of the world's gold output. With California it produced such wealth that the United States of America and the United Kingdom were able to adopt the gold standard for their currencies and thus underwrite their financial dominance. The gold rush transformed the Australian colonies. In just two years the number of new arrivals was greater than the number of convicts who had landed in the previous seventy years. The non-Aboriginal population trebled, from 430,000 in 1851 to 1,150,000 in 1861; that of Victoria grew sevenfold, from 77,000 to 540,000, giving it a numerical supremacy over New South Wales that it retained to the end of the century. The millions of pounds' worth of gold bullion that was shipped to London each year brought a flow of imports (in the early 1850s Australia bought 15 per cent of all British exports) and reinforced the proclivity for consumption. The goldfield towns also provided a ready market for local produce and manufactures. In this decade the first railways were constructed, the first telegraphs began operating, the first steamships plied between Europe and Australia.

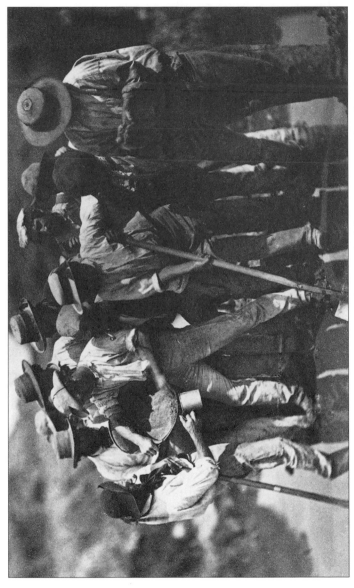

5.1 The writer and photographer Antoine Fauchery worked for two years on the Victorian goldfields in the early 1850s. His carefully composed tableau of alluvial prospectors, with shovels and pan, conveys the excitement of the early gold rush. (La Trobe Picture Collection)

'This convulsion has unfixed everything', wrote Catherine Spence, an earnest young Scottish settler in Adelaide who visited Melbourne at the height of the gold fever. 'Religion is neglected, education despised, the libraries are almost deserted; ... everybody is engrossed by the simple object of making money in a very short time.' Many shared her concern. Gold acted as a magnet for adventurers from all round the world, with a preponderance of single men who imbued the diggings with masculine excitement. Most of them were British but there was a substantial proportion of 'foreigners': Americans, with a knowledge of water-races and a fondness for firearms; French, Italian, German, Polish and Hungarian exiles who had been swept up in the republican uprising of 1848 that had shaken the crowned heads of Europe. The Chinese, 40,000 of them, made up the largest foreign contingent and were subjected to ugly outbreaks of racial violence. At the head of Port Phillip Bay, where most goldseekers disembarked, heaps of abandoned possessions alongside the forest of masts testified to the exorbitant prices for transport and accommodation. Seamen deserted their ships, shepherds abandoned their flocks, labourers quit their masters and husbands their wives to seek fortunes with pick and shovel. Small wonder that critics saw the gold rush as a levelling inundation and denounced the mania that turned settlers into wanderers, communities into mobs.

These fears came to a head as the surface gold at Ballarat was worked out and the diggers, who now had to labour for months in wet clay to reach the deep leads, became resentful of the bullying and corruption associated with the collection of the monthly licence fee. Agitators such as the Prussian republican, Frederick Vern, the fiery Italian redshirt, Raffaelo Carboni, and the blunt Scottish Chartist, Tom Kennedy, harangued them:

> Moral persuasion's all a humbug,
> Nothing convinces like a lick i' the lug!

They came together in a Reform League under the leadership of an Irish engineer, Peter Lalor. At the end of 1854 a thousand men assembled at Eureka, on the outskirts of Ballarat, and unfurled their flag, a white cross and stars on a blue field, to proclaim their oath: 'We swear by the Southern Cross to stand truly by each other, and fight to defend our rights and liberties.' Troops from Melbourne overran the improvised stockade on the slopes of the Eureka goldfield and killed twenty-two of its defenders. But the Eureka rebels were vindicated. Juries in Melbourne refused to convict the leaders put on trial for high treason; a royal commission condemned the goldfields administration; the miners' grievances were remedied and even their demands for political representation were soon conceded, so that within a year the rebel Lalor became a member of parliament and eventually a minister of the Crown.

The Eureka rebellion became a formative event in the national mythology, the Southern Cross flag a symbol of freedom and independence. Radical nationalists celebrated it as a democratic uprising against imperial authority and the first great event in the emergence of the labour movement. The Communist Party's Eureka Youth League invoked this legacy in the 1940s, and the industrial rebels of the Builders' Labourers Federation adopted the Eureka flag in the 1970s; but so did the right-wing National Front, while revisionist historians have argued that the rebellion should be seen as a tax revolt by small business. More recently, the open-air museum at Ballarat has recreated 'Blood on the Southern Cross' as a sound-and-light entertainment for tourists. Rebellion might be too strong a term for a localised act of defiance. Like the officials who overreacted, its celebrants saw it as a belated counterpart to the Declaration of Independence of the American colonists eighty years earlier, without which a transition to nationhood was incomplete. Even for a conservative historian, writing in the early years of the Australian Commonwealth, it was 'our own little rebellion'. Long before then, however, the Southern Cross had been hoisted anew as an emblem of protest, the Eureka legend incorporated into radical action.

The Victorian gold rush was followed by subsequent discoveries and rushes. Forty thousand headed for the South Island of New Zealand in the early 1860s, and as many more crossed into New South Wales when fresh finds occurred there. Next came major discoveries further north in Queensland, including Charters Towers in 1871, the Palmer River in 1873 and Mount Morgan in 1883, and over the Coral Sea into the Pacific islands. Then there was a movement into the dry Pilbara country of Western Australia and

west of the Nullarbor Plain where major finds at Coolgardie in
1892 and Kalgoorlie 1893 completed an anti-clockwise gold circuit
of the continent. Meanwhile, in 1883, rich lodes of silver and lead
had been found inside the circle by Charles Rasp, a sickly German
boundary rider on a pastoral station in far western New South
Wales, which became the mining town of Broken Hill; he died a rich
man. The mineral trail was marked by land stripped bare of trees to
line the workings and fuel the pumps and batteries, by polluted
waterways, heaps of ransacked earth and chemical residues, and
also by churches, schools, libraries, galleries, houses and gardens.
The impulse to atomistic and single-minded cupidity that dismayed
Spence when the hunt for gold began was quickly tempered by
collective endeavour and civic improvement.

The repeated movements drew on an accumulation of knowledge
and skill, though in the process there was a perceptible change.
Later mining fields offered more limited opportunities close to the
surface. Their greatest wealth lay deeper in reefs that required expensive machinery and more complex metallurgical processes. So
the lonely prospector gave way to the mining engineer, the independent digger to the joint-stock company and wage labour. Mining
communities are always beset by a consciousness of impermanence
that is inherent in their dependence on a non-renewable resource,
and the nostalgia for a past heroic era was captured in 1889 by a
child of the diggings, Henry Lawson. Lawson wrote as a young
poet, already captivated by the golden age:

> The night too quickly passes
> 　And we are growing old,
> So let us fill our glasses
> 　And toast the Days of Gold;
> When finds of wondrous treasure
> 　Set all the South ablaze,
> And you and I were faithful mates
> 　All through the Roaring Days.

The mateship of the roaring days was kept alive in sentiment and
action. The goldfields were the migrant reception centres of the
nineteenth century, the crucibles of nationalism and xenophobia,
the nurseries of artists, singers and writers as well as mining engineers and business magnates. The country's great national union of

bush workers had its origins on the Victorian goldfields. Its founder was William Guthrie Spence, as earnest and as improving as his compatriot and namesake who had lamented the gold frenzy.

The gold rush coincided with the advent of self-government. In 1842 Britain allowed New South Wales a partly elected legislative council, a concession it extended to South Australia, Tasmania and Victoria by 1851. In 1852, as ships laden with passengers and goods departed British ports for Australia on a daily basis, the minister for the colonies announced that it had 'become more urgently necessary than heretofore to place full powers of self-government in the hands of a people thus advanced in wealth and prosperity'. An empire of free trade required free institutions. He therefore invited the colonial legislatures to draft constitutions for representative government and in the following year his successor allowed that these could provide for parliamentary control of the administration under the system of responsible government.

The colonies proceeded accordingly, and in 1855 the British parliament enacted the constitutions of New South Wales, Tasmania and Victoria. South Australia received its constitution in 1856, and Queensland was separated from New South Wales in 1859 and similarly endowed. Henceforth the colonies enjoyed self-government along the lines of the British constitution: the governors became local constitutional monarchs, formal heads of state who acted on the advice of ministers who in turn were members of and accountable to representative parliaments. The imperial government retained substantial powers, however. It continued to exercise control of external relations. It appointed the governor and issued him instructions. Any colonial law could be disallowed in London and governors were to refer to the Colonial Office any measure that touched the imperial interest, such as trade and shipping, or threatened imperial uniformity, such as marriage and divorce.

These restrictions were of less immediate concern to the colonists than the composition of their parliaments. Following the British model of the Commons and the Lords, they were to consist of two chambers, an Assembly and a Council. The Assembly would be the popular chamber, elected on a wide male franchise. South Australia provided at the outset that all men could vote for the Assembly, and the other colonies followed in the next few years. The Council was to be the house of review and a bulwark against excessive democracy. But how? Those who feared unfettered majoritarian rule favoured the installation of a colonial nobility, a device mooted earlier in Canada and now proposed for New South Wales by the ageing William Wentworth with support from a son of John Macarthur, but ridiculed by a fervent young radical, Daniel Deniehy. Since Australians could not aspire to 'miserable and effete dignity of the worn-out grandees of continental Europe', this 'Boy Orator' supposed that it would be consistent with 'the remarkable contrariety which existed at the Antipodes' that it should be favoured with a 'bunyip aristocracy' – the bunyip being a mythical monster. As for John Macarthur's son, Deniehy proposed that he must surely become an earl and his coat of arms would sport a rum keg on a green field.

Deniehy's mockery helped defeat the proposal. New South Wales and Queensland fell back on an upper house consisting of members appointed for life by the governor. As the governor acted on the advice of his ministers, this proved a less reliable conservative brake than was created in South Australia, Tasmania and Victoria, where the upper house was elected on a high property franchise with an even higher property requirement for members. Since those Councils had to agree to any change to their unrepresentative composition, they proved impregnable to the popular will. Furthermore, since the constitutions gave the Councils near equality with the Assemblies in the legislative process (in contrast to Westminster, where the relationship between the two houses of parliament was uncodified and tilting in practice in favour of the representative branch of the legislature), the men of property were able to veto any popular measure that threatened their interests.

The frequent legislative deadlocks produced occasional but grave constitutional crises, notably in Victoria, where advanced liberals mobilised widespread support for reform in the 1860s and again in the late 1870s. The insistence of the Colonial Office that the governor maintain strict neutrality in the first of these confrontations strained the limits of self-government. George Higinbotham, the unbending champion of the colonial liberals, claimed that 'the million and a half of Englishmen who inhabit these colonies, and who during the last fifteen years have believed they possessed self-government, have really been governed during the whole of that time by a person named Rogers', who was the permanent head of the Colonial Office. Since lesser men shrank from the consequences of Higinbotham's obduracy, his efforts to put an 'early and final stop to the unlawful interference of the Imperial government in the domestic affairs of this colony' proved unsuccessful.

These flaws were obscured in the first, heady phase of self-government by the rapid advance of democracy. In the 1840s a popular movement had formed in Britain around democratic principles embodied in a People's Charter. Chartism terrified the country's rulers and many Chartists were transported to Australia. Yet in the 1850s four of the six demands of the Chartists were secured in the three most populous south-eastern colonies. The Assemblies were elected by all men, in secret ballots, in roughly equal electorates and with no property qualification for members. While the fifth Chartist objective of annual elections found little support, most colonies voted every three years; and by 1870 Victoria embraced the sixth, payment of members.

The people governed, and yet they remained dissatisfied with the results, for in their triumph they had created a new tribulation – the popular politician. As their representative he was expected to serve them, and constituents importuned their local member to make the government meet their needs. They demanded roads, railways and jobs for their boys. The member of parliament in turn pressed these claims upon the ministry and, if they were not satisfied, sought to instal a more amenable alternative. Under such pressures democratic politics was bedevilled by patronage and jobbery. Elections took on the nature of auctions in which candidates outbid each other with inflated promises to voters. Ministries formed and dissolved in quick succession as the result of shifting factional allegiances. Parliamentary proceedings became notorious for acrimony and opportunism. Public life was punctuated by revelations of corruption, vitiated by cynicism.

Colonial politics, then, operated as a form of ventriloquism whereby the politician spoke for the people. Those who made a career from this activity were artful, theatrical and above all resilient – none more so than Henry Parkes, five times premier of New South Wales between 1872 and 1891, who had arrived as a young English radical and ended as the arch-opportunist Sir 'Enery. If in principle the system of government was democratic and the parliamentarians were the servants of the people, then the working of the representative institutions left a gulf between the state and its subjects. The politicians shouldered the blame for this unpalatable paradox and Australians quickly developed a resentment of the inescapable necessity of politics. They erected grandiose parliamentary buildings to express their civic aspirations and despised the flatterers and dissemblers they installed there.

The colonial state grew rapidly. In the 1850s it inherited a restricted administrative apparatus of officials, courts, magistrates and local police, which proved quite inadequate for the fresh demands created by the gold rush, and was almost immediately expected to perform important new functions. In addition to the maintenance of law and order, colonial governments embarked on major investment in railways, telegraphic and postal communications, schools, urban services and other amenities. They continued to spend heavily on assisted immigration. They employed one in ten of the workforce and their share of national expenditure rose from 10 per cent in 1850 to 17 per cent by 1890. The public provision of utilities, in striking contrast to the pattern of private enterprise in the United States, is held up as an exemplar of national difference between dependence on the state and entrepreneurial initiative. The circumstances that confronted the Australian colonies allowed no alternative. They sought to develop a harsher, more thinly populated land by creating the necessary infrastructure for producing primary export commodities. The colonial governments alone could raise the capital, by public borrowing on the London money market, and alone could operate these large undertakings. More than this, they were expected to foster development in all its publicly recognised forms – economic, social, cultural and moral – for this was an age that believed in progress as both destiny and duty.

The enhanced role of the colonial state had further effects. When the colonies took charge of their own affairs, they became competitors for immigration and investment. The separation of Queensland

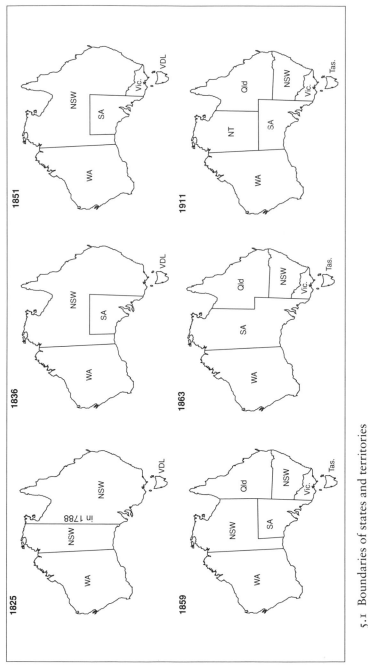

5.1 Boundaries of states and territories
(NSW: New South Wales; NT: Northern Territory; Qld: Queensland; SA: South Australia; Tas.: Tasmania; VDL: Van Diemen's Land; Vic.: Victoria; WA: Western Australia). In 1911 the Australian Capital Territory was excised from New South Wales.

from New South Wales in 1859, followed by boundary adjustments in 1861 and the allocation of administrative responsibility for the Northern Territory to South Australia in 1863, completed the parcelling up of the continent. Except for the excision of an Australian Capital Territory in 1909, these divisions have remained ever since. The devolution made for important differences in public policy (symbolised by the adoption of different railway gauges) and accentuated regional variations of economy and demography, though a common constitutional, legal and administrative heritage was always apparent.

Yet self-government also created highly centralised polities. The colonies had previously followed the English practice of appointing local magistrates to conduct the courts, supervise the police, grant licences to publicans, control public works and generally act as the eyes and ears of the administration. Local school boards were responsible for the provision of education. Now these activities were turned over to centralised agencies and directly funded by colonial revenue rather than rates. Local initiative languished. While urban and rural authorities were established on an elective basis, they were mere statutory creations of the colonial legislatures so that local government remained a stunted creature with residual responsibilities. The police station, the courthouse, the post office and the school, all were agencies of a bureaucratic hierarchy controlled from the capital city by regulation and inspection, post and telegraph, in a career structure that ensured uniformity.

The issue that dominated the first colonial parliaments and animated colonial politics was the campaign to unlock the lands. The former Chartists who flocked to the goldfields brought with them a hunger for the freedom and independence of an agricultural smallholding, as did Irish tenants, Americans seized with the doctrines of Jeffersonian democracy, and other Europeans with memories of rural communities broken up by commercial landlords. The newcomers found that the fertile south-eastern corner of Australia was occupied by several thousand pastoralists who were meanwhile entrenching their privileges in the unrepresentative upper houses of the colonial parliaments. The campaign to gain access to the land was therefore simultaneously a campaign to democratise the constitutions. In Victoria a Land Convention assembled in Melbourne in 1857, under a banner with the motto *vox populi* inscribed on a Southern Cross, to protest against a bill that would renew the tenure of the squatters. In 1858, when the Council rejected electoral reform, the Convention assembled a crowd of 20,000 to march on Parliament House and nail to it a sign, 'To let, the upper portion of this house'. In New South Wales the Council's rejection of a land reform proposal provided the liberal premier with the justification to purge that nominee chamber of its diehard conservative members.

If the land campaign was thus a source of contention and a means of confronting the inequality of wealth and power, it was inspired by a dream of agrarian harmony.

> Upset squatterdom domination,
>   Give every poor man a home,
> Encourage our great population,
>   And like wanderers no more we'll roam;
> Give, in mercy, a free scope to labour,
>   Uphold honest bold industry,
> Then no-one will envy his neighbour,
>   But contented and happy we'll be.

The land reformers envisaged a society of self-sufficient producers that would channel the energies of the people into productive contentment. It would replace the vast tracts of grassland with crops and gardens, the squalid huts of the shepherd with smiling homesteads, the restlessness of the single man with the satisfactions of family life, the improvised pleasures of the bush shanty with the amenities of civilisation. The yeoman ideal that exerted a powerful influence from this time until well into the next century was an essentially masculine one. It anticipated what a liberal newspaper described in 1856 as a 'pleasant, patriarchal domesticity' with the patriarch 'digging in his garden, feeding his poultry, milking his cow, teaching his children'. That his wife was likely to undertake most of these tasks was passed over. Having acquired the right to govern the state, men assumed equal rights to govern their families.

Selection Acts were passed in all colonies, beginning with Victoria in 1860 and New South Wales in 1861. They provided for selectors

to purchase cheaply up to 250 hectares of vacant Crown land or
portions of runs held by pastoral lessors. Their immediate effect was
the opposite of that intended by the land reformers. Squatters kept
the best parts of their runs, either by buying them or using dummy
agents to select them on their behalf. By the time the defects in the
early legislation – some of them the result of bribery and some
inadvertent – were closed, the squatters had become permanent
landowners. The genuine selectors, meanwhile, struggled to earn a
living as farmers on holdings that were often unsuited to agriculture. Lack of expertise, shortage of capital and equipment, and
inadequate transport defeated many of them. Those who survived
found the yeoman ideal of self-sufficiency turned women and
children into unpaid drudges who worked long hours in primitive
conditions and subsisted on a restricted diet. The need to supplement income with wage labour took men from their homes and
impeded the development of their farms. The revival of bushranging
in the 1860s drew on the discontent of the rural poor, and the
young men who joined Ned Kelly, the most legendary bushranger
of them all, were sons of struggling or unsuccessful selectors.

The Kelly gang cultivated local celebrity in the rugged country of
north-east Victoria as flash larrikins who stole horses as casually
and as recklessly as latter-day delinquents steal cars – until in 1878
they ambushed a police patrol and killed three officers. The gang's
subsequent exploits were the stuff of legend: a series of audacious
bank robberies; a long statement of self-justification that joined the
ancestral memories of Ned's Irish convict father to the grievances of
an oppressed rural underclass; the beating of ploughshares into
armour for the final shootout when the gang sought to wreck a train
carrying police from Melbourne; and then Ned's studied defiance
through his trial and passage to the gallows. His supposed final
words, 'Such is life', ensured immortality. Just as the Kelly gang
sang the ballads that commemorated earlier gallant bushrangers,
so they too became folk heroes. Sympathisers sustained them in
mountain hideouts beyond the reach of the railway, local informers
operated a bush telegraph by word of mouth to set against the
electronic telegraph of the authorities. More than this, the symbol-
ism of making agricultural implements into helmets and breastplates proved irresistible to journalists and press photographers

who carried the story to a national audience, as well as to the writers, artists, dramatists and film-makers who have repeatedly reworked it. Vicious killer or social rebel, Ned Kelly is a product of a countryside on the cusp of modernity.

Those selectors who prospered did so as large-scale commercial producers who bought additional labour and combined farming with grazing. Agricultural success came first in the 1870s among wheatgrowers of South Australia and western Victoria, where the advent of the railway and farm machinery made for productive efficiency. Prominent among them were German settlers, law-abiding, devout and industrious. Other farms were hacked out of the dense rainforests along the eastern coast: those in the south used the cream separator and refrigerator to establish a dairy industry, while in the north a thriving sugar industry emerged on plantations. The area of cultivated land increased from less than 200,000 hectares in 1850 to more than 2 million by the end of the 1880s.

Wool production also increased tenfold, but from a much larger base. By the early 1870s it once more led gold as the country's major export, and sales to Britain during the 1880s amounted to one-tenth of the national product. The increased output was made possible by substantial investment in improvements: larger sheep with heavier fleeces on better pastures that were now fenced and watered by dams and underground bores. Before 1850 a traveller could have proceeded through the pastoral crescent of eastern Australia without opening a gate. Now lines of posts spanned with fencing wire marked the grazier's transition from squatter to landowner. The enclosed paddocks were dotted with the ghostly trunks and limbs of trees devoid of leaves, killed by ringbarking to augment the pasture; the native wildlife was already losing out to imported flora and fauna such as thistles and rabbits, which would become serious pests.

For the time being, the owner rejoiced in the remaking of the habitat. His simple homestead was replaced by an imposing replica of the English country house, and probably also a townhouse in the capital city where he educated his children and spent much of the year. Behind the owner's residence was the manager's quarters, and a small village of workshops, yards, dams, gardens and accommodation for the workforce as well as the woolshed – misleadingly named, for it was a great hall with stands for fifty shearers or more to strip the fleece that afforded these wool kings their dynastic comforts.

Wool prices remained high until the mid-1870s and then turned down. Caught in a cost–price squeeze, the graziers responded by increasing production, pushing further inland into the arid grassland and saltbush and mulga country beyond. Abandoned properties testified to the perils of excessive optimism. Newcomers pressed too far into Queensland in the 1860s and too far west in New South Wales in the 1880s. These advances ended in retreat. Cattle could survive in the low-rainfall zone – they could walk further to water, were less vulnerable to attack by dingo, and could be driven long distances to market – but they were less profitable because experiments with canning and refrigeration had yet to succeed and beef producers were still restricted to the domestic market.

The movement into the interior brought a revival of exploration, and yielded new heroes in a more grandiose, high-Victorian mode of epic tragedy. In 1848 the German Ludwig Leichhardt, famous for an earlier overland journey to the Northern Territory, set off for the west coast from Queensland and disappeared with six companions; among the conjectures of his fate in the wilderness is Patrick White's novel *Voss* (1957). In the same year Aborigines speared another explorer, Edmund Kennedy, in the far north Cape York Peninsula. In 1860 Robert Burke, an officer on the Victorian goldfields, and William Wills, a surveyor, were seen off at Melbourne on a lavishly appointed expedition to cross the continent from south to north. Scattering equipment behind them, they reached the muddy flats of the Gulf of Carpentaria but died of starvation on the return journey at Coopers Creek, near the border of Queensland and South Australia. The colonists made heroes of them in verse and art, and there have since been histories, novels, plays and several films. The pencilled diary of their final days holds pride of place in the State library. A statue was unveiled in Melbourne in 1865, the first great monument to inhabitants of that city; its repeated relocation attests to an uncompleted journey.

It was a South Australian, John Stuart, who succeeded in the following year and his return journey was a near-run thing with partial paralysis and temporary blindness – but unlike Burke and Wills, whose bodies were recovered for a state funeral, Stuart left Australia embittered at the lack of recognition. His journey provided the route for the Overland Telegraph line, completed in 1872, which established direct electronic communication from Europe, and the repeater stations became bases for prospectors and pastoral pioneers in Central Australia. Further expeditions traversed the Gibson Desert to the west and the Nullarbor Plain that stretched between Adelaide and Perth. Alexander Forrest's journey from the north coast of Western Australia to the Overland Telegraph found grazing lands in the Kimberley district that were taken up in the 1880s by overlanders from Queensland such as the Durack family.

Another South Australian explorer in the spinifex country of the western desert crested a hill some 300 kilometres from the Overland Telegraph in 1873 and saw a great monolith more than 2 kilometres long and 350 metres high. The explorer named it Ayers Rock, after the colony's premier. In 1988 it was returned to its traditional owners and its original name of Uluru was restored. Red in colour, it transmits a spectacular light at sunrise and sunset. For its owners it is a sacred place, and for the many tourists who now flock to Uluru and the New Age visitors who journey there as a spiritual pilgrimage, it is the epicentre of the country's Red Heart. It is also a place of mystery and dark secrets. The disappearance in 1980 of a baby, Azaria Chamberlain, joined the powerful tradition of the child lost in the bush to rumours of devil worship and ritual sacrifice at a site of sinister mystery.

These are recent transformations. Earlier European Australians spoke not of a Red Centre but a Dead Centre. The inland frontier of settlement was known as 'the outback' or 'the Never-Never', a place of confrontation with inhospitable nature. In 1891, the year before he hanged himself with his stockwhip, the drover and poet Barcroft Boake wrote of the city comforts provided to absentee pastoralists by the men and women of the outback:

> Out on the wastes of the Never Never –
>   That's where the dead men lie!
> There where the heat-waves dance for ever –
>   That's where the dead men lie!

In contrast to the westward occupation of North America, the European occupation of Australia was never completed, the inland frontier never closed.

As they moved north, the Europeans encountered further challenges. Geographically, the upper third of the Australian continent above the Tropic of Capricorn presents extreme variations of landforms, rainfall and habitat: from the arid north-western coast, across stretches of red sand dunes, claypans, baked floodplains and broken, rocky country to the dense rainforests, mangrove beaches and coral reefs that run along the eastern shore. Physically, the region called into question the coloniser's capacity to adapt: habituated to a temperate climate, newcomers were slow to shed their flannel underwear, Crimean shirts and moleskin trousers, or give up their diet of meat, flour and alcohol. Psychologically, it confronted them with the presence of other people more at home in an alien environment. On both sides of the Torres Strait and Coral Sea, where European Australia converged with Asia and the Pacific, the white man was outnumbered by other races.

The Chinese encountered the greatest hostility. For more than a century they were the largest non-European national group in Australia, distinctive in appearance, language, religion and customs. From their arrival on the multinational diggings in the early 1850s, they were singled out for criticism. The overwhelming majority were indentured, recruited from Kwantung province by emigration agents in Hong Kong to work in large groups and repatriate their earnings. All but a handful were single men, so that they were condemned as both an economic and a social threat. 'We want no slave class amongst us', a Melbourne newspaper insisted in 1855. The Victorian government imposed special entry taxes and appointed protectors to separate them on the goldfields, though this did not prevent a major race riot on one field in 1857. The New South Wales government introduced similar restrictions after another attack on a Chinese encampment there in 1861. From this time onwards there was a racist strain in popular radicalism.

The Chinese came when the gold rush moved into north Queensland in the 1860s and the Northern Territory in the 1870s, but they were unwelcome competitors on the diggings and quickly moved into horticulture, commerce and service industries. Gold in turn took European Australians into New Guinea, and the British government was startled to learn in 1883 that Queensland had annexed the territory. London disallowed the action but did declare most of the eastern half a protectorate on condition that the Australian colonies covered its costs. Earlier, in 1872, Queensland's northern border had been extended into the Torres Strait to encompass islands that were rich in pearl, trochus, turtle-shell, *bêche-de-mer* and sandalwood. The trade in these natural resources extended both east and west, from Broome to the outer Coral Sea, and proceeded along quite different lines from industry in the south. The work was performed by local or imported labour, using systems of employment developed on the ship and beach communities of the Pacific.

Whereas pastoralism spread workers thinly over grasslands and agricultural selection spawned the family farm, the labour needs of the more intensive enterprises in the north called for additional assistance. Whether the white man was incapable of sustained physical effort in the tropics, as contemporary science suggested, or simply unwilling to become a plantation labourer, it was clear that some other source was needed. The sugar plantations that were established in north Queensland from the 1860s used the Pacific islands as a labour reserve. At first they drew on the New Hebrides (Vanuatu), whence the common term 'Kanakas'; later they turned to the Solomons and other island groups off the east coast of New Guinea for men and women to clear the forest, plant and weed the cane, then cut, crush and mill it into sugar. Sixty thousand of them were recruited over forty years, some voluntarily and some at the point of a gun. Initially they worked as indentured labourers under close restriction for a fixed term and returned with the fruits of their labour; by the 1880s a sizeable proportion settled with a substantial measure of freedom as part of the local working class.

Well-publicised cases of abuse brought growing criticism of the Pacific island labour trade from humanitarians in the south. The ruthless behaviour of the 'blackbirders' who recruited the islanders, the harsh discipline of the planters, the high mortality rate and low rates of payment suggested a form of bond labour akin to slavery. A comparison might be drawn with penal transportation, which resumed in Western Australia between 1850 and 1868, for this too incurred the odium of eastern colonists. That the Western Australians had invited London to send convicts to ease their labour shortage did not remove the stigma. But the west could be seen as a delinquent laggard on a recognised path of development – it used convicts to construct public works and foster pastoralism and agriculture – whereas the plantation economy of the north suggested a more polarised and regressive social order. More than this, it threatened the growing concern for the racial integrity of Australia.

The Aborigines of the north played little part in the plantations but were substantially involved in maritime and other resource-gathering industries such as woodcutting. Through links with Torres Strait and Melanesian islanders, they were incorporated into the colonial economy far more extensively than further south. Their recruitment into the pastoral industry followed a process of invasion that was even more fiercely contested than that which had gone before, and more shocking to the invader because it cost the lives of white women and children. At Fraser's Hornet Bank Station a party of nine was massacred in 1857, and at Cullinlaringo (inland from Rockingham) nineteen in 1861. Here and elsewhere, the whites did not spare Aboriginal women and children. By the 1860s the sheep were giving way to cattle, but still the fighting continued. At Battle Mountain, in far west Queensland, as many as 600 Aboriginal warriors confronted settlers and the native mounted police in 1884. During the 1880s perhaps a thousand Aborigines were killed in the Alice Springs pastoral district of the Northern Territory.

So difficult was the European occupation of the north, and so demanding the circumstances of its pastoral industry, that the occupiers had no alternative but to employ Aboriginal labour. The incorporation of Aboriginal communities into the open-range cattle industry occurred at the point of a gun, but it gave participants a significant role. They constituted a pool of labour from which pastoralists drew the drovers, servants and companions who sustained them and maintained their enterprise. Their situation has generated substantial discussion and debate. Descendants of the pastoral pioneers recalled them as wayward children. Later critics of racial inequality saw them as oppressed and exploited. More recently still, as the northern cattle industry has declined, historians have drawn on the memories of Aboriginal informants to suggest how Aboriginal men and women 'workin' longa tucker' managed both the land and the stockowners as well as the stock.

Further south, where the spread of agricultural settlement reduced these possibilities, Aborigines were becoming wards of the state. The Victorian Board of Protection, established in 1859, saw them as victims to be protected and confined: 'they are, indeed, but helpless children whose state was deplorable enough when this country was their own but is now worse'. Edward Curr, a pastoralist and sympathetic student of *The Australian Race: Its Origins, Languages, Customs* (in four volumes, 1886–87), told a subsequent inquiry that 'The blacks should, when necessary, be coerced, just as we coerce children and lunatics who cannot take care of themselves.' At Coranderrk, in the upper Yarra valley east of Melbourne, 2000 hectares were set aside in 1863 as a self-contained rural settlement under the direction of a white manager. Its residents ran stock, grew crops, operated a sawmill, a dairy and a bakery; but days were set aside for hunting, and artefacts were produced for white purchasers in an early anticipation of cultural tourism.

The urge to collect was premised on an anticipation of imminent disappearance. In Tasmania, the death in 1869 of an Aboriginal man who was taken (and believed himself) to be the last male of his island people resulted in a macabre contest for possession of his skull between the local Royal Society and a doctor working for the Royal College of Surgeons in London. His widow, Truganini, was greatly disturbed by the mutilation and anxious that her body be protected from the men of science; but when she died seven years later, her remains were soon exhumed and the skeleton was put on display at the Tasmanian Museum in 1904. In novels, plays, films and postage stamps she appeared as the 'last Tasmanian', the representative of a sad but inevitable finality. Seventy years later Truganini's skeleton was restored to the Tasmanian Aboriginal community, cremated and the ashes scattered over the waterway in the lands her people had occupied. A British museum returned a shell necklace belonging to her in 1997.

Among those who lived at Coranderrk was Barak, a man of the Wurundjeri clan of the Woiworung people, who as a small boy had witnessed the signing of Batman's 'treaty'. Those associations were now regarded as quaint antiquities, for the custodial regime obliterated the territorial divisions of the indigenous peoples and submerged their distinct identities, languages and social structures into the common category of Aborigines. Given the Christian name 'William' and the title of the 'last king of the Yarra Yarra tribe', Barak produced drawings of aspects of traditional life: corroborees, with figures in possum-skin cloaks; hunting, with men pursuing emus, echidnas, snakes and lyrebirds; ritual fighting between warriors wielding boomerangs and parrying-shields. These closely patterned drawings embodied an ordered social structure integrated with the natural world. Corroborees were not permitted at Coranderrk; in 1887 the governor wished to see one but had to settle for a drawing by Barak. But this was not the only form of

5.2 Barak drew many versions of the corroboree. At the top of the drawing are two rows of dancers with boomerangs. Below them are two fires and in the lower section seated spectators keep the time by clapping, with two men standing over them in possum-skin cloaks. The design echoes the rhythmical pattern of the ceremony. (National Gallery of Victoria)

Aboriginal self-representation. In 1868 Thomas Wills, the inventor of Australian rules football and a survivor of the Cullinlaringo massacre, took a team of Aboriginal cricketers from western Victoria to England. They alternated displays of their prowess with bat and ball with exhibitions of boomerang throwing and dancing. Whether by imitation of the white man's ways or maintenance of their own, a powerful syncretism was resisting absorption and extinction.

Up to 1850 the increase in the European population of Australia matched the decline in the Aboriginal population. After 1850 the number of inhabitants rose rapidly, to over three million by 1888. A torrent of immigration during the first heady years of the gold rush slowed to an irregular stream that again flowed rapidly in the 1880s. The rate of natural increase was also high: a woman who married in the 1850s was likely to bear seven children, one who married in the 1880s, six. Three million humans were more than the land had ever supported and required a more single-minded exploitation of its resources than had previously been attempted.

It was achieved by continuous improvement in the production of commodities for overseas markets. That improvement was in turn made possible by transfers of capital, labour and technology. The heavy investment by British financiers in the pastoral industry and the ready subscription of British savings to public loans raised by the colonies to finance their railways and other utilities allowed for a rapid build-up of the capital stock. The decision of ambitious individuals and families to try their luck in Australia brought additional savings as well as new skills and energies. The introduction of new methods and techniques to pastoralism, agriculture, mining and smelting stimulated a more general dynamic of adaptation and modification.

Sustained over three decades, the cumulative effect of these improvements brought remarkable material prosperity. Australians earned more and spent more than the people of the United Kingdom, the United States or any other country in the second half of the last century. The necessities of life were cheaper, opportunities greater and differences of fortune less pronounced. Not all shared in the bounty. Low wages and irregular earnings pinched the lives of those without capital or work skills, but the capacity to set the working day at just eight hours indicated an economy operating well above subsistence level. First won by building workers in Melbourne in 1856, the eight-hour day was never general. It served rather as a touchstone of colonial achievement. In the global economy created by European expansion, the imperial powers commanded the resources and exploited the populations of Africa, Asia and Latin America for their own benefit. In these colonies of sojourn, the European coloniser was concerned to extract raw materials for his factories; the colonised peoples were at the mercy of changes in technology and products, and the gap was widening. By contrast, settler colonies such as Australia were able to close the gap, to increase local capacity and enjoy its benefits.

The efficiency gains of rural industries left the majority of the workforce free to pursue other activities. Some processed food and made clothing, some were employed in construction and some in the widening range of service industries. An increasing number went into workshops that produced a growing range of items formerly imported from Britain. The growth of towns was a distinctive feature of these prodigious settler colonies. Even during the gold rush and the wave of agricultural settlement that followed, two out of every five colonists lived in towns of 2500 or more inhabitants. By the 1880s towns encompassed half of the population, a far higher proportion than in Britain, higher also than in the United States or Canada. Even smaller towns of perhaps a thousand residents supported a range of urban amenities: hotel, bank, church, newspaper, mill, blacksmith and stores. No less than international trade, the Australian town created an economy of market-minded specialist producers.

In every colony the capital city consolidated its dominance. It was the rail terminus and the principal port, the place where the new-comer disembarked and, after the gold rush, usually stayed. It was the commercial, financial and administrative hub, and used its political leverage to augment control over the hinterland. Brisbane, Sydney, Melbourne, Hobart, Adelaide and Perth, each one of them a coastal city established before the settlement of its inland districts, were separated from each other by at least 800 kilometres and

5.3 Shearers at work on a station near Adelaide. These men
use blade shears, which were replaced by machine shearing at
the end of the century. Some 50,000 men were employed
during the shearing season. (State Library of South Australia)

movement between them was by sea. Perth, the most isolated, was
still hardly more than a township with 9000 inhabitants in 1888;
Hobart languished with 34,000. Brisbane and Adelaide had grown
into large regional towns of 86,000 and 115,000 respectively.
Melbourne, with 420,000, and Sydney, with 360,000, were the
behemoths. For a brief period in 1888 Melbourne boasted the
tallest building in the world. Of the North American cities, only
New York, Chicago and Philadelphia exceeded it.

   Each of the colonial capitals presented the visitor with its own
appearance and atmosphere: torpid Perth on the sunlit estuary

of the Swan River; trim Hobart beneath a brooding mountain; vigorous Brisbane with airy bungalows in lush tropical splendour; the orderly cottages of Adelaide framed by spacious parklands; Sydney's crooked sandstone terraces on the slopes around its majestic harbour; the single-minded flat grid of Melbourne. Pressed for an admiring response to these various places, the visitor was more likely to register their common features. Each metropolis sprawled over a large area with low population densities. Each was surrounded by extensive suburbs, linked to the centre by public transport and served by other utilities, though all but Adelaide lacked sewerage and the primitive sanitation was noisome during the long summers. The houses were more spacious than those of older cities (four rooms or more was now the norm) and there was a higher rate of ownership (half or more were owned by their occupants). This generous residential provision absorbed a high proportion of private capital and cost the occupiers a considerable part of their incomes, but food was cheap and families took pleasure in their own house and garden. The small scale of most enterprises, the infrequency of large factories and the absence of the crowded tenements typical of the great nineteenth-century cities with their teeming masses of peasants-turned-proletarians, all testified to the modest comfort of the Australian commercial city.

Such reflections would scarcely satisfy the colonial need for affirmation. The colonists of the New World, as they increasingly thought of themselves, wished both to emulate and surpass the models of the Old. The cities were their showplaces and they expected the increasing numbers of celebrities, travel writers and commentators who came out to Australia to praise their achievement. Hence Melbourne's Parliament House had to be the grandest in the Empire outside Westminster, the ballroom of its Government House had to be larger than that in Buckingham Palace. 'Marvellous Melbourne', a title conferred by a visiting British journalist, embarked during the 1880s on a heady boom. Its pastoralists had expanded across the Murray River into the southern region of New South Wales, and they spearheaded the Queensland sugar and cattle industries. Its manufacturers took advantage of protective tariffs to achieve economies of scale in the largest local market and sell to other colonies. Its merchants created plantations in Fiji and demolished kauri forests in New Zealand. Its financiers seized control of the rich Broken Hill mine, its stock exchange buzzed with flotations on other minefields. The ready availability of foreign investment inflated a speculative bubble of land companies and building societies.

There was a strong Scottish presence among Melbourne's business class and, in the words of an emigrant Scot, 'There are few more impressive sights in the world than a Scotsman on the make.' Single-minded in the pursuit of wealth, these calculating men marked their success with flamboyant city offices and suburban palaces. Morally earnest, they worshipped in solid bluestone churches and raised stately temperance hotels. Confident and assertive, they assumed their capacity to guide social progress and took pleasure in sport and display. An unsympathetic observer suggested that

in another hundred years the average Australian will be a tall, coarse, strong-jawed, greedy, pushing talented man ... His religion will be a form of Presbyterianism; his national policy a Democracy tempered by the rate of exchange. His wife will be a thin, narrow woman, very fond of dress and idleness, caring little for her children, but without sufficient brain power to sin with zest.

That observer was Marcus Clarke, a literary bohemian who complemented the boastful achievements of Marvellous Melbourne with the exotic images of low life in Outcast Melbourne. The squalor and crime of the inner-city slums, the gambling dens of Chinatown, the dosshouses and brothels of the lanes and alleyways, all just a short distance from the clubs and fashionable theatres, provided bohemians and moral reformers alike with a repertoire of city life as compelling in cosmopolitan ambience as the stock exchange or the sporting oval. Fergus Hume's crime novel, *The Mystery of a Hansom Cab* (1886), became an international bestseller with its interplay of the bright diurnal respectability of Marvellous Melbourne and the shadowy nightlife of Outcast Melbourne, both in their own ways places where people cast off their pasts to assume new identities: 'Over all the great city hung a cloud of smoke like a pall.'

The same process of reinvention was apparent in those more intimate literary products of a settler society, the diary and the letter.

5.4 The man of the house at ease with a magazine while the woman reads the Christmas mail. The lush fernery frames the verandah of their urban villa and the light clothing emphasises the summer warmth of the antipodean setting. (*Illustrated Sydney News*, 23 December 1882)

More than a million people made the voyage out between 1851 and 1888, the great majority by sailing-ship in a passage lasting up to a hundred days. The shipboard journal filled the gap between leaving and arriving. Most diarists displaced the fears and anxieties of the venture into the unknown by composing a record of uneventful routine among unlikely companions forced into temporary contiguity. With disembarkation, this state of suspended animation ended and the journal was set aside. Henceforth the letter became the chief link between separated kith and kin. Letters of introduction were presented to influential patrons, and new arrivals eagerly sought out even the most remote connection. Distance thickened ethnic ties: hence the popularity of Burns suppers, the Welsh *eisteddfod* and the German *liedertafel*. It cost sixpence to send a letter home, and took months for it to reach its destination, but 100,000 were sent back monthly during the 1860s and as many arrived here from Britain and Ireland. At both ends of the oceans, a circle of family, friends and neighbours formed at the arrival of the mail to share the news from the other side of the world.

Uncollected letters at the colonial post offices bore mute testimony to the fragility of these threads. Death, disgrace or despair might terminate communication with relatives back home; alternatively, a long silence might be broken decades later by a despatch from the backblocks or even a dramatic reunion. For Charles Dickens, writing in the middle of the nineteenth century, Australia served as a device to despatch a redundant character, including two of his own sons. For Arthur Conan Doyle, at the century's close, it offered a ready supply of enigmatic returnees suitable either as victim or culprit, whom Sherlock Holmes invariably detected through their recourse to the shrill cry of 'cooee' or some other colonial hallmark. The lost inheritance of the antipodean exile and the windfall legacy from a long-forgotten colonial relative became a stock-in-trade of fictional romance. Within Australia, the restless motion of arrival and departure presented particular problems for those in dependent relationships: special laws and special arrangements were needed for deserted mothers and children.

Colonists responded to these uncertainties by reproducing the familiar forms of civil society. Here they displayed a marked preference for voluntarism, not so much as a check on government as a supplementation of it. For all their reliance on state support in the pursuit of economic development and material comfort, they built their economy and satisfied their needs through the market. The market rewarded those who helped themselves and encouraged exchanges based on self-interest; when extended to other areas of social life in a settler society committed to advanced democracy, the impulse for gratification opened an enlarged space for personal choice. The freedom of the individual, however, was premised on the expectation that it would be exercised responsibly. If the logic of the market posited an impersonal, utility-maximising individualism, those who were incorporated into the market appealed to the popular norms of moral economy to assert their claims for a reasonable share in the fruits of progress. Hence the appeal of the eight-hour day as a protection of labour against excessive toil. That expressive national phrase 'fair dinkum' derives from the English midlands where 'dinkum' means an appropriate measure of work. 'Fair dinkum' and 'fair go' took on wider meaning in Australia to mark out a normative code that applied more widely to other aspects of social interaction.

The social norms were expressed most fully in voluntary dealings where individuals dealt with each other as equals united in common purpose. Voluntarism combined the expectation of individual autonomy with the need for mutuality that was all the more urgent in a land of strangers. Clubs and societies provided for their interests and recreations, sporting associations for their games, lodges for companionship, learned societies for the advancement of knowledge and literary societies for its display, mechanics institutes for self-improvement, friendly societies and mutual benefit organisations for emergencies.

The family, the most intimate form of association, was bound tightly. Both the reduction in the numerical imbalance of men and women, and the continuing legal and economic imbalance between the sexes, made for high rates of family formation. Holy wedlock was now the norm, reinforced by laws that controlled a wife's property and offspring, and provided few opportunities for her to escape an oppressive husband. The couple's fortunes usually depended upon his capacity as a provider and hers as a domestic manager. Yet even within this unequal partnership the voluntary principle still operated. Both bride and groom chose each other freely and quickly established autonomy from parents and in-laws in their own household. In the colonial family, furthermore, the wife typically played a more active role and was more closely involved in crucial decisions. Children, similarly, carried greater responsibilities and enjoyed greater licence.

Even in worship the same tendencies were apparent. It was already established that there was no established religion in Australia, and that all were entitled to worship as they chose. This was in part a recognition of ethnic diversity: most Catholics were Irish, most Presbyterians Scottish, and they demanded equality of status with the Church of England. The colonies had formerly encouraged the activities of the principal Christian denominations with financial support, but even this form of religious assistance was now withdrawn under challenge from the voluntarists. While the Catholic and Anglican churches struggled to provide priests and places of worship over a greatly extended field of activity, the Protestant Nonconformists were quicker to do so. Their more localised, less hierarchical forms of government, and the greater involvement of their laity made for higher rates of worship. The Evangelical religion of the dissenters became the majority faith of active Christians during the second half of the nineteenth century.

In Victoria and South Australia, where Presbyterians, Methodists, Congregationalists, Baptists and Lutherans were strongest, they exerted a powerful influence on society at large: pubs and shops closed on Sunday, few trains ran and public amusements were prohibited. Yet even this stern puritan discipline was under challenge. As early as 1847 the poet Charles Harpur detected an 'individualising process' at work in colonial religious life that could not be stopped. The growing challenge of science and reason weakened the hold of dogma. Some clung to their religion, some cast it off and others felt the loss of faith as a painful but inescapable necessity. The crucial point was that all these alternatives were available. By 1883 even the devout George Higinbotham could see no alternative but to 'set out alone and unaided on the perilous path of inquiry'.

Up to the middle of the century the churches had been the chief providers of education; henceforth the state assumed that role. The withdrawal of state aid from church schools was hastened by rancorous denominational particularism. The creation of an alternative system of elementary education – secular, compulsory and free – was prompted by a desire to create a literate, numerate, orderly and industrious citizenry. 'The growing needs and dangers of society', declared George Higinbotham in 1872, demanded 'a single centre and source of responsible authority in the matter of primary education'; it must of necessity be the responsibility of the state. The provision of state schools in every suburb and bush settlement made a heavy call on the public outlays of the Australian colonies; the teachers and administrators comprised a substantial part of the public service. Centralised, hierarchical and rule-bound, the education departments were prototypes of the bureaucracy for which Australians demonstrated a particular talent.

The universities that were established in Sydney (1850), Melbourne (1853) and Adelaide (1874), similarly, were civic institutions, set up by acts of parliament, supported by public appropriations and controlled by councils largely appointed by government. Melbourne even prohibited the teaching of theology. Their founders hoped that a liberal education in a cloistered setting would smooth rough colonial edges and elevate public life. In practice the universities quickly developed a more utilitarian emphasis on professional training. Preparation of lawyers, doctors and engineers became the chief justification of a restricted and costly higher education.

For that matter, the expectation that the 'common', 'public' or 'state' school (the various cognomens conveyed a wealth of meaning) would redeem the rising generation of colonial children, enhance their capacity and nurture a common purpose proved illusory. Some teachers brought the centrally prescribed curriculum to life. Some pupils caught from it a spark that fired their imaginations. For the most part, however, the government school operated as a custodial institution. The ringing of the bell and marking of the roll instilled habits of regularity. Ill-trained and hard-pressed teachers drilled their charges in the rudiments of reading and writing, instructed them with moral homilies, and released them into the workforce in their early teens. Nor was the goal of a common education, secular, compulsory and free, ever achieved. Catholics insisted on maintaining their own schools. Parents withheld their children so that they could contribute to the family income. Fee-paying Protestant schools filled the gap between elementary and higher education, and in turn reproduced economic and social inequalities.

The state persisted, nevertheless, in its promotion of a common culture. Museums, galleries, libraries, parks, botanical and zoological gardens were among the sites of rational recreation and self-improvement. While imitative of established models (Melbourne's public library began with a blanket order for all the works cited in Gibbon's *Decline and Fall of the Roman Empire*, its gallery with plaster casts of classical friezes and statuary), the civic emphasis gave such institutions a distinctive character, at once high-minded, didactic and popular. Their public function in turn shaped cultural forms. The privately commissioned portraits and domestic paintings of earlier colonial artists gave way to the romantic landscapes of Conrad Martens and Eugene von Guérard and the monumental history canvases of William Strutt. The proliferation of commercial theatre, sport and other recreational activities testified to the extent of discretionary expenditure as well as the time and space to enjoy it.

An English visitor to Melbourne in the late 1850s was struck during her morning perambulations by the sight of a newspaper on every doorstep. The newspaper extended the process of voluntary association far beyond the limits of the public assembly and the spoken word. It exploited technological improvements – the overseas telegraph, the mechanised press, cheap pulp-based paper and rapid, regular transport – to reach a mass audience. It was itself a commodity and enabled buyers and sellers to operate in a market that was no longer confined to a place. It both reported events and interpreted them, mobilised the public as a political force and constituted the reader as a sovereign individual.

The power of the press was unmistakable: more than one Victorian premier submitted the names of his ministers for the approval of David Syme, the majority owner of the Melbourne *Age*. Some thought of journalism as constituting a fourth estate of government, or, since the colonies lacked lords spiritual and temporal, their newspapers might claim an even higher precedence. Even this was not enough for Syme: a lapsed Calvinist and trainee for the ministry, he exercised stern moral vigilance over every aspect of colonial life. 'What a pulpit the editor mounts daily', the *Age* boasted, 'with a congregation of fifty thousand within reach of his voice.' A forthright secularist, land reformer and advocate of protection, he was the most advanced in his liberalism, but other newspaper owners with similar Nonconformist connections lent their support to schemes of material and moral progress as befitted a property-owning democracy. John Fairfax, the owner of the *Sydney Morning Herald*, was a Congregational deacon, and the founder of the Adelaide *Advertiser* a Congregational minister.

The colonies marked their progress in bricks and mortar, but also in amenities, achievements and anniversaries. In 1888 Sydney marked the centenary of the arrival of the First Fleet with a week of celebrations. There was a civic procession and a banquet with portraits of Wentworth and Macarthur looking down on the table of dignitaries. A statue of Queen Victoria was unveiled in the city and a new Centennial Park opened in swampy land to the south. Parcels of bread, cheese, meat, vegetables and tobacco were distributed to the poor, though not to the Aborigines. 'And remind them we have robbed them?' was Henry Parkes's sardonic retort to this suggestion. Parkes himself wanted to raise a pantheon in the new park to house the remains of the nation's honoured dead and the relics of both European and Aboriginal Australia, but his idea met a fate similar to William Wentworth's earlier call for a colonial peerage. 'We have not advanced to that stage of our national life when we have any great heroes to offer', observed a radical critic.

Parkes also proposed that New South Wales be renamed Australia, but this too was mocked into oblivion: one Victorian suggested 'Convictoria' would be more apt. Victoria responded later in the year with a Centennial Exhibition, the most ambitious and expensive of these exercises in colonial promotion modelled on London's Great Exhibition of 1851. Two million visitors inspected the pavilions where every imaginable kind of produce was on display along with decorative and applied arts. There was also a cantata that dramatised the colonial progress from rude barbarity to urban splendour:

> Where the warrigal whimpered and bayed
> Where the feet of the dark hunter strayed
> See the wealth of the world is arrayed.
> Where the spotted snake crawled by the stream
> See the spires of a great city gleam
> Is it all but the dream of a dream?

5.5 The Melbourne international exhibition of 1880–81 was the grandest of all the colonial exhibitions, with two million visitors. The temporary pavilions were subsequently removed, leaving the principal domed building as a lasting monument to 'Marvellous Melbourne'. (National Library of Australia)

Such affirmative comparisons of then and now were a stock-in-trade of colonial writing. That a note of uncertainty should be struck in the centennial year and at the very height of colonial vainglory suggests a remarkable foresight.

6

National reconstruction, 1889–1913

The Jondaryan station occupied 60,000 hectares of grazing country in the Darling Downs district of south Queensland in the 1880s, and employed seventy hands. Twice a year, in late spring and early autumn, some fifty contract workers would assemble there and cut the fleece of more than 100,000 sheep. They lived in primitive quarters close to the shearing-shed, where six days a week from sun-up to sun-down they bent down over the animals and plied their shears. Charges for rations and fines for improperly shorn sheep or other infractions were deducted from their earnings. In the late 1880s the Queensland shearers formed a union to secure better pay and conditions, and by December 1889 it had enrolled 3000 members. The union demanded that pastoralists employ union members only; the Darling Downs employers refused.

The shearers gathered at Jondaryan in September 1889 and set up camp till the manager acceded to their demands. The manager sought non-union labour to break the strike: as one shearer put it, the station 'got a lot of riffraff from Brisbane who "tommy-hawked" the wool off somehow'. But when the wool bales were railed to Brisbane for shipment to England, the waterside workers refused to handle them and declared the wool would 'stay there till the day of judgement and a day or two after' if the owners of Jondaryan did not concede the union conditions. The station manager met with other members of the Darling Downs Pastoralists Association in May 1890, which sent representatives to a conference in Brisbane of pastoralists and shippers who agreed they would employ only union shearers. The 190 Jondaryan bales were then released for shipment.

The victory of the Queensland Shearers Union encouraged the Australian Shearers Union, which covered the southern colonies. It too was challenging the tyranny of the wool kings and pressing for exclusion of non-union labour from the woolsheds. But the pastoralists and shipowners were determined to resist the union demands, and responded to the alliance of rural and urban workers with their own unions of employers. 'The common saying now is the fight must come', announced the president of the Sydney Chamber of Commerce in July 1890, 'and most employers add the sooner the better.' The fight came in the following month when the shipowners told the recently formed Marine Officers Association that, before its wage claims could be discussed, the association's Victorian members must end their affiliation with the Melbourne Trades Hall Council. The marine officers walked off their ships, the waterside workers refused to load them, the coalminers refused to supply coal to ships, the colliery owners locked them out, the pastoralists broke off negotiation with the shearers.

The Maritime Strike, as it became known, spread further. The owners of the Broken Hill mine locked out their workers; the transport workers, who linked the wharf and the railhead to the factory and the shop, were brought out by the Labour Defence Committee; the gas stokers, who provided the city with its power and illumination, refused to work with coal cut by strikebreakers. A city without light! What forces of disorder might that release? 'The question' for Alfred Deakin, the chief secretary of Victoria, 'was whether the city was to be handed over to mob law and the tender mercy of roughs and rascals, or whether it was to be governed, as it had always been governed, under the law in peace and order.' He called out the part-time soldiers of the local defence force, who confronted union pickets at the port of Melbourne and were instructed by their commander that if necessary they should 'fire low and lay them out'. In Sydney the government of Henry Parkes sent special police with firearms to Circular Quay to clear a passage for wool-drays through a menacing crowd. In Queensland, where the pastoralists seized the opportunity in early 1891 to renege on their earlier agreement with the shearers,

6.1 In this contemporary depiction of the Maritime Strike, Capital and Labour confront each other across a precipitous divide. Capital appears as an overbearing Mr Fat, Labour as a lean and resolute working man. (*Bulletin*, 16 August 1890)

Samuel Griffith as premier also called out the defence force and read the riot act.

The employers, the police, the troops and the courts broke the great Maritime Strike before the end of 1890. In 1891 and again in 1894 the pastoralists again defeated the shearers, as did the mine-owners of Broken Hill repeat their victory in 1892 and the coal-owners theirs in 1896. Other, less organised workgroups simply crumbled before their employers' demands: perhaps one in five wage-earners belonged to a union in 1890; by 1896 scarcely one in twenty did. The confrontation between the unions, with their demand for a 'closed shop', and the employers, who insisted on 'freedom of contract', had ended with a decisive victory for the latter. The colonial governments' interpretation of 'law and order' ensured that all attempts to prevent the introduction of non-union strikebreakers failed.

Yet the events of the early 1890s had a lasting effect. The unrest in the cities frightened liberal politicians such as Deakin and Griffith into alarmed repression. The conflict in the countryside resulted in a far more draconian punishment. The Southern Cross flag flew over the camps of striking shearers, who in revenge for their victimisation burned grass, fences, buildings and even riverboats. The bush was put under armed occupation, the ringleaders rounded up and imprisoned for sedition and other crimes. An era of liberal consensus that reconciled sectional interests in material and moral progress had passed. One reason for the alarm was the suddenness of the polarisation of employer and employee. Local associations of masters and craftsmen in particular trades had dealt with each other for decades within a framework of mutual obligations and shared values. Then, in the late 1880s, new unions sprang up to enrol all workers in their industries, and proclaim solidarity with other workers, not just here but around the world – in 1889 the Australian unions subscribed £36,000 to the strike fund of the London dockers. Employers formed their own combinations and they too abandoned the language of moral suasion for the rhetoric of confrontation. An illusion of harmony gave way to open antagonism as the two sides faced each other across the barricades of class warfare.

The liberals were not alone in their disillusionment. For Henry Lawson, a boy from the bush who had joined his mother in Sydney and was caught up in the radical fervour, the attack on workers was shocking and the response defiant:

> And now that we have made the land
> A garden full of promise,
> Old greed must crook his dirty hand
> And come to take it from us.

But Freedom's on the Wallaby,
    She'll knock the tyrants silly,
She's going to light another fire,
    And boil another billy.
We'll make the tyrants feel the sting
    Of those that they would throttle;
They needn't say the fault is ours
    If blood should stain the wattle.

His mother, Louisa Lawson, had fled an unhappy marriage and published Henry's first verse in her magazine, the *Republican* – its mission, 'to observe, to reflect, and then to speak and, if needs be, to castigate'. For mother and son, the need was urgent.

For William Lane, an English migrant who edited the newspaper of the Queensland labour movement, the defeat was final. He had come to Australia as a place of redemption from 'the Past, with its crashing empires, its falling thrones, its dotard races'. Now the serpent of capitalism had invaded the Edenic new world, and the racial and sexual integrity of *The Workingman's Paradise* (as he entitled his novel of the strike) was defiled. In 1893 Lane set sail with more than 200 followers to start anew in Paraguay, where his messianic puritanism soon brought discord in the socialist utopia he called New Australia. One of Lane's followers was a young school-teacher, Mary Cameron, linked romantically to Henry Lawson before she sailed across the Pacific:

O, women of New Australia,
    As our hands were clasped this day,
We knew that the Lord was with us
    And had led us all the way.

She returned in 1902 as Mary Gilmore and accompanied her husband to his family's rural property. Writing sustained her from this 'descent into hell', and in 1908 she became the contributor of a woman's page for the principal union paper, the *Australian Worker*. As poet, commentator and correspondent, Mary Gilmore fashioned herself into a national bard.

For W. G. Spence, the founder of the Australian Shearers Union, the actions of 1890 revealed a different lesson. As he set them down in his memoirs, they brought about *Australia's Awakening*.

6.2 The bush poet, Henry Lawson, is shown humping his swag, with waterbag and billy. Although Lawson had gone briefly up-country in the summer of 1892–93, he lived most of his adult life in Sydney. (National Library of Australia)

First there was stirring of Australian manhood into the fraternity of unionism, which elevated mateship into a religion 'bringing salvation from years of tyranny'. Then came the industrial war, 'which saw the Governments siding with the capitalists', and revealed the true nature of both. This in turn 'brought home to the worker the fact that he had a weapon in his grasp' that could defeat them and bring final emancipation: the vote. Within a year of their defeat in the Maritime Strike, the trade unions of New South Wales formed a Labor Electoral League that won thirty-five of the 141 seats in the Legislative Assembly. Similar organisations emerged in the other colonies and came together at the end of the decade as the Australian Labor Party. By 1914 the Labor Party had held office in every state. Spence himself wrote *Australia's Awakening* from the federal parliament.

It was a dramatic reversal of fortune. Long before the British Labour Party achieved more than token representation, even while the socialist parties of France and Germany were still contending for full legitimacy, the stripling Australian Labor Party won a national electoral majority. New laws allowed a rapid recovery of union membership to one-third of all wage-earners by 1914, a level unprecedented in any other country. That precocious success stunted the Australian labour movement. The achievement of office while still in its infancy turned the Labor Party into a pragmatic, majoritarian electoral organisation. Its socialist founders either moderated their principles or were pushed aside. Its inner-party rules, designed to ensure democratic control, were used to consolidate the dominance of the politicians. As early as 1893 the Queensland shearer Thomas Ryan, who had been charged with conspiracy in 1891 and elected to parliament in 1892, proclaimed the results: 'The friends are too warm, the whiskey too strong, and the seats too soft for Tommy Ryan. His place is out among the shearers on the billabongs.'

Ryan had been chosen as the Labor candidate by workers gathered under a spreading gum tree that stood at the entrance to the railway terminus at Barcaldine in central Queensland, where just a year earlier striking shearers and shed-hands congregated to read the jeremiads of William Lane. It was known as the Tree of Knowledge and its forbidden fruit was parliamentarism. The tree still stands, a hallowed symbol of Labor mythology, though its remaining boughs are thinly covered with leaves and the decrepit trunk is now reinforced by concrete. For when Ryan returned to his workmates, there was no lack of volunteers to take up the burden of parliamentary duties. The creation of this political movement out of the wreckage of a crushing industrial defeat presaged a new force that would in turn impel the earlier factional groupings to form a single anti-Labor Party. The mobilisation of class loyalties affected every aspect of public life: the differences so clearly emphasised in the events of the Maritime Strike produced a solidarity that was almost tribal in its intensity, the workers determined that they should prevail, the capitalists adamant that they should not. The prescient Alfred Deakin predicted accurately in 1891 that 'the rise of the labour party in politics is more significant and more cosmic than the Crusades'.

The wave of strikes and lockouts occurred as the years of prosperity and growth ran out. Wool prices had been slipping since the 1870s (the drive of the pastoralists for greater productivity underlay the conflict in that industry) and exports fell from nearly 30 per cent of domestic production to less than 15 per cent by the late 1880s. There was an increased reliance on British investment both for government expenditure on public works and for private urban construction. Both were marked by excessive optimism, cronyism and dubious business practice, for the same promoters were active in the cabinet and boardrooms, and easy credit fuelled the land boom that reached its peak in Melbourne. By 1890 the cost of servicing the foreign debt had reached 40 per cent of export earnings. After the London money market learned in that year that defaults by several South American governments were jeopardising a leading merchant bank, it refused new loans to Australia. Then some of the riskier land companies failed, and the drain on bank deposits became a run. In the autumn of 1893 most of the country's banks suspended business, plunging commerce and industry into chaos. To add insult to injury, many of the principal financiers had new laws introduced to escape their creditors. A deep suspicion of the 'money power' was a lasting legacy of the depression of the 1890s.

Between 1891 and 1895 the economy shrank by 30 per cent. Unemployment reached 30 per cent of skilled labour in 1893. Among the unskilled the proportion thrown out of work was higher, but no statistics were kept since there was no systematic provision for their support. Rather, there was charitable assistance for women and children, and work schemes for men, both pitifully inadequate to cope with the need. Some fled to Western Australia, where the discovery of new gold deposits brought fresh British investment and attracted 100,000 easterners. Some tramped the bush in search of work or handouts, some stayed in the city to eke out a living from intermittent earnings supplemented by scavenging, recycling and cultivating their domestic plots (for there were high vacancy rates in the housing market). Immigration came to a halt after 1891: there was a net increase of just 7000 during the rest of the decade. Australian incomes did not regain their pre-depression level until well into the following decade. A sharp decline in rates of marriage and childbirth indicated the extent of poverty and insecurity. An entrenched caution and aversion to dependence were additional long-term effects of the depression.

After depression came drought. From 1895 to 1903 a run of dry years parched the most heavily populated eastern half of the continent. The land was already under pressure as the result of heavy grazing and repeated cropping. After supporting human life for tens of thousands of years, the country had been conquered and remade in less than a century. The sudden change of land use from subsistence to gain, the introduction of new species and practices determined by an international flow of credit, supplies and markets, brought drastic environmental simplification, imbalance and exhaustion. The signs were already apparent in habitat destruction by exotic plants and animals. By the 1880s rabbits, which had ruined pastoral properties in Victoria, South Australia and New South Wales, spread north into Queensland and in the 1890s they crossed the Nullarbor Plain into Western Australia. When drought killed off the last of the ground cover, the land turned to dust that swallowed up dams, buried fences and rose into the air. The largest dust storm in late 1902 covered the eastern States with a red cloud that blotted the sun and even crossed the Tasman to envelop New Zealand, 3000 kilometres to the east. Between 1891 and 1902 sheep numbers were halved.

Discord, depression, drought. The horsemen of the apocalypse rode over the continent and trampled the illusions of colonial progress. Yet from these disasters arose a national legend that exercised a powerful hold on succeeding generations. It was created by a new generation of writers and artists who adapted received techniques into consciously local idioms for local consumption. In their search for what was distinctively Australian they turned inwards, away from the city with its modern ills of a derivative civilisation, to an idealised interior. This place was no longer a tranquil Arcadian retreat. In the paintings of Tom Roberts and Fred McCubbin it was a landscape of dazzling light. In the ballads and stories of Henry Lawson it was harsh and elemental. The green tones of the pastoral romance gave way to the brown of the bush; the squatter and the homestead were overtaken by the shearer, the boundary riders, and other itinerant bush workers, whom a visiting Englishman described in 1893 as 'the one powerful and unique national type produced in Australia'. With the nomad bushman were associated fierce independence, fortitude, irreverence for authority, egalitarianism and mateship – qualities that were no sooner punished in the war against the bush unions than they were claimed for the nation at large.

The weekly *Bulletin* magazine was the chief medium of this national self-image. Founded in 1880, it practised an exuberant and irreverent mockery of bloated capitalists, monocled aristocrats and puritan killjoys, while it championed republicanism, secularism, democracy and masculine licence. From 1886, when the *Bulletin* threw its pages open to readers, thousands of the beneficiaries of mass education were drawn into an enlarged republic of letters. Here Lawson and A. B. Paterson jousted in verse, the one a refugee from the horrors of the outback, the other a pastoralist's son turned city lawyer who extolled its plenitude – though Paterson also wrote 'Waltzing Matilda', the song of the tragic swagman who probably plunged into the billabong to evade the troopers because he was an organiser of the striking shearers. Here too appeared Steele Rudd, with his bucolic jocularity at the expense of the hapless Dad and Dave on their selection; Barbara Baynton, a selector's wife, who wrote of the malevolence of the bush and the brutality of its men, and John Shaw Neilson, who spun songs of spare beauty out of his grim lot as a failed selector's son.

The outback is never kind to women and children. Lawson's laconic irony sustains the idealism and sentimentality of masculine bonding, but his most powerful stories tell of women with absent husbands who are left to fight the terrors of the bush. Nature in Australia has a dark side that eventually drives everyone mad, and defies ordinary logic. Just nineteen years old, Miles Franklin related

My Brilliant Career (1901) as a rebel against her fate as the daughter of a dairy farmer: 'There is no plot in this story, because there has been none in my life.' Joseph Furphy, failed selector, bullock-driver and finally a wage-worker in his brother's foundry, opened *Such Is Life* (1903), the most complexly nomadic of the novels of the period, with the exultation 'Unemployed at last!' He sent the manuscript to the editor of the *Bulletin* in 1897 with the characterisation 'temper democratic: bias, offensively Australian'. Yet even Lawson, the most gifted of the radical nationalist writers, soon retreated into the platitudes of 'The Shearers' (1901):

> No church-bell rings them from the Track,
>   No pulpit lights their blindness –
> 'Tis hardship, drought and homelessness
>   That teaches those Bushmen kindness ...
>
> They tramp in mateship side by side –
>   The Protestant and 'Roman' –
> They call no biped lord or 'sir',
>   And touch their hats to no man!

The bush legend was just that, a myth that enshrined lost possibilities, but one that could be tapped repeatedly for new meaning. Even in the 1980s it allowed an unsophisticated crocodile hunter to triumph over hard-boiled New Yorkers in a Hollywood feature film.

Crocodile Dundee was the creation of a street-wise former maintenance worker on the Sydney Harbour Bridge. The bush legend of the 1890s, similarly, was shaped by an emergent urban intelligentsia, men who clung to the city despite their dissatisfactions with its philistine respectability. Lawson had grown up in the bush but his knowledge of the outback derived from a brief foray in the summer of 1892–93 into south-west Queensland. 'You have no idea of the horrors of the country out here', he wrote to his aunt; 'Men tramp and beg and live like dogs.' The *plein air* artists of the Heidelberg school ventured just a few kilometres beyond the suburbs of Melbourne to set up camp and paint the scrub. Tom Roberts executed the iconic pastoral work, 'Shearing the Rams', in his city studio after a short trip up-country. Charles Conder used Sydney Harbour and its adjacent waterways for his impressionist paintings. The *Bulletin* was known as 'the bushmen's bible' but created and produced in Sydney by alienated intellectuals who projected their desires onto an imagined rural interior and allowed city readers to partake vicariously in the dream of an untrammelled masculine solidarity.

All settler societies have their frontier legends. Whether it be the sturdy independence found in the American West by Frederick Jackson Turner, or the escape from bondage that Boers commemorated in their Great Trek, the white men attach themselves to the land in a nationally formative relationship. In challenging such national myths, revisionist historians do not dispel the aura of national origins so much as rework them to discover alternative foundations. Thus the Australian feminist historians who contest the misogyny of the legend of the 'nineties still see the nomad bushman as emblematic, only they interpret his freedom as a repudiation of domestic responsibilities. The masculinity the *Bulletin* celebrated was a licence to roam. Its writers and cartoonists mocked those who would hobble the lone hand: the nagging housewife, the prim parson and the assembled forces of wowserdom (wowser was an expressive local term for those who sought to stamp out alcohol, tobacco and all other pleasures). The principal contest at the turn of the century, these feminist critics suggest, was not the class conflict between capitalists and workers but rather the more elemental conflict between men and women.

The women's movement that emerged alongside the labour movement at the end of the century shared many of its assumptions. Early feminists such as Louisa Lawson, with early socialists, dwelt on the progressive character of Australian society. They celebrated the egalitarianism of Australian men and the comparatively good position of women. They also regarded Australia as free of the Old World evils of class, poverty or violence, and correspondingly free to explore novel possibilities. Just as local republicans drew on American precedents, agrarian radicals on the ideas of Henry George and socialists on the writings of Edward Bellamy, so the women's movement was strongly influenced by the Woman's Christian Temperance Union, which crossed the Pacific in the early 1880s. The movement sought to advance women and reform society by purifying domestic and public life of masculine excess. It thus sought a range of measures – temperance, laws against gambling, control of prostitution, an increase in the age of consent, prevention of domestic violence – to protect women from predatory men. Conscious of their lack of political power, these women campaigned for female suffrage, and between 1894 and 1908 they won the right to vote for the national and every colonial legislature.

The leaders of this suffrage movement were educated and independent women. Rose Scott in Sydney and Vida Goldstein in Melbourne acquired organisational skills in public philanthropy that they then applied to the cause of sexual emancipation. For both of them it was a full-time activity that precluded marriage and motherhood. Mary Gilmore explained her own lapse from participation in the campaign as the consequence of domesticity:

> I gang nae mair t'lecture ha'
>   I sit nae mair 'neath Mistress Scott;
> I mak' a denner jist f'r twa,
>   An' sit beside a bairnie's cot.

There were strains, also, between the feminists of the labour movement, who sought a more equal partnership to redeem the working-class family from hardship, and the more assertive modernism that would remove the impediments to autonomy. Higher education, professional careers, less constrictive clothing and even the freedom of the bicycle were among the hallmarks of the 'new woman'.

The appearance of the 'new woman' signalled a contest as fierce in its conduct and far-reaching in its consequences as that fought out between labour and capital. It did not give rise to a new political party, and all early attempts by women to win parliamentary representation failed, for the sex war was fought out on different terrain. The leader of Labor Party announced in 1891 that his comrades had entered the New South Wales legislative assembly 'to make and unmake social conditions'; the women's movement stayed out of parliament to remake the family and sexual conditions. In both cases a fierce assault brought home the illusory character of customary expectations. A heightened consciousness of distinctive interests produced a movement that sought to recover just entitlements with novel demands. The labour movement fought for the rights of labour, the women's movement for control of women's bodies.

An infamous rape case in 1886 on waste land at Mount Rennie in Sydney, close to the site of the Centennial Park, served as the Jondaryan incident in this contest between the sexes. A sixteen-year-old orphan girl searching for work was waylaid by a cab driver, taken there and pack-raped by eighteen men. There was an upsurge in such crimes in the 1880s, suggestive of heightened sexual tension, but this one was unusual in that the culprits were prosecuted, four hanged and seven others sentenced to hard labour for life – the Mount Rennie case was as unusual and as controversial as the Myall Creek case fifty years earlier. Those who sought to curb the animal instincts of men did not rest there but extended their campaign to crimes against women within the home. From denouncing the evil of domestic violence they moved to question the very basis of marriage as a trade in sexual labour, and to demand that women should have control over their fertility. Here they were swimming with the demographic tide – there was a marked decline in marriage during the depression decade, and an even sharper decline in reproduction – though that did not prevent the men who conducted a royal commission on the birthrate in 1903 from blaming women for neglecting their national duty as breeders and domesticators.

Women had an effective response to that accusation. The interests of the nation would best be served by ensuring that children were born voluntarily and raised in homes purged of men's irresponsibility and excess. It was for this reason that feminists sought to restrain the men who frittered their earnings on gambling, tobacco and alcohol, and returned from the pub to tyrannise their dependants. Masculinity had to be tamed of its selfish, aggressive qualities in order for the lone hand to be brought to his duty as a reliable breadwinner and helpmate. Femininity had to be heeded for its superior moral status to purify the family circle and exalt national life. Not all Australian feminists followed this domestic logic to its extreme conclusion of separate spheres. They still argued for women's rights of education, employment and public participation. They also created their own voluntary associations that infused civic life with nurturing maternalist values celebrated by the Woman's Christian Temperance Union:

Queen of the Home, true friend and help meet,
    Guide and mother of the race;
Wide her sphere, and great her mission.
    Naught her influence can efface.

The contest between the sexes at the turn of the century did not displace men from positions of dominance in politics, religion and business, but it decisively altered their prerogatives.

The labour and the women's movements were movements of protest. With the end of an era of uninterrupted growth, the belief in progress faltered. With the failure of existing institutions to maintain harmony, the liberal consensus fractured. An optimism grounded in common interests and shared values yielded to disillusionment and conflict. Socialists and feminists called on the victims of oppression to rise up against the masters and men who exploited and abused them. The goal was to reconstruct society and heal the divisions of class and gender; the effect was to mobilise powerful collectivities with separate and distinctive loyalties – socialism and feminism were universal in scope and international in operation. In response to these challenges an alternative collectivity was asserted, that of the nation. It was institutionalised during the 1890s through a process that produced a federal Commonwealth with restricted powers, but behind that limited compact lay the stronger impulses of tradition and destiny. Out of the crisis of colonial coherence, a binding Australian nationhood was created.

Australians can hardly be accused of rushing into federation. The process can be dated back to the early 1880s, when the designs of the French and Germans in the South-West Pacific alarmed the colonies, but New South Wales's suspicion of Victoria prevented anything more than a weak and incomplete Federal Council. In 1889 the aged and previously obstructive premier of New South Wales, Henry Parkes, made a bid for immortality as the father of federation by issuing a call for closer ties. That brought representatives of the colonial parliaments to a Federal Convention in Sydney in 1891. They drafted a constitution, but their colonial parliaments failed to approve it. Federation revived when the colonies authorised the direct election of delegates to a new convention and agreed in advance to submit its proposals to popular referendum. The second Federal Convention met from 1897 to 1898, but only the four south-eastern colonies proceeded to referendums and only three produced the necessary affirmative vote. Further concessions were required before New South Wales did so in a second referendum and the outlying laggard colonies of Queensland and Western Australia came in. The proclamation of the Commonwealth on 1 January 1901 in Centennial Park, Sydney, came more than a decade after Parkes had appealed to 'the crimson thread of kinship'.

For Alfred Deakin, the leading Victorian who pursued union as a sacred duty, 'its actual accomplishment must always appear to have been secured by a series of miracles'. For Edmund Barton, the champion in New South Wales and the first national prime minister, the winning of 'a nation for a continent and a continent for a nation' was a surpassing achievement. Federation was heralded in song and verse. It stimulated the capacity for grandiloquence on

6.3 Edmund Barton and Alfred Deakin were the leaders of the federal movement in New South Wales and Victoria, and the first two prime ministers of the new Commonwealth. Barton sits on the left in marmoreal dignity, while Deakin's informal pose suggests a more mercurial temperament. (National Library of Australia)

which Australians draw whenever they stand to make public pronouncements with an eye to posterity.

The actual compact was far more modest. The constitution blended the British system of responsible government with the United States model of federalism: the colonies (henceforth States) assigned certain specified powers to a bicameral national parliament, the House of Representatives representing the people and the Senate the States, with the government responsible to the popular lower house. Much of the protracted federal debate was taken up with enumerating those powers and balancing the fears of the less populous States with the ambitions of the more populous. All of the States made elaborate calculation of the effect of the union on their own fortunes. Merchants, manufacturers and farmers considered how they would fare when Australia was turned into a common market. As Deakin recognised, 'Few were those in each colony who made genuine sacrifices to the cause without thought or hope of gain.'

Nor did the colonists wrest independence from imperial control. During this period the British government encouraged the settler colonies of Canada, New Zealand, Australia and South Africa to amalgamate into more coherent and capable dominions, self-governing in their internal affairs while consistent in their imperial arrangements. The new designation, Dominion, was adopted in 1907 at a colonial conference in London that determined these gatherings would henceforth be known as imperial conferences. So London fostered Australian federation, the Colonial Office shaped its final form, and the Commonwealth constitution took legal force as a statute of the British parliament. That fact alone alienated local republicans, while the process of federation was initiated too early for members of the labour or women's movement to participate and shape it. In contrast to the earlier confederations of the United States and Germany, Australia undertook no war of independence or incorporation. Unlike the Italians, it experienced no Risorgimento. The turnout in the federal referendums was lower than for parliamentary elections; in only one colony, Victoria, and that narrowly, did a majority of eligible citizens cast their votes in favour of federation.

Yet for the federal founders and for those present-day patriots who would revive the civic memory, those plebiscites were all-important. They installed the people as the makers of the Commonwealth and popular sovereignty as its underlying principle – a principle the courts have now come to recognise in their interpretation of the constitution. According to this view, the politicians had been entrusted with the national task but botched it. The work of the first Federal Convention of 1891 languished in the colonial parliaments. Then came an unofficial gathering in 1893 at the Murray River town of Corowa, on the border between New South Wales and Victoria, of representatives of local federal leagues and branches of the Australian Natives Association, a voluntary society restricted to some of those born in the country. That gathering devised the alternative procedure that would bring success: the people themselves would elect the makers of a new federal arrangement, the people would adopt it, the people would be inscribed in its preamble and included in the provisions for its amendment. This was a unique achievement. In the words of one celebrant, it was 'the greatest miracle of Australian political history'.

Perhaps it was, but it was also expressive of national prejudices. The unofficial gathering at Corowa was orchestrated by politicians. The man who proposed the new approach there and enunciated the principle 'that the cause should be advocated by the citizen and not merely by politicians' was himself a politician. All but one of the delegates elected to the second Federal Convention had parliamentary experience; two-thirds had ministerial experience, a quarter as premiers. Federation was an inescapably political act but one that Australians, with their disregard for politics, preferred to see otherwise, and their representatives were happy to perform through a sleight of hand. The politicians, having impugned their own calling, called forth a voice that could restore its legitimacy: they reinstated the people as a disembodied presence capable of an altruism that they themselves could not achieve.

These people were Australians but that national identity was itself undergoing reconstruction to become more prescriptive. The new nation was shaped by external threat and internal anxiety, the two working together to make exclusive racial possession the essential condition of the nation-state. The external threat came initially from rival European powers. Spain and the Netherlands had preceded the British into the Pacific in the earlier era of imperial expansion; now France, Germany and the United States staked their claims as the principal powers scrambled to take possession of the last unclaimed portions of the globe. The Australian colonies, which had their own sub-imperial ambitions in the region, pressed Britain to forestall the interlopers but Britain was already feeling the strain of its imperial burden.

The maintenance of the British Empire absorbed an increasing effort. As Britain faced sharper competition from the manufacturers, traders and financiers of ascendant industrial economies, it turned to easier fields in its colonies and dominions. But cheap colonial produce, ready dominion markets and lucrative careers in imperial administration imposed their own cost. A free-trade empire required a large military expenditure. The cost of the Royal Navy constituted an effective tariff on the cheap imports that sustained the workshop of the world. That cost increased as European powers stepped up the pace of the arms race, and Britain was forced to concentrate more of its naval strength closer to home. It therefore expected its settler dominions to become more self-sufficient. In 1870 it had withdrawn the last garrisons from Australia, leaving the colonies to raise their own troops; an adverse British report in 1889 on the capacity of these militia forces was one stimulus for federation. The Royal Navy remained as the guarantor of Australian security, and forts constructed at the entrance of major ports were meant to hold off an attacking force until relief arrived. In 1887 the colonies agreed to meet part of the cost of a British squadron in Australian waters. The British Admiralty was so unimpressed by the colonies' own superannuated warboats that they denied them the right to fly the White Ensign.

If the Empire no longer extended to the antipodes as securely as the nervous settlers wanted, they must offer themselves in its overseas service. They had begun to do so in the 1860s as volunteers alongside British troops and pakeha New Zealanders in a war against the indigenous Maori. Their next act of assistance, to a British expeditionary force in Sudan in 1885, was insubstantial and inglorious. The contingent sent to South Africa between 1899 and 1902 was more substantial – 16,000 Australian troops assisted the British in putting down Dutch settlers there – but scarcely earned martial glory. Again in 1900 the colonies sent a contingent to China to assist the international forces to quell a rebellion against the European presence. All four of these overseas wars, it should be noted, began as local risings against foreign control, and in all four the Australians fought on the imperial side against national independence.

The last of them was the least remarked and probably the most eloquent of Australian fears. By the early twentieth century Asia had displaced Europe as the source of military threat in the national imagination. A rash of invasion novels appeared at this time in which the country was no longer besieged by French or Russian battleships but rather overrun by hordes of Orientals. The fear was fed by the growing economic and military power of Japan, which imitated Western techniques to defeat China and occupy Korea in 1895. An Anglo-Japanese treaty in 1902, which allowed Britain to reduce its own naval strength in the Pacific, increased the Australian concern. The Japanese navy's destruction of a Russian fleet in 1905 increased it further. Thwarted in his efforts to increase the British presence in the Pacific, Alfred Deakin as prime minister invited the 'Great White Fleet' of the United States to visit Australia and began the construction of an expensive Royal Australian Navy. By 1914 it was established, along with a system of compulsory military training.

More than this, the Australian fear of invasion played on the Asian presence in Australia. There had been earlier explosions of racial violence, most notably against the Chinese on the goldfields. Antagonism revived in 1888 with the arrival of a vessel from Hong Kong carrying Chinese immigrants who were turned away under threat of mob action from both Melbourne and Sydney. The controversy touched national sensitivities because Hong Kong was a British colony and the Colonial Office was antagonistic to immigration restriction based on overt racial discrimination. For nationalists, the alien menace therefore served as a reminder of imperial control; hence the adoption by the *Bulletin* in this same year of the slogan 'Australia for the Australians'. For trade unionists, the Chinese were cheap labour and a threat to wage standards. For ideologues such as William Lane, they were sweaters and debauchers of white women. Even the high-minded Alfred Deakin judged that the strongest motive for federation was 'the desire that we should be one people, and remain one people, without the admixture of other races'.

Yet racial exclusion did not require a break with Britain, nor did it rely on Commonwealth legislation. Racism was grounded in imperial as well as national sentiment, for the champions of the Empire proclaimed the unity of the white race over the yellow and the black. Hence the claim of Charles Pearson that 'we are guarding the last part of the world in which the higher races can live and increase freely for the higher civilization'. Pearson, a costive English intellectual who migrated to Australia for his health and practised both education and politics with a melancholic rectitude, sounded the alarm in a global survey that he proposed to call *Orbis Senescens* – for he was convinced that civilisation was exhausting the vitality of the European peoples. His London publisher thought that title too gloomy so it appeared in 1893 as *National Life and Character: A Forecast*, and impressed the future United States president Theodore Roosevelt with the urgency of its warning. Hence also the claim of Alfred Deakin, Pearson's former pupil, that the visit of the Great White Fleet showed that 'England, America and Australia will be united to withstand yellow aggression.' Australians did not invent this crude xenophobic terminology – it was, after all, an imperial bard who warned of 'lesser breeds without the law' – but their inclination to overlook the multiracial composition of the Empire was a domestic indulgence that only a dutiful Dominion could afford.

In 1897 the Colonial Office persuaded the Australian premiers at a conference in London to drop explicit discrimination against other races in favour of an ostensibly non-discriminatory dictation test for immigrants, a device used by other British dominions to achieve the same result. Since a foreigner could be tested in any European language, the immigration official need only select an unfamiliar one to ensure failure. This was the basis of the Immigration Restriction Act passed by the new Commonwealth parliament in 1901, but by then Asian immigration was negligible. White Australia was not the object of federation but rather an essential condition of the idealised nation the Commonwealth was meant to embody. Deakin spelt it out during the debate on the Immigration Restriction Act:

The unity of Australia is nothing, if that does not imply a united race. A united race means not only that its members can intermix, intermarry and associate without degradation on either side, but implies one inspired by the same ideas, an aspiration towards the same ideals, of a people possessing the same general cast of character, tone of thought . . .

The founding conference of the federal Labor Party adopted White Australia as its primary objective; in 1905 it provided the rationale with its commitment to 'The cultivation of an Australian sentiment based upon the maintenance of racial purity and the development in Australia of an enlightened and self-reliant community'.

Ideals, character, tone of thought, sentiment, enlightenment, self-reliance, community. These virtues sound as desirable at the end of the twentieth century as they were at the beginning. The dissonance comes from their association with racial exclusiveness. We might better grasp their plausibility if we transfer them from race to culture. Our respect for the language, beliefs, customs and cohesiveness of ethnic groups is a pluralist one and purged of biological undertones of genetic determinism, but it still accepts these markers as supporting a collective identity that provides meaning and purpose to those who share it.

White Australia was therefore an ideal but it was also a falsehood. The Immigration Restriction Act was used to turn away non-European settlers but it left substantial numbers of Chinese, Japanese, Indians and Afghans already here. Commonwealth legislation passed in 1901 provided for repatriation of Pacific islanders from the Queensland sugar industry but long-term residents were allowed to stay as the result of protests. New immigrants from Java and Timor were allowed to enter the pearling industry. Non-European traders, students and family members continued to land at Australian ports. Since racial uniformity was an illusion, the promise of equality was also a lie. Discriminatory laws denied naturalisation to non-Europeans, excluded them from welfare benefits, shut them out of occupations, and in some States refused them land tenure.

Above all, White Australia was a denial of the country's original inhabitants. They were absent from the ceremonies that marked the advent of the Commonwealth. They were eliminated from the art and literature that served the new national sentiment: while earlier landscape painters had frequently incorporated groups of natives to authenticate the natural wilderness, the Heidelberg school removed them to attach the white race to its harsh and elemental patrimony. Aborigines were even deprived of their indigeneity by the members of the Australian Natives Association, who appropriated that term for the locally born Europeans. Yet they remained to discomfort the white conscience. Compassion came more readily to the usurper than acceptance, for fatalism lightened the burden of charity. Earlier humanitarians had been prepared to ease the passing of those they had wronged. In gloomy anticipation they proclaimed a duty to smooth the pillow of the dying race.

Now, as Darwinian science displaced evangelical Christianity and natural law as a source of authority, the scientist provided new confirmation of this forecast. Seen from the perspective of evolutionary biology, Australia had been cut off from the process of continuous improvement brought about by the competition for survival, and constituted a living museum of relic forms. Separated by such a wide gulf from the march of progress, its original people were incapable of adaptation and therefore doomed to extinction. Census data seemed to support this theory. They presented a downward trend, to just 67,000 Aboriginal natives in 1901. But several of the States failed to enumerate all their Aboriginal inhabitants and the Commonwealth constitution excluded them from the national census (so that their numbers would not be used for purposes of electoral representation). More than this, the State counts excluded a significant proportion of the Aboriginal population that was incorporated into the larger society – in effect, these governments confirmed the expected disappearance of the indigenous people by defining some of them out of existence.

Again, the process enlisted science to validate coercion. Between 1890 and 1912 every State government took over what remained of the mission settlements by making Aborigines wards of the state. New agencies, usually called protection boards, were empowered to prescribe their residence, determine conditions of employment, control marriage and cohabitation, and assume custody of children. The actual use of these powers varied – Queensland and Western Australia, with the largest Aboriginal populations, had the most extensive reserves and settlements and the most authoritarian regimes – and many Aborigines minimised their exposure to them. The forcible separation of children from parents ensured that. In this horrifying practice the government drew on the doctrine of race as a genetic category. If Aborigines were held incapable of supporting themselves, those born of Aboriginal and European parents were believed to possess a greater capacity. If denied assistance and removed from the reserves, they might be expected to support themselves and even produce progeny no longer recognisably Aboriginal within a couple of generations. It would thus be possible to reduce or close down the reserves as the residual numbers held there declined. In making these judgements the protectors employed a vocabulary of 'full-blood', half-caste', 'quadroon' and 'octoroon'; more often they worked by estimations of degrees of 'whiteness', which was taken as synonymous with capacity and acceptability. They did not encourage miscegenation – several of the protectors insisted that their staff must be married men – but once it occurred they believed it would 'breed out' the Aboriginal blood.

Such a programme was beset by contradictions. Ostensibly protective, the settlements and missions were premised on the demise of their residents. Others, on the other hand, were forcibly evicted and expected to interact and intermarry with non-Aborigines. In sharp contrast to other white-supremacist settler societies, there was no uncrossable barrier between black and white. All of this was premised on the elimination of Aboriginality, the abandonment of language, custom and ritual, and the severing of kinship ties so that absorption could be complete. It was an impossible condition, and for present-day Aborigines it constitutes a policy of genocide. So it was in the literal sense, except that the genes were to be diluted rather than the basis of mass execution in the manner made infamous by the Holocaust. The more common accusation is of cultural genocide, meaning the destruction of a distinctive way of life, and that undoubtedly was intended, though it is a further irony that the scientists who justified this objective were also the collectors and recorders of Aboriginal culture who made it possible for some of the Aboriginal survivors to reclaim that culture as their own.

The proclamation of the Commonwealth on the first day of the new century fused national and imperial ceremony. In a competition to design a national flag that drew 32,000 entries, five people shared the prize by imposing the British one on the corner of a Southern Cross. A coat of arms, supported by a kangaroo and emu, also had to wait until 1908, backed after 1912 by two sprays of wattle. First the Test cricket team and then other sporting representatives adopted the green and gold of the gum tree and the wattle as the national colours. Australian flora and fauna were popular decorative motifs in the federation period, with the wattle to the fore as an Australian equivalent of the Canadian maple. The golden wattle went with golden fleece, golden grain, golden ore and the gold in the hearts of the people. According to the Wattle Day League, it stood for 'home, country, kindred, sunshine and love'. But Empire Day had been introduced some years earlier as part of a conscious strengthening of imperial links. Nationalism and imperialism were no longer rivals. You could, like Alfred Deakin, be an 'independent Australian Briton'.

Britain provided this independent Australia with a portion of its own imperial responsibilities when it handed over its portion of New Guinea as the Commonwealth territory of Papua in 1902. South Australia did the same with the Northern Territory in 1911. Meanwhile federal parliamentarians selected a site for a national capital on a grassy plain in the high country between Sydney and Melbourne and the members of the cabinet considered various names for it: Wattle City, Empire City, Aryan City, Utopia. In the end they settled on a local Aboriginal word, Canberra. An American architect, Walter Burley Griffin, won the competition to design the capital. He conceived a garden city with grand avenues linking its governmental and civic centres, and concentric patterns of residential suburbs set in forest reserves and parks. But bureaucrats hampered the execution of his design, which was still incomplete in 1920 when responsibility was transferred to a committee. Melbourne, a monument to nineteenth-century mercantile imperialism, remained the temporary national capital for the first quarter of the twentieth century.

6.4 These trade marks for soap, wine, poison, sporting goods and baking powder were all devised in the early years of the twentieth century when the new nation fashioned native symbols. (Mimmo Cozzolino and G. Fysh Rutherford, *Symbols of Australia*, Ringwood, Vic.: Penguin, 1980)

The Australian nation was shaped by the fear of invasion and concern for the purity of the race. These anxieties converged on the female body as nationalist men returned obsessively to the safety of their women from alien molestation, while doctrines of racial purity, no matter how scientific, rested ultimately on feminine chastity. Women participated in this preoccupation with their own maternalist conception of citizenship, which took emancipation from masculine tyranny as a necessary condition of their crucial contribution to the nation-state. A woman's personal and bodily integrity thus served as a further condition of her admission to civic status, as in the Commonwealth legislation in 1902 which gave all white women the vote. But the same legislation disenfranchised Aborigines, who were deemed to lack both the autonomy and the capacity to make such a contribution. Some feminists regretted this Faustian compact, just as they criticised the treatment of Aboriginal women who were subjected to sex slavery of a particularly clear and offensive nature. The vulnerability of Aboriginal women to white predators and the denial of their children, the very devices that were expected to bring about a White Australia, were for these white women intolerable iniquities against the institution of motherhood. Here again maternalist citizenship was at odds with the masculine nationalism proclaimed by the *Bulletin* when in 1906 it changed its slogan 'Australia for the Australians' to 'Australia for the White Man'.

White Australia, Alfred Deakin stated in 1903, 'is not a surface, but it is a reasoned policy which goes to the roots of national life, and by which the whole of our social, industrial and political organisation is governed'. He spoke as leader of the Protectionist Party, which held government with the support of the Labor Party. There were three parties in the national parliament until 1909, Protectionist, Free Trade and Labor, and none commanded a majority. Except for a brief interval, the Protectionists and Labor alternated in office with the qualified support of the other, and a sufficient measure of agreement on policy to cause the Free Traders to rename themselves the Anti-Socialists for the 1906 election, though with no greater success. The social, industrial and political forms of the new

Commonwealth were therefore worked out by a consensus that spanned the manufacturing interests and progressive middle-class followers of protectionist liberalism with the collectivism of the organised working class.

The task undertaken by these political forces was to restore the prosperity lost in depression and drought, heal the divisions opened by strikes and lockouts, and reconstruct a settler society to meet the external and internal dangers to which it felt itself vulnerable. The external threats, strategic, racial and economic, were also internal, foreshadowing loss of sovereignty, degradation, poverty and conflict. The search for security and harmony produced a coherent programme of nation-building.

Some of the elements of this programme have already been described. The threat of invasion was met by military preparations within the framework of imperial protection. While Australia felt it necessary to assert its own interests in imperial forums, the intention was always to ensure that London was conscious of the needs of its distant dominion: the independence of 'independent Australian Britons' was premised on the maintenance of the Empire. Australia relied on the Royal Navy not just to defend its shores but to keep open the sea routes for trade. Three-fifths of its imports came from Britain, half its exports went there. British finance underwrote the resumption of growth in the early years of the new century as the pastoral industry was reconstructed and the agricultural frontier expanded.

The fear of racial mixing was met with the White Australia Policy, which closed Australia to Asian immigration. But the regime of migration control was more than simply exclusionary. Overseas labour recruitment, along with foreign investment in public works and private enterprises, was a motor of growth. Immigration resumed in the times of prosperity that returned by the end of the first decade of the century. Forty thousand settlers were assisted to come to Australia between 1906 and 1910, 150,000 more between 1911 and 1914, when the population passed 4.5 million. Conversely, migrants were discouraged when unemployment was rife and new entrants had a depressive effect on the labour market: there were fewer than 4000 assisted settlers between 1901 and 1905. The counter-cyclical pattern of government migration activity helped secure the labour movement's acceptance of this aspect of nation-building.

Jobs were also safeguarded by tariff duties on imports that competed with Australian products. This arrangement secured the alliance of the Protectionist and Labor parties, representing the employers and their workers in the manufacturing industries. By the time that alliance lapsed and the Protectionist and Free Trade parties merged in 1909 to create the Liberal Party in order to combat the growing success of the Labor Party, the tariff (with lower duties on imperial products) was a settled feature of national policy. Protection allowed local producers to expand their output and increase manufacturing employment from fewer than 200,000 in 1901 to 330,000 by 1914. The Commonwealth's protection of local industry had a novel dimension: it was available only to employers who provided 'fair and reasonable' wages and working conditions. As Deakin explained, 'The "old" Protection contented itself with making good wages possible' but the New Protection made them an explicit condition of the benefits.

The determination of a fair and reasonable wage was the task of the Commonwealth Arbitration Court, which was an additional component of the national programme. The endemic conflict between employers and unions was to be resolved by State tribunals with powers to arbitrate disputes and impose settlements. Several States had created such tribunals in the aftermath of the strikes and lockouts of the 1890s, and the federal one was established in 1904 after prolonged parliamentary argument. In 1907 it fell to its president, Henry Bournes Higgins, to ascertain the meaning of a fair and reasonable wage in a case concerning a large manufacturer of agricultural machinery. He determined that such a wage should be sufficient to maintain a man as a 'human being in a civilized community'; furthermore, since 'marriage is the usual fate of adults', it must provide for the needs of a family. He therefore used household budgets to work out the cost of housing, clothing, food, transport, books, newspapers, amusements, even union dues, for a family of five, and declared this a minimum wage for an unskilled male labourer. It took some years to extend this standard (which became known as the basic wage and was regularly adjusted for changes in the cost of living) across the Australian workforce, but the principles of Higgins's Harvester judgement became a fundamental feature of national life. Wages were to be determined not by bargaining but by an independent arbitrator. They were to be based not on profits or productivity but human need. They were premised on the male breadwinner, with men's wages sufficient to support a family and women restricted to certain occupations and paid only enough to support a single person. Women contested the dual standard for the next sixty years.

Around these arrangements a residual system of social welfare was created. The great majority of Australians were expected to meet their needs through protected employment and a legally prescribed wage. They were also expected to provide for misfortune through accident or illness: Higgins's basic wage included the cost of subscription to a voluntary society that offered coverage for medical costs and loss of earnings. It was recognised that some were not so provident – and State governments supported the private charities – but dependence was discouraged and self-sufficiency a hallmark of masculine capacity. That many mothers were denied the benefit of a husband's earnings was recognised only in the restriction of charitable assistance to women and children; for a man to accept a handout was to forfeit his manliness. To this logic of the male breadwinner there were allowed special cases where the state offered direct assistance: the old-age pension, from 1908, and an invalid pension, from 1910, for those outside the workforce, and a maternity benefit, from 1912, to assist mothers with the expense of childbirth. Australia came early to the payment of benefits for welfare purposes, but it stopped short of the general systems of social insurance developed in other countries where the operation of the labour market imperilled social capacity. Rather, Australia provided protection indirectly through manipulation of the labour market in what one commentator has described as 'wage-earners' welfare state'.

Such were the components of a system that was meant to insulate the domestic economy from external shocks in order to protect the national standard of living. Contemporaries took great pride in its generous and innovatory character. Social investigators came from Britain, France, Germany and the United States to examine the workings of this 'social laboratory' that had apparently solved the

problems of insecurity and unrest. Seen from a late-twentieth-
century vantage-point, as its institutional forms were dismantled, it
was judged more harshly. An economic historian suggests that a
system of 'domestic defence' meant to provide protection from risk
lost the capacity for 'flexible adjustment' and innovation. A political
commentator sees the 'Australian Settlement' as a premature lapse
into an illusory certainty that left 'a young nation with geriatric
arteries'.

These judgements give priority to the economic aspects of the
national reconstruction. They construe the national reconstruction
as one that sacrificed efficiency to equity. They make insufficient
recognition of the fundamental inequities of race and gender it
institutionalised, and they exaggerate its amelioration of class
divisions, for the Australian Settlement did not settle conflict between capital and labour, which continued to generate major
disputes in defiance of industrial arbitration. But the principal
object of the national reconstruction was not the economy, nor
social justice, but the nation. The makers of the Commonwealth
sought to modify the market to create national mastery of material
circumstances, to weld a thinly peopled continent with distant
centres and regional differences into a secure whole, and to regulate its divergent interests to serve national goals. That was not
simply a defensive or protective project; it was an affirmative and
dynamic one.

This can be seen in the impressive record of technological
innovation. Colonial Australians had cultivated the reputation of
improvisers. The rule of thumb prevailed over formal knowledge,
the mechanics institutes and schools of mines were more closely
attuned to industrial requirements than the fledgling universities. By
the end of the century there was an enhanced scientific effort.
Miners found new methods of extracting minerals: the flotation
process developed at Broken Hill was copied around the world.
Farmers used fertilisers and new varieties to extend into the low-
rainfall zones beyond the Great Dividing Range; the mechanical
harvester that gave rise to the basic wage was as advanced as
that used on the North American plains. Governments built substantial irrigation works to support more intensive horticulture.
Factories, shops and offices were quick to embrace new machines

or techniques that increased productivity. Australians took up the pocket-watch, the typewriter and the telephone with the enthusiasm they showed later for the personal computer. This, moreover, was a society that was equally innovatory in its leisure: from the 1880s the Saturday half-holiday became common and a biblical division of the week into six days and one gave way to five and two. Australians might not have invented the word 'weekend' but they certainly made good use of it.

They were quick also to adopt the gospel of efficiency. The striving for improvement in every corner of national life accorded with the new understanding of progress, no longer as the fruits that came from planting civilisation in an empty continent but as a conscious task of national survival in an uncertain, harshly competitive world. 'The race is to the swift and strong, and the weakly are knocked out and walked over', warned a leading businessman. Thus employers applied the methods of scientific management to industry through simplification of the labour process, careful measurement of each task and close supervision of its performance. The domestic market was too small for these techniques to be applied fully to any but the biggest companies, and their impact was probably greater in public enterprises, such as railway workshops, and major government departments, which dwarfed private-sector organisations in scale and complexity. Both federal and State governments were expanding to take on new tasks, administrative, infrastructural, financial, industrial and even commercial. Public transport, communication, gas, electricity, banks, insurance, and coalmines, timber-yards, butchers, hotels and tobacconists when the Labor Party held office, provided essential services, checked profiteering and acted as pacesetters for wages and conditions.

Beyond industrial and administrative efficiency lay the goal of social efficiency. This was pursued through a range of reforms aimed at reinvigorating the race and strengthening its capacity to contribute constructively to national goals. The reformers were modernists, seized with the pace of change and the powerful currents that ran through human conduct, and they were experts, confident that they could harness the creative impulse and instil purposeful order. They were concerned with the ills of modernity, the slum, the broken home, social pathology, degeneracy. They worked through professional associations and voluntary bodies, and they embedded their plans in public administration. They styled themselves progressives, after the American progressivist movement on which they drew. Progressivism found application in town planning and national parks, community hygiene, 'scientific motherhood', kindergartens, child welfare and education. The New Education replaced the old rote learning with an emphasis on individual creativity and preparation for the tasks of adulthood: manual skills, nature study, health and civics, to promote an ethic of social responsibility.

The Australian Settlement, then, was not a settlement. The reconstruction of the Australian colonies came in response to challenges that jolted established arrangements and assumptions. In their search for security the colonists adopted the forms of the race and nation, both artefacts of the modern condition of uncertainty and constant change. White Australia bound the country more tightly to Europe in its external relations. Internally, it made the country seem to have been almost uninhabited before the European conquest, so that European capital, labour, technology and culture could work on it more fully. With these resources as the basis of a new nation came the problems of dependence and economic vulnerability, the old quarrels over rank and religion, and further ones over class and gender. William Lane had sought to preserve the innocence of the New World with his New Australia, a forlorn endeavour. Alfred Deakin used New Protection to provide a measure of autonomy and harmony. But the New World was tethered to the Old and could not escape its effects.

7

Sacrifice, 1914–1945

In the space of thirty years the circumstances of Australian nationhood changed irrevocably. The country's strategic dependence on Britain drew it into two wars. Both originated in European rivalry and together they exhausted the dominance of the European powers. The first sapped the political stability of the combatants and cut the flows of trade and investment that sustained their prosperity. The second destroyed their empires, leaving an impoverished rump of a continent divided and bound by the two superpowers to its east and west. Britain, a victor in both wars, was perhaps the most diminished by their cumulative effects. Australia, as the largest British outpost in the Pacific, also incurred heavy war losses. The fading of imperial certainties created doubt and division. The nation-building project faltered under the weight of debt and increased dependence. Only as the second war spread to the Pacific, and Australia found itself isolated and in danger of invasion, came a belated recognition of the need to reconstruct the nation for changed circumstances.

The first of these wars was known as the Great War by contemporaries who had never experienced such a catastrophe and could not imagine that another would follow so soon. After the conclusion of the Napoleonic Wars in 1815 Europe had enjoyed a century of peace✗— although it waged repeated wars of colonial conquest, at home there were only occasional and restricted conflicts that were quickly settled by a decisive encounter of professional armies. The Great War involved mass conscript armies

✗ Ugh? What do you call the war of 1870?

and absorbed the entire resources of the combatants in a prolonged contest of attrition that lasted from 1914 to 1918. When Germany supported Austria-Hungary in its ultimatum to Serbia, and Britain and France joined with Russia to resist them, the war extended from the Atlantic seaboard to the eastern regions of Europe. Soon it drew in Turkey and Italy. The United States came late, but the global reach of the combatants made this a world as well as a European war.

After Germany overran Belgium and repulsed a Russian advance, the initial movement of the combatants bogged down in static trench warfare. Both on land and at sea the application of industrial technology to warfare gave defenders supremacy over attackers. Mines and submarines paralysed the offensive potential of battleships; massive land fortifications, barbed wire, machine guns, gas and flame-throwers cut down the waves of advancing soldiers. Although commanders sacrificed millions of troops, the outcome was determined ultimately by the capacity of the two sides to maintain their war machines and sustain their populations. Hunger weakened Russia and allowed revolutionaries to seize power with their slogan of 'peace, bread and land'. Shortage of food played a critical role in Germany's final collapse. The farmlands of Britain's overseas Dominions provided a granary that sustained its effort. The merchant ships that carried Canadian and Australian produce contributed to the final Allied victory as much as the troopships that brought their young men to the battlefield.

The young men went first. At the outbreak of war a federal election was in progress and party leaders vied in their enthusiasm for Australian participation: Joseph Cook, the Liberal prime minister, declared that 'all our resources in Australia are in the Empire and for the Empire'; Andrew Fisher, the Labor leader, pledged 'our last man and our last shilling'. Labor won and affirmed the outgoing government's offer to despatch a force of 20,000 troops. That Australia would participate was not in question – it was still constitutionally bound to follow Britain and the announcement of war was relayed to the prime minister by the governor-general – the question at issue was the form that participation would take. The answer was given by the formation of the expeditionary force. It was raised by recruitment of volunteers and named the Australian

Imperial Force. Behind that decision lay a protracted argument in the years leading up to 1914 between those who sought a citizen militia on the Swiss model for purposes of national defence and those who wanted an army under British control that could serve abroad. The dispute was resolved by blending the voluntary principle with the imperial design. The Australian Imperial Force would be commanded by British generals until the last year of the war, and consist predominantly of front-line troops reliant for most support functions on the British Army. The Royal Australian Navy, similarly, was placed under control of the Royal Navy from the beginning of the war.

There was first a local task. In 1914 the German empire in the Pacific stretched from north-east New Guinea through a chain of Pacific islands that extended north almost to the Chinese coast. These territories provided radio bases to intercept naval communications and direct German cruisers to intercept Allied shipping. The British Admiralty therefore instructed the Australians to occupy New Guinea and the New Zealanders to capture German Samoa. This they did, and the Australians were preparing to proceed further north when the British told them not to bother: the German territories above the equator had been occupied already by Japan. The Japanese navy was to police the Pacific, thereby freeing British ships to serve closer to home. In exchange, the British government assured Japan that it would retain control of these northern islands, an arrangement initially concealed from Australia because of the alarm it would cause there. The governor-general was instructed to 'prepare the mind' of his ministers for the unwelcome news and urged that no anti-Japanese agitation should 'during the progress of the war be allowed to arise in Australia'. Here already a divergence of imperial strategy and national interests was opening.

A further strain became apparent when the Dominion troops completed their initial training and departed for service at the end of 1914. They joined with their New Zealand counterparts to form the Australian and New Zealand Army Corps: from that cumbrous title the acronym soon entered general usage as Anzac, signifying a citizen soldier with the distinctive qualities of the settler societies from which he sprang, resourceful and willing. A more colloquial term, 'digger', was also quickly adopted, harking back to the egalitarian fraternity of the goldfields. There was no room for the Anzacs in the training camps of England, so they disembarked in Egypt where the Australians quickly impressed the British officers responsible for licking them into shape with their raw turbulence. The reluctance to salute was an affront, the roughneck treatment of the Egyptian hosts a scandal. These uncouth colonials were needed, however, to repel the Turkish army from its advance on the Suez Canal, a vital imperial thoroughfare. Subsequently the Light Horse Brigade participated in the Allied advance through Palestine, Lebanon and Syria, where they fought some of the last great cavalry battles in military history.

Before then the Anzacs were employed in an attempt to forestall that campaign and knock Turkey out of the war. The idea was to force the straits at the eastern shore of the Mediterranean that opened to the Turkish capital. Once that was taken, the expeditionary force could enter the Black Sea and link with the Russian forces. It was first necessary to secure the Gallipoli peninsula, upon which Turkish troops commanded the strait. In the early morning of 25 April 1915 British, French and Anzac forces therefore made separate landings on the peninsula. The Australians and New Zealanders scrambled ashore at Anzac Cove and stormed the precipitous slopes before them. Checked in their advance, they dug in and defied all attempts to dislodge them, but were unable to capture the heights despite repeated attempts to do so. With the onset of the winter, they abandoned Gallipoli and left behind 8000 dead. The withdrawal, five days before Christmas 1915, was the most impressive operation in the eight-month campaign.

The Australian casualties were a fraction of those incurred during the war and fewer than the British suffered at Gallipoli. Although the Anzacs had performed creditably under fire, the campaign revealed errors of command and execution. Even so, their exploits on the Turkish peninsula quickly gave rise to an enduring legend of martial valour. The Anzac legend began with the reports of the initial landing given by the official war correspondent: 'there has been no finer feat in this war', this British journalist assured Australian readers. It was fostered by Australian correspondents, one of whom linked the prowess of the Anzacs to the incompetence of their British commanders – his name was Keith Murdoch, and his son Rupert, who entered the British newspaper industry as the 'Dirty Digger', would exact a painful colonial revenge. The legend dealt with sacred themes: baptism under fire in the pursuit of an unattainable objective, sacrifice, death and redemption through the living legacy of a nation come of age. It told of courage and stoicism in the ultimate test of mateship and thus converted a military defeat into a moral victory. Within a year the Australian servicemen commemorated the anniversary of the landing and Anzac Day was quickly established as a public holiday, marked ever since by a dawn service when the immortality of the fallen is proclaimed.

The principal Australian correspondent, C. E. W. Bean, did most to codify the legend. A journalist before the war, after it the official war historian and director of the Australian War Memorial, he attributed the qualities of the Australian soldier to the stimulus of local conditions. 'The Australian is always fighting something', he had written in 1907. 'In the bush it is drought, fires, unbroken horses, wild cattle; and not unfrequently strong men.' Wrestling with man and nature made the Australian 'as fine a fighting man as exists'. Within a few days of the Gallipoli landing Bean was able to confirm that 'the wild pastoral independent life of Australia, if it makes rather wild men, makes superb soldiers'. He quickly produced a popular tribute, *The Anzac Book*, an anthology of stories, verse and skits he collected from the troops at Gallipoli. Their testimony celebrated the individuality of front-line soldiers who collectively affirmed the legend. As the official war historian Bean would expand this technique into a vast encomium to the national character.

After their withdrawal from Gallipoli, the Australian infantry divisions were reinforced and deployed in the defence of France. Here they participated in the mass offensives against the German line during 1916 and 1917 that inflicted many more casualties and called for new qualities of endurance.

> We stumble, cursing, on the slippery duck-boards,
> Goaded like the damned by some invisible wrath,
> A will stronger than weariness, stronger than animal fear,
> Implacable and monotonous.

The horrors of this ordeal exceeded participants' powers of description; the most notable war novels appeared many years later.

There was already a sharp disjuncture, however, between the response to war by those on the Western Front and the representations created for domestic consumption. The lurid propaganda posters that showed the bestial Hun violating Australian womanhood contrast with the sombre paintings of the war artists selected by Bean, or Will Dyson's battlefield drawings of human extremity. In 1916 the demotic poet C. J. Dennis had a scruffy, undisciplined larrikin from the Melbourne slums answer 'the call of the stoush' and affirm the values of the digger in Turkey, but an Australian serving in the French trenches a year later had no such certainty:

> Adieu, the years are a broken song,
> And the right grows weak in the strife with wrong,
> The lilies of love have a crimson stain,
> And the old days will never come again.

The Western Front was lethal. There were 14,000 deaths in 1916, 22,000 in 1917, and the much greater numbers of non-fatal casualties constantly thinned the ranks. The rate of enlistment rose after Gallipoli, from 52,000 volunteers in 1914 to 166,000 in 1915, but then declined to 140,000 in 1916 and just 45,000 by 1917. The first recruits were predominantly young and single, many of them attracted by the pay which was equivalent to average earnings and higher than other countries offered their servicemen. As these enthusiasts ran short, it became necessary to appeal to the patriotic duty of older, married men. The leadership of the country had passed at the end of 1915 from Andrew Fisher, a Labor moderate uncomfortable with the demands of war, to Billy Hughes, his bellicose deputy. Hughes was a union organiser turned politician with an authoritarian streak, who directed Labor's socialist sentiment into a nationalist crusade to impose the collective interest on business and labour alike. A nation at arms provided him with the licence to strengthen the hand of government. Diminutive and deaf, a wizened firebrand with a rasping voice and rancorous manner, he travelled to England to press the British to remedy Australian grievances.

The war had also exacted a heavy economic toll. It cut the inflow of labour and capital, and deprived Australia of German, French and Belgian markets that accounted for 30 per cent of the country's exports. The shortage of shipping also restricted imports, and allowed an expansion of local manufactures, but it created a stock-pile of rural produce. The economy contracted by 10 per cent in the first year of the war. Unemployment increased. Price rises ran ahead of wages, and Hughes's abandonment of a referendum to control prices angered the labour movement. He therefore wanted Britain to underwrite the output of wool, wheat, meat and minerals, and in this he eventually prevailed. It was perhaps a pyrrhic victory, for it froze the existing economic structure. Even though heavy industry developed around the country's first major steelworks, which opened in 1915, the opportunity for more substantial diversification was lost.

In pressing his country's needs Hughes called for a renewed war effort, yet the number of Australian volunteers was flagging. He returned to Australia in mid-1916 committed to conscription. Opposition could be expected from a labour movement that was increasingly critical of the slaughter, and the Labor parliamen-tarians were most unlikely to pass the necessary legislation. Accordingly the prime minister appealed over the heads of his party to the country with a referendum. He had the support of the press, the Protestant churches, business and professional leaders. The principal opposition came from socialists, radicals and feminists, all of whom challenged the assumption of a unified national interest in war and the supposed equality of sacrifice embodied in military conscription.

These critics were already hampered by draconian restrictions on freedom of information, expression and activity. Under the War Precautions Act passed in 1914 the federal government was em-powered to proclaim regulations necessary for public safety and the defence of the Commonwealth. It had interned 7000 enemy aliens with little regard to their circumstances or sympathies: they included eminently respectable German-Australians, migrants from the Balkans who were unwilling subjects of the Hapsburg empire, even Afghan camel-drivers who had come from well beyond the ambit of the Ottoman empire. Here the government had popular support: an upsurge of anti-foreign behaviour swept the country as the passions released by war hardened the identification of nation with race, and narrowed the boundaries of acceptable difference.

So too with dissidence. Anti-war meetings were broken up, anti-conscription speakers prosecuted, offices and homes raided. The most forthright opponent of the war was the Industrial Workers of the World, and some of its members were framed in 1916 on charges of arson and treason.

The government's response to feminist opposition was also severe. War accentuated sexual divisions. In separating men from women, it licensed a masculine aggression that spilled over into disturbing irregularity. The marked wartime increase of sexually transmitted diseases became a metaphor for national insecurity, which in turn brought closer regulation of women. Such circumstances allowed an intensification of the moral reform movement, though some of its principal achievements – six o'clock closing of pubs, for example – were regulation *by* women. Women were excluded from the armed forces (even the 2000 nurses who served abroad were denied official military rank) and in contrast to other combatant countries few Australian women were brought into the paid workforce (while those who were remained on lower wages). Their war effort was channelled into voluntary activities, and their greatest service was to provide and sustain fighting men. The transgression of the radical feminists, who challenged this expectation of maternal sacrifice with violent street protests, was punished with special severity.

The excessive censorship of news from the front and the heavy-handed domestic repression probably rebounded on the Australian government. The British government's military bombardment of Dublin to repress an Irish nationalist uprising in Easter 1916 certainly disturbed the substantial minority of Australians of Irish descent. The men at the front were divided; some were disenchanted, and some who remained ardent believed their volunteer status should not be sullied by compulsion. When the country voted in October 1916 in the referendum, it narrowly rejected the proposal to conscript Australians for overseas military service.

Hughes tried again a year later, and his second referendum campaign was even more divisive. By now the prime minister cast his opponents as traitors. The labour agitators were doing the work of the Bolshevik revolutionaries who had seized power in Russia and taken it out of the war; they were agents of Germany, said

Hughes. The workers who increasingly turned to strike action were wreckers. The women who refused to give up their sons were emasculating the nation. The Irish Catholics who criticised the war – most notably the Irish archbishop of Melbourne, Daniel Mannix – were preaching the separatist disloyalty of the Sinn Fein; in English, that meant 'ourselves alone' but in practice it meant stabbing the home country in the back. The prime minister, who now carried his own revolver, brooked no opposition. He personally led a raid on the printing office of the Queensland government to seize copies of an anti-conscription speech by the State premier that had been censored from publication in Hansard. Pelted with eggs on the return journey, he created his own Commonwealth police force. The second referendum failed by a slightly greater margin than the first. Australia remained one of the few combatants to maintain a volunteer force and the only one to have rejected conscription.

This did not reduce its toll. Out of a population of five million the armed forces voluntarily recruited 417,000 men, more than half of those who were eligible. Of the 331,000 who served abroad, two out of every three were killed or wounded. The 60,000 war dead represented a higher proportion of enlistments than any other contingent of Britain and its Empire (though countries with a conscript army lost a higher proportion of the total population). Long before the final victory at the end of 1918, the common enthusiasm for war gave way to grim resignation. Not even the prominence of the Australian Corps in resisting Germany's last offensive and then leading a decisive advance under the command of its own general, John Monash, could restore the purposeful unity of 1914.

Armistice Day eventually became Remembrance Day, but in memory of what? Sacrifice in the service of Empire and the defence of freedom was the best explanation contemporaries could provide, usually by rehearsing stories of German atrocities in occupied Belgium and portraying Germany as a military state bent on world domination. In hindsight, some historians have cast doubt on Germany's intentions and capacity. It did not seek war, the revisionists argue, and only struck when a powerful combination threatened it on both sides. German aims stopped short of swallowing up the British Empire, as indeed its grim struggle for survival suggested was far beyond its capacity. Germany was no more despotic than Russia, its circumscription of liberties for the purposes of war no different from the methods adopted by the Allies.

If so, was it Australia's war? As Australia has drifted further away from Britain and Europe, it has become increasingly difficult for later Australians to understand why an earlier generation travelled half-way round the world to fight a distant foe. We forget that many Australians believed Britain was endangered, and rallied out of ethnic loyalty as well as self-interest to its support – they might now be almost extinct, but Anglo-Australians were once a legitimate ethnic group. The heroism of the Anzacs is now recalled in pilgrimages to Turkey, France and Belgium, where the ravaged landscape is healed and all that remains is ordered rows of graves. There are memorials in almost every Australian township and suburb, but most of these bear mute testimony to those named on them – and it is a distinctive feature of the Australian war memory that they record the names of the survivors as well as the dead. The most common forms are the obelisk and the lone digger on a pedestal, typically a private who stands with head bowed and rifle reversed. Younger Australians are hard-pressed to distinguish the combatants, much less the passions that animated them.

Those passions were apparent at the Paris peace conference where the victors divided the spoils. Hughes joined with France in demanding a Carthaginian peace, a punishment of Germany so severe that it could only imbalance the international economy and poison international relations. He took issue with the United States for wanting to replace the old order of empire with a new system of liberal internationalism that would encompass free trade, national self-determination, and settlement of differences through a League of Nations. He affronted the Japanese with his opposition to a declaration of racial equality in the Covenant of the League of Nations. He importuned the British with his insistence that Australia should retain control of New Guinea; in the end a special category of mandated territories was created to ensure that the former German colony would be administered as an 'integral portion' of Australia, with full control over trade and immigration.

British support was essential. With it Australia secured New Guinea; without it, Japan could not be denied the northern islands.

In his public confrontation with the United States, Hughes could take the high ground of brutal realism. 'I represent sixty thousand dead', he told the idealistic President Wilson. In private arguments with Britain he might well have added that he spoke for a public debt of £700 million, half of it owed in London, but Britain had incurred deaths and debts of much greater magnitude. The overriding purpose of the war, for Hughes, was to maintain the Empire on which Australian security depended. His chief goal at the peace conference was to hold Britain to its Empire. He therefore sought a greater role in imperial affairs through direct access to the British government (so that the practice of communication through the governor-general and the Colonial Office was abandoned) and separate representation at Paris. He wanted to go further with closer co-ordination of imperial affairs but the fellow-Dominions of Canada, South Africa and, after 1921, Ireland would not have that. They were loosening the ties with Britain; Hughes with his idiosyncratic methods of aggressive dependence was holding to them. Behind this parapet, moreover, he could be franker in his racial exclusivism, more reckless in his disregard of Japanese sensitivities, than the other English-speaking nations of the Pacific. The United States, Canada and New Zealand also restricted Asian immigration, but none advertised their prejudice as provocatively as the empty island-continent of the south.

At home this assertive loyalism drove deep divisions. An immediate political effect of the first conscription referendum was a split in the Labor Party. At the end of 1916 Hughes led his supporters out of a meeting of its federal parliamentarians; in early 1917 he joined with the non-Labor forces to form a National Party, which was returned to office in a federal election four months later. Similar splits brought down Labor governments in New South Wales and South Australia. Betrayed by its leaders, vilified for its failure of national duty, the labour movement turned for a period towards the militant class rhetoric of direct action. Even when moderates reimposed control of the federal Labor Party, they were unable to regain the initiative they had enjoyed before it. For a quarter-century after 1917, Labor remained in opposition in federal politics except for two disastrous years during the economic emergency of the Depression.

Those who left the Labor Party called themselves Nationalists and the nation they upheld was loyal to the Empire. They retained connections to the ancestral homeland in sentiment, recreation and worship. The sectarian animosities fanned during the argument over conscription confirmed the Protestant ascendancy in its religious prejudices, while Catholics were estranged from the new forms of national ceremony: their Church did not participate in the post-war commemoration of Anzac Day, and it was absent when the foundation stone of the national war memorial was laid in Canberra in 1929. The gendered division of protector and protected also persisted, hardening the aggressive qualities of masculinity, emphasising the vulnerability of femininity. The 60,000 who had fallen in the service of the Empire gave the alignment of loyalty with conservative, Protestant men a sacral force, yet the nation that came of age in war was more resentful, less confident of its capacity for independent experiment.

War is sometimes regarded as a regenerative force, rather like the Australian bushfire that galvanises energy, burns away the outmoded accretion of habit, and allows new, more vigorous growth to occur. The Great War brought no such national revitalisation. It killed, maimed and incapacitated. It left an incubus of debt that continued to mount as the payments to veterans and war widows continued; even in the depths of the Depression of the early 1930s there were more Australians on war benefits than in receipt of social welfare. So far from strengthening a common purpose, it weakened the attachment to duty; to live for the moment was a common response to the protracted ordeal. The war increased rather than lessened dependence, hardened prejudices, accentuated divisions.

Capitalising on his exploits at the Paris peace conference, Hughes presented himself to the electorate at the end of 1919 as the 'Little Digger' and renewed the Nationalist majority. At the next election, three years later, he faced greater opposition. A Country Party had formed to represent the disgruntled farmers, and city businessmen were becoming restless under Hughes's erratic regimen of state control. The Nationalists lost their parliamentary majority and in early 1923 overthrew Hughes to form a coalition with the Country

7.1 Billy Hughes, the bellicose Labor prime minister, split his
party during the First World War when he campaigned for
military conscription. The 'Little Digger' is shown here on the
shoulders of soldiers at the end of the war. (National Library
of Australia)

Party. The new Nationalist prime minister, Stanley Bruce, and his
Country Party deputy, Earle Page, held office till the end of the
decade. They were an unlikely pair, the one a patrician Melbourne
business leader educated in England, the other an excitable doctor
from rural New South Wales, and their administration made little
use of the new broom that its supporters hoped would sweep away
the excesses of the little imp they had ejected. The lines of national
policy were too firmly established, the problems too persistent.

Hughes had sought to rebuild national capacity within the
imperial fold. He looked to Britain for the sale of primary products,
import replacement for the expansion of secondary industries, state
activity to augment population and state regulation to maintain
living standards. Without some corresponding gains in productivity,
however, these protective devices would increase the cost structure
of producers. A substantial extension of tariff protection at the end

of the war gave impetus to the newly formed Country Party, while urban business interests expected Bruce to curtail the profligacy of government expenditure and regulation. These expectations were dashed. Rather than reducing the tariff, the Bruce–Page government extended assistance to the primary producers. Instead of curtailing public expenditure, it increased it. The new administration was locked into a policy of 'protection all round'.

Bruce is the only businessman to have made a successful transition to national politics. Displaying a politician's grasp of the effectiveness of striking phrases, he explained the elements of that policy to an Imperial Conference in 1923 with an alliterative jingle: 'Men, money and markets'. Men from Britain were needed, along with women and children, to fill up the empty spaces, but most of all men to make the land productive – the British government financed a new wave of more than 200,000 assisted migrants during the decade. Money was required from British investors so the Australian government could undertake the necessary development projects and Australian producers could expand their capacity – the Commonwealth and the States, now co-ordinating their borrowing, returned to the City of London in the 1920s and borrowed £230 million with a further private inflow of £140 million. Markets had to be found for the increased primary production – Britain remained the principal customer for Australian wool and wheat, along with shipments of dairy produce, meat, fruit and sugar.

The policy was premised on rural growth. When officials selected British emigrants, they looked for those who would go onto the land. When treasurers raised loans, they spoke of extending railways to the new farm districts, of irrigation projects, of the schools, hospitals and other facilities associated with land settlement. The principal form of assistance to returned servicemen was soldier settlement, a scheme whereby the government set up 40,000 diggers on their own farms. Government marketing schemes were designed to persuade the British consumer to buy Australian butter; the Commonwealth's scientific institute applied its efforts to the eradication of pests and the improvement of stock. The popular phrase 'Australia Unlimited' denoted an abundant resource, land, which needed only capital and labour to blossom; the very word development was synonymous in the 1920s with land settlement and its associated public works.

Closer settlement revived the yeoman ideal of self-sufficiency. Some of the new farms were established at the limits of settlement, consolidating the wheat belt in the hinterland of Western Australia and carving dairy holdings out of the dense forests in the south-west of that State, while on the other side of the continent large runs were cut up into agricultural blocks, thus pushing graziers further inland. The family farm was consolidated as the operational unit of primary industry and rural life. These farmers were largely self-sufficient in labour (though the assisted migrants included 20,000 'farmboys') but otherwise tied to the operation of the market, for they were engaged in commercial enterprises with substantial entry costs and dependent on machinery, fertiliser and other inputs. Many of the entrants incurred heavy debts as they struggled to clear the land and bring it into production. It was their misfortune to do so just as European farmers recovered from the war along with other New World producers who competed for export sales. When prices stalled after the middle of the decade, the mounting dissatisfaction of the farmers strengthened the Country Party.

Rural hardship increased the drift to the cities. They grew rapidly (Sydney passed the million mark in 1922, Melbourne in 1928, when together they held more than one-third of the country's inhabitants) and absorbed much of the investment. Residential construction accounted for nearly half of private capital formation during the decade; provision of transport and utilities to the spreading suburbs drew heavily on public funds. These investments in turn supported a wide range of industries. Real estate transactions boosted the finance sector. Building, servicing and fitting out the new homes stimulated brickyards, timber mills, pipemakers, paintmakers, textile mills, furniture manufacturers. The highways and city streets carried motor traffic – by 1929 the rate of car ownership was surpassed only by the United States, Canada and New Zealand. The new electricity grids allowed Australian factories to turn out novel domestic products: although few homes yet boasted an electric stove or refrigerator, most had an iron, vacuum cleaner and radio. With labour-saving devices came greater opportunities for leisure and a move in domestic design towards the modern and the convenient. The cigarette replaced the pipe, the beard gave way to the cleanshaven chin, the long skirt to the light frock. Radio and the cinema increased the impact of advertising and commerce.

From flickering images of modernity and the syncopated strains of pleasure the idea took hold of the 1920s as a time of growth and renewal, a release from wartime hardship.

Yet there remained deep unease. With the return of the soldiers, jobs were scarce. The labour market improved in the early 1920s, but increased mechanisation shrank the demand for unskilled workers and unemployment remained at over 5 per cent for the remainder of the decade. With no job security and no public assistance when laid off, casual labourers were excluded from the new forms of consumption. The larger, more cohesive groups of manual workers in vital industries such as mining and maritime transport were best able to express their dissatisfaction: a wave of post-war industrial disputes paralysed the economy for lengthy periods. Then the demand that ex-servicemen be given preference over unionists added a further strain: all too often the volunteer for military service became a volunteer to jump a queue or even to break a strike. In a series of further confrontations at this time former members of the AIF attacked radical demonstrators: the title of their organisation, the Returned Soldiers and Sailors Imperial League of Australia, testified to their traditional loyalty.

The most common cause of dispute was display of the red flag, a familiar symbol of the labour movement now associated with communist revolution. The Bolshevik seizure of power in Russia at the end of 1917 had been followed by further uprisings elsewhere and then by the formation of the Communist International, which appealed to workers around the world to make common cause against the capitalist ruling class and urged colonial peoples to rise up against their imperial masters. Although the newly formed Communist Party of Australia remained tiny, its very existence was an affront to conservatives. The association with the Russian Bolsheviks conjured up the threat of a foreign conspiracy led by rootless Jewish malcontents to impose an alien despotism on Australia.

While the Australian Labor Party rebuffed the Communist Party's attempt to affiliate in 1924, the Nationalists used the trade union links to make the 1925 national election an anti-communist crusade, and followed its victory with new criminal sanctions against the unions. During the 1920s the Red Menace displaced the Yellow

Peril as the source of imminent danger. More than this, Russia's abandonment of the war against Germany revived the memory of the conscription plebiscite and the domestic electorate's failure of national duty. Could the fickle voters be trusted? It seemed to conservatives that democracy itself might have to be qualified in the defence of God, King and Empire. Former officers of the AIF formed secret armies to be ready in the hour of need.

All this occurred at a distance from the dance-halls and beaches. The Nationalist election posters that showed brutal Cossacks shooting down Australian fathers, mothers and children as they fled from a burning church established a nightmare connection that seldom impinged directly on national life. The hard-faced men who trained under cover of darkness maintained strict security. The maimed veterans were not encouraged to dwell on their loss; the diggers who survived found it difficult to share their experience with those who had not been there – until in old age they finally relaxed their stoical reticence. From a safe distance there has been an upsurge of interest in Australian military history that is affirmative in a less divisive register, less concerned with the causes and effects, more reflective of the human dimension.

In the 1920s the memories were still fresh and raw, anaesthetised in a sonorous diction of chivalry that carried over into the crusade for development:

> The bush in all its beauty,
>   The wheat lands in their pride,
> The forest in its freedom,
>   The sand plains far and wide —
> They are waiting, waiting, waiting
>   With their struggles and their joys;
> They are waiting to be conquered
>   At the hands of British boys.

The images that circulated were those of a clean, white, cheerful and resolute country. As government publicists lured immigrants with the promise of rural plenty, so artists returned to an Arcadian imagery of forest and field.

That most striking symbol of modern science, the aeroplane, excited public attention with epic flights from England and the United States. A Queenslander and former war pilot, Bert Hinkler, completed the first solo flight between England and Australia in 1928. In the same year a merchant prince, Sidney Myer, supplemented a government grant for Charles Kingsford Smith and Charles Ulm to make the first flight across the Pacific. Myer had arrived in Australia from a Russian shtetl; Kingsford Smith was born in Canada, Ulm's father was French; their plane was designed by a Dutchman, built in the United States and christened the *Southern Cross* – aerial flight joined Australia to the world. A Yorkshire lass, Amy Johnson, failed narrowly to eclipse Hinkler's record when she landed at Darwin on Empire Day, 1930, but her reception was even more acclamatory: 'not only has she spanned the distance between England and Australia; she has cleared the Sahara which still lay between the sexes'. The aeroplane found its apotheosis in the Flying Doctor Service, taking medicine to the bush.

New societies frequently confuse novelty with freedom. Earlier generations of Australians had thought they could forsake the past in order to blaze a new trail, but never with such fearful premonition. The past now signified a cumulation of ills that wracked Europe and the rest of the world, an exhaustion of old civilisation and an atavistic madness that might well overwhelm Australia itself. 'This modern movement is loaded with the leprosy of the ages', warned an Australian artist on his return from abroad in 1927. The idea of Australia as threatened by foreign evils was symbolised by the influenza epidemic that struck Europe at the end of the war. Despite efforts to quarantine its carriers, influenza carried off 12,000 Australians in 1919. As with the virus, so with other pathogens. Seditious and obscene publications were censored, degenerate art condemned, undesirable aliens deported. The Commonwealth imposed new restrictions on Australian nationality in 1920. In procedures for both immigration and naturalisation of immigrants, it developed an exhaustive system of classification of different races and nationalities. Entry quotas were introduced for southern Europeans and other undesirable immigrants, naturalisation procedures made contingent on a test of political loyalty administered by the Commonwealth security agency, which was another product of the war.

The policy of exclusion was both vainglorious and timorous. Protection of local manufacturers had extended though the New

Protection to wage-earners, then through marketing and assistance schemes to the farmers. Protection of racial purity had spread to keep Australia from all foreign dangers to civic and moral virtue. Australia was not alone in this stance. After championing internationalism at the Paris peace conference, the United States had turned its back on the League of Nations; but it did so from a position of strength. In a report to Washington in 1925 an American diplomat was struck by the similarities and differences. White Australia was about as old as his own country when it threw off British rule, but it seemed quite unprepared to take that step. 'Selfishness would seem to be the dominating motive in most people's lives.' They showed no capacity for initiative, lived for the moment and acted only when there was no alternative. More people went to the races on 25 April than attended the Anzac Day ceremony. 'There is little spirit in the people ... there is nothing in their past that really stirs them nationally.' His country's isolationism was affirmative and confident, the Australian version cramped and defensive. Despite the higher duties on non-imperial products, American imports increased to more than a quarter of all foreign trade. Despite the call for restrictions, American films, comics and jazz were avidly consumed. By comparison, British culture seemed stilted, local work provincial. Life appeared more glamorous, more real, on the other side of the Pacific.

As a small, vulnerable, export-dependent country, an Australia that retreated into isolation became more reliant on Britain; but Britain's own capacity was weakened, its willingness to sustain the old imperial arrangements uncertain. Britain represented Australia at an international conference in Washington, where it was agreed in 1921 that the major Pacific powers would maintain a ratio of naval strength in the Pacific: five British and five American for every three Japanese vessels. Australia welcomed the agreement, which replaced the much-resented Anglo-Japanese treaty, but overlooked the fact that the British and American navies would operate outside the Pacific. Much would depend on the new British naval base to be constructed at Singapore.

Meanwhile at a 1926 Imperial Conference Britain devised a new formula for its Dominions. They were to be autonomous, equal, united by common allegiance to the Crown and freely associated as members of what was now called 'the British Commonwealth'. The formula was a concession to Canada and South Africa, a rebuff to Australia which wanted no part of it and did not ratify the measure that enacted it until a new world war forced acceptance of an established fact. Even the economic links were straining now that Britain was no longer the world's financial centre; its attempt to regain that status by returning to the gold standard in 1925 added to its trading difficulties. Australia was more than ever committed to the production of raw materials and food – fully 95 per cent of its exports were primary products – but Britain was no longer the workshop of the world.

That left the financial links, and Australia was the principal public borrower from the City of London in the 1920s, but most of those funds went not to building rural export industries but to the further growth of swollen cities. The imbalance caused unease, for the city was the site of social problems and its pleasures seemed to sap the national character, but there was no alternative. The bush could not absorb a population growth of one million persons during the decade, for it no longer provided sufficient jobs: at the turn of the century one in three was employed in farming and mining; by 1929 less than one in four worked in those occupations. Since maintenance of the standard of living was an established condition of national policy, the Commonwealth protected the workers in city factories with tariffs on competing imports and the States provided additional jobs in government enterprises and public works. Wage regulation through industrial arbitration allowed modest increases in earnings, and the employer's additional costs were passed on to the consumer through an adjustment of the tariff.

It was a fortuitous arrangement that permitted investment without saving. As Australians responded to the new forms of household credit, they discarded habits of thrift learned in the depression of the 1890s. As the country increased its foreign borrowing, it was able to pursue growth without having to stint on consumption. Lenders provided these funds, however, in the expectation of returns. As export prices slipped, they began to question the profligacy of the borrower. The tariff, the arbitration system and the application of loans to urban construction all came under criticism. Among these construction works was the Sydney Harbour

Bridge, a heroic project to link the city to the north shore that was awarded to an English firm using Australian materials and Australian labour. Work began in 1925 and by 1929 the two halves of the 500-metre arch were creeping across the harbour, when Australia's credit collapsed. Before the span was completed, a toll was introduced to pay for its cost.

Even before the Wall Street crash in October 1929 made further borrowing impossible, the government attempted to stem a mounting imbalance of payments by reducing the cost of Australian exports. Having stacked the Arbitration Court with new appointments and introduced new laws against strikes, it welcomed a series of industrial awards designed to get more work for less pay. Three groups of workers resisted the new awards, and each one was bludgeoned into submission after long, violent disputes. The first were the waterside workers, who from August 1928 to the winter of 1929 tried in vain to prevent strikebreakers from taking their livelihood. Next were the timber workers, who picketed the sawmills and lumber-yards for most of 1929. Last and most bloody was the dispute on the coal district of New South Wales, which began in February 1929 when the owners locked out the miners for refusing to accept wage reductions. Armed police occupied the Hunter Valley, broke up all assemblies, bashed protesters, fired on pickets and killed one of them.

The miners held out until 1930, but by then the wave of industrial conflict had brought down the federal government. Bruce, the prime minister, decided to go the whole hog and abandon the field of arbitration along with its floor under wages. Billy Hughes, the man he had supplanted, gathered together a group of government malcontents to combine with the Labor parliamentarians and defeat the measure in parliament late in 1929. Bruce called an election. Labor won an overwhelming victory. During the 1920s, then, Australia embarked on a dash for growth that relied heavily on favourable external circumstances and increased the country's vulnerability. It was the misfortune of the labour movement, excluded from most of its benefits and vilified for criticising its inequalities, to assume responsibility just as the growth stalled.

Labor took office in the week the New York stock exchange on Wall Street crashed. Already the prices of wool and wheat were falling; in the following year they would fall even more steeply. This meant that more than half the country's exports were needed just to meet the payments due on foreign loans. After the collapse of the international financial system, there could be no new borrowing. On the contrary, the Bank of England sent a senior official to Australia in 1930 to prescribe the economies that would be necessary to restore Australia's credit. The Commonwealth and State governments would have to balance their budgets by reducing outlays on both public works and welfare payments. Wages would also have to come down, and in January 1931 the Arbitration Court cut them by 10 per cent. In the same month the currency was devalued by 25 per cent.

With the sharp reduction of export income and foreign funds, the Australian economy contracted. The new government resorted to the conventional methods of economic protection – an increase in tariffs and a halt in immigration – but without money for consumers to spend, these devices brought no relief. Unemployment increased, from 13 per cent at the end of 1929 to 23 per cent a year later and 28 per cent at the end of 1931. The Labor ministry could not even force the mineowners to re-employ the miners they had illegally dismissed. The new prime minister, James Scullin, was a decent but ineffectual man overwhelmed by forces beyond his grasp. He pleaded that the government was hamstrung by the absence of a majority in the Senate and the refusal of the head of the Commonwealth Bank to accept its decisions. In fact it was paralysed by its own irresolution, hopelessly divided between those who could see no alternative but to follow the bankers' demands and those who demanded that human needs come before obligations to foreign lenders.

As a debtor and a primary exporter, Australia was hit hard by the Depression. Its unemployment level was higher than that of Britain and most other industrial economies, the level of distress closer to Canada or Argentina. Unlike Argentina and despite the urging of Labor radicals, Australia did not repudiate its debts. Instead the Commonwealth and six States (three of them also governed by the Labor Party) agreed in 1931 to implement the economies needed to meet the bankers' insistence on balanced budgets: higher taxes, reduced expenditures. Conversion of domestic public loans to lower interest rates and a voluntary conversion of private borrowings were the sole concessions to the principle of 'equality of sacrifice'. The agreement estranged the unions and aggravated divisions within the Labor Party. After defections from both its right and left wings, the federal Labor government fell at the end of the year to a revitalised conservative party, the United Australia Party, led by the former Labor treasurer, Joseph Lyons. Similar splits brought down State Labor governments in New South Wales, Victoria and South Australia.

Labor failed both to protect jobs and to protect the jobless. The calamity of mass unemployment overwhelmed the existing charities. State governments resorted to distribution of ration vouchers. Some compelled breadwinners to work for their meagre allowance, and some despatched single men to work camps in the country where they were less of a threat. City-dwellers who could not keep up rent payments were likely in any case to take to the bush in search of casual jobs or handouts, hitching a ride or jumping a train but always moving on. Shanty towns sprang up on waste land and river banks, with a constant turnover of inhabitants. Some farmers also abandoned their unequal struggle to keep up mortgage payments but most stayed on the land until it was taken from them, for it was possible to eke out a living by falling back on subsistence agriculture. The gulf between the employed and unemployed was a striking feature of the 1933 census, which revealed that unemployed men had on average been out of work for two years. The Depression widened inequalities of wealth and income. There was compassion for those in need and there was rejection. They were objects of pity and fear.

Prolonged unemployment strained social bonds and family links, sapped confidence and capacity. The Depression gave rise to a literature and art that responded to human extremity with a grim realism; it depicted men and women tossed about by inexorable forces, stripped of dignity by constant humiliation and reduced by hunger to passive stupor. Yet some victims responded with defiance rather than despair, and an Unemployed Workers Movement, formed by the Communist Party in 1930, provided them with

7.2 As victims of the inter-war Depression lost their homes, shanty towns sprang up on waste land. This improvised dwelling in the docklands of Melbourne uses a water tank as a chimney and bedsteads for a front fence. (Victorian Department of Human Services)

leadership. Initially it organised demonstrations at suburban ration depots and led marches on government offices in the State capitals, but these were broken up and the leaders gaoled; the party's national conference had to be postponed at the end of the year because most of the delegates were behind bars. The Unemployed Workers Movement turned next to campaign against eviction. By assembling local residents, it sought to prevent landlords from putting tenants onto the street. The activists also channelled the discontent of the itinerant unemployed as they gathered seasonally, and brought communal purpose to the shanty towns. These activities were episodic in character, difficult to sustain, and the 30,000 nominal members of the Unemployed Workers Movement were far in excess of the 2000 members of a Communist Party characterised by doctrinal excess and repeated expulsions. But as one of them put it, 'we've got to make a stand. Do something! Don't cop it passively.'

The economic and social emergency of the early 1930s was also a political emergency that strained the country's democratic institutions. Both left and right believed that representative govern-

ment had failed. For communists, the state was an instrument of
class rule and Labor politicians and union leaders were forced by
the capitalist crisis to abandon their pretence to represent the
workers and reveal themselves for the traitors they were. Conservatives, on the other hand, saw parliament as a talking-shop of
self-serving parasites, Labor as irresolute and unfit to govern. Its
reluctance to impose cuts, talk of repudiation and failure to quell
communist agitation among the unemployed prompted a right-wing
mobilisation.

It began during 1930 when prominent figures appealed over the
heads of the political parties for a programme of unity that would
set the country's affairs in order. Their solution to the emergency,
sound finance and self-sacrifice, presented a conservative course
of action as uncontentious common sense, the fulfilment of debt
obligations a matter of national honour. The rejection of politics
was a recurrent feature of political life in a country where democracy was compulsory and there were three levels of government.
Part of this upswell came from resentment against the growing
power of a remote federal government at the expense of the States.
Western Australia voted to secede from the Commonwealth in
1933, though by then that possibility had closed. Some felt the same
about the concentration of State activities in the capital cities, and
separatist New State movements sprang up in outlying regions.
The principal national organisation with 100,000 members, the All
for Australia League, used an anti-political politics to promote a
spurious consensus. Ostensibly non-partisan, it joined with the
National Party to form the United Australia Party and shared in the
spoils of office when that reinvigorated force won an election at
the end of 1931.

Behind this electoral strategy lay more forceful preparations. The
secret armies of the right, formed after the war, took the activity of
the Unemployed Workers Movement as their cue for action. In
country centres they broke up unemployed camps and ran trouble-
makers out of town. In the cities they closed down meetings and
assaulted public speakers. The old hands increased their readiness
for the expected revolutionary insurrection, but it was a New
Guard, formed in New South Wales following the election of a
more radical Labor government at the end of 1930, that took the

offensive. Motorised detachments of the New Guard descended on working-class neighbourhoods of Sydney to do battle for control of the streets. 'Nothing more lethal than a pick handle', was their commander's instruction, though he 'noted with amusement many a bulge on the hip'. The New Guard's most celebrated success came in early 1932 when one of its officers, mounted on a horse, slashed the red ribbon with his sabre to open the Sydney Harbour Bridge before the Labor premier could cut it with scissors. The incident was theatrical, but it came as the demagogic premier, Jack Lang, was defying the national agreement to reduce public expenditure and street violence was building an atmosphere of public hysteria. Only when the governor dismissed Lang in May 1932 did the unrest subside.

Economic recovery began with improved export sales and a recovery of manufacturing, both assisted by the cheaper currency. An imperial trade conference in Canada in 1932 increased the preferential tariff for British imports in return for greater access to British markets for Australian farmers. The public foreign debt stabilised, private investment flowed back into the industrial sector, and there was substantial construction around regional iron and steel centres in New South Wales and South Australia. Employment lagged behind the increased production, however, and even in the late 1930s 10 per cent of the workforce remained without jobs. Wage increases were also resisted, and it was only as the unions rebuilt their membership that they could press their demands for improvement.

In this process the unemployed activists turned into industrial militants. Mostly young, they found positions in manual occupations such as mining, transport, construction and heavy industry, and applied their organisational zeal to the improvement of pay, conditions and job security. Their earlier experience was formative both in firing their determination and honing their capacity. They were class warriors, linking the bread-and-butter issues of working life to the iniquity of capitalist exploitation and its generation of imperialism, fascism and war. By the end of the decade communists held leading positions among the miners, waterside workers, seamen, railway workers, ironworkers and a host of smaller occupational groupings. The radicalisation of the unions was a lasting effect of the Depression.

Recovery from the physical and social effects of the Depression was more protracted. The birthrate dropped to a new low, immigration did not resume until the end of the decade, and population growth slowed. On the other hand, infant mortality also fell and public health improved. Fewer children, more widely spaced, more carefully nurtured, marked the extension of government and medical influence over the family, as well as the increasing attention of the housewife to nutrition, hygiene and domestic management. The temporary interruption of customary roles during the Depression, when men were more likely to be at home and women to be working (because female employment held up better and recovered sooner), did not reduce female domestic responsibilities or soften male attachment to the privileges of the breadwinner.

In the aftermath of the Great War Australian feminists had sought to expand citizenship. They pressed for increased participation in public life and equality in the workplace. Instead of providing that all adult males be paid a family wage, a device that one Labor woman said treated women and children as mere 'appendages of men', it would be better to distinguish the different needs of households and supplement workplace earnings with direct state support for families. Those who campaigned for increased welfare provision sometimes drew on the strengthened rhetoric of martial citizenship. They likened the ordeal of childbirth to the perils of combat, and they appealed to the chivalry of a nation of warriors. While feminists stressed the maternal contribution to the nation, they also participated in international forums that affirmed a common sisterhood – and were prominent critics of barbarous treatment of Aboriginal women and children.

Their endeavour to expand social welfare foundered on the conservative aversion to higher taxes and the trade union attachment to the basic wage. Only in New South Wales was a limited system of child endowment introduced in 1927. The Depression turned attention back to safeguarding men's employment through closer regulation of workforce patterns and disqualification of married women from more occupations. In response, feminists concentrated on the demand for equal pay with a campaign that slowly gathered momentum among left-wing unions. Even so, women's wages rates remained pegged at little over half those of men.

The existing lines of public policy remained intact. As other countries responded to the failure of the market with new forms of welfare provision, Australia held fast to the threadbare protective devices of the wage-earners' welfare state. The inter-war difficulties seemed to have smothered an earlier talent for innovation. Or perhaps the resumption of established patterns of sport and recreation suggested the underlying resilience of popular habits. Cricket, football, horse-racing and cinema held attention in the Depression and soon rebuilt attendances. Sporting champions came to occupy an exalted place for their affirmation of grace and fortitude, but the most celebrated heroes were those betrayed by unscrupulous foes. Thus Les Darcy, the boy boxer forced to leave Australia in 1916 because he would not volunteer for the AIF, dead within six months; or the chestnut horse Phar Lap who won the Melbourne Cup in 1930 but also died in America, 'poisoned by the Yanks'; or Don Bradman, the wonder batsman, against whose incomparable skills the English had to bend the rules of cricket during the 'Bodyline Tour' of 1932–33.

There was a vacuum of national leadership. The new prime minister, Joseph Lyons, was a homely, avuncular man who shied away from controversy, his United Australia Party ministry anything but united as the senior conservatives jostled for influence. One of its younger, more principled members resigned within a year from what he described as 'a sort of government of the feeble for the greedy'. The admission of the Country Party back into coalition after the 1934 election only aggravated divisions, while the inclusion of new talent accentuated leadership rivalries. The ablest and most impatient was Robert Menzies, a Melbourne barrister; among his many qualities a seemly modesty was conspicuously absent.

A series of resignations traced the dissatisfaction with policy. In 1935 Hughes was forced to resign when he published a book critical of the government's foreign policy. As the fascist regimes in Germany and Italy embarked on a policy of military belligerence, and the Australian government clung tightly to Britain in its initial reliance on collective security through the League of Nations, Hughes demanded military readiness. Restored to office in 1937 as minister for external affairs, he continued to attack Hitler and Mussolini: to yield to their territorial claims, he said, would be 'like giving a snack of sandwiches to a hungry tiger'. But this was precisely what the Lyons government did. From the Italian invasion of Ethiopia in 1935 to the German dismemberment of Czechoslovakia in 1938, Australia's appeasement of the dictators was as abject as Britain's, partly because it was desperate to avoid another war and partly out of admiration, if not sympathy, for the aggressors' achievements. 'There is a good deal of really spiritual quality', Menzies declared on his return from Germany in 1938, 'in the willingness of young Germans to devote themselves to the service and well-being of the State.'

In 1937 another minister resigned in protest against the government's trade policy. Concerned that a decline in Australian purchases of British manufactured goods might imperil the privileged access of primary producers to the British market, the government had imposed new restrictions on non-British imports. In doing so, it singled out textiles from Japan, a country with which Australia had a substantial trade surplus. The Japanese retaliated with damaging sanctions against Australian woolgrowers. Apart from the loss of export income, the trade diversion dispute set back earlier attempts to build closer relations in the region. A growing body of Australian diplomats, commentators and business leaders recognised the signs of an emergent nationalism in Asia. If Australia still offered few concessions in its immigration policy, they hoped that trade links would promote regional co-operation. Now Australia affronted the most powerful and expansive of the Asian countries; along with British and American rebuffs to Japan, it was one more slight from the colonial *gaijins*.

Finally, in early 1939, Menzies resigned in protest against the government's retreat from a scheme for social insurance. This was scarcely a radical or comprehensive measure, for it covered just medical benefits and pensions, but it offended the doctors and insurance societies. The irresolute prime minister died in the following month, and Menzies quickly succeeded him, but by now a decade of conservative supremacy was drawing to a close. The inability to proceed with social insurance was a signal demonstration of the paralysing grip of sectional interests.

The government was most resolute in dealing with dissidents. The Labor Party, still suffering from the divisions created in the

Depression and hopelessly split on foreign policy between isolation-ism and anti-fascism, was not an effective opposition. Communist unions took the lead in resisting appeasement and imposed a boycott on Japan following its invasion of China. After waterside workers refused to load a shipment of iron, that trade was curtailed but in the course of the dispute the government shut down a critical radio station. Isolationism and appeasement extended from foreign policy to immigration and cultural life. The Lyons government censored criticism of the foreign dictators, and allowed a limited number of refugees to enter Australia only on the payment of a substantial fee. It imposed a special quota on Jewish victims of the Nazis. The most celebrated critic of the fascist regimes was Egon Kisch, a Czech journalist. Denied entry to speak at a conference of the Movement Against War and Fascism in 1934, he jumped ship and appealed to the High Court so that he could tour the country.

Despite the government's endeavours to shut it out, the ferment and strife of the outside world pressed in on Australia. During Kisch's visit a Writers League was formed to affirm an alternative, experimental literature, a literature of commitment in the service of humanity. It merged in 1938 with the Fellowship of Australian Writers, concerned to validate the national experience. From a Book Censorship Abolition League, formed in 1935 to reduce the long index of prohibited literature, there came a Council for Civil Liberties, contesting other infringements on freedom. Against the attempt in 1937 to establish a traditional Academy of Art with a royal charter, the Contemporary Art Society embraced the modern styles. The Australian Broadcasting Commission, established in 1932, supported orchestral music and provided a forum for current affairs. The six dilapidated universities, still teaching fewer than 10,000 undergraduates, flickered with fresh energy. Across these various sites of creative endeavour there was a mood of progressive engagement and critical unrest with established orthodoxies. The gulf between these intellectuals and the mistrustful, practical men who exercised authority had never been wider.

The two groups came together, however, to lay down the policies that regulated how others lived. The inter-war years were the heyday of the expert as the determining intelligence of official policy, still unencumbered by considerations of consultation and

7.3 A large blackboard advertised the meeting of Aborigines in Sydney on the 150th anniversary of white settlement as a Day of Mourning. (*Man*, March 1938)

consent. In urban planning, public administration, health, education, industry and finance, these experts prevailed, and at the end of the 1930s they were extending their reach to native policy. By this time the earlier forms of knowledge that defined Aboriginal Australians as a primitive race were losing their authority, the regime of protection demonstrably failing. The Aboriginal communities of south-eastern Australia had formed their own organisations, which reworked the terms protection and advancement to demand the abolition of the protection system and seek new ways of advancement. As Sydney staged a re-enactment of Governor Phillip's landing on 26 January 1938 to commemorate the 150th anniversary of European occupation, the Aborigines Progressive Association observed a Day of Mourning for 'the Whiteman's seizure of our country' and enslavement of their people. It called for a 'new policy which will raise our people to full citizen status and equality'.

A week later these activists met with the prime minister and a new minister for the interior, who turned for advice from the administrators to the anthropologists. A national meeting of administrators in 1937 had affirmed the policy of biological assimilation;

the anthropologists offered an alternative expertise that replaced biology with culture. Culture was both universal and particular: it was an organising principle of all peoples but distinctive to each one of them. Accordingly, any attempt to assist Aborigines should be based not on the imposition of alien practices but rather on what A. P. Elkin, the professor of anthropology at the University of Sydney and chief adviser to the minister, described as 'helping them to develop further along their own cultural lines'. Elkin therefore called for an Aboriginal administration informed by anthropological expertise. He saw such a regime operating in Papua, where benevolent paternalism protected the indigenous people from expatriate exploitation, in contrast to the mandate territory of New Guinea, where the plantation *mastas* enforced obedience from indentured native labour. These two territories, however, were exotic places of exile and adventure for a thin sprinkling of white men and women; the indigenous Australians were an occupied minority, aliens in their own land.

Elkin's recognition of cultural difference was qualified. While softening the rigid definitions of racial capacity that distinguished the savage from the civilised, he still discerned a hierarchy of racial development: the role of the anthropologist was to guide administrators with insights that would assist in 'raising primitive races in the cultural scale'. While expounding the rich complexity of Aboriginal culture, he believed that it was fragile and unlikely to withstand exposure to European culture. He thought that those in the settled districts and towns had already lost much of their cultural identity. Other anthropologists in northern Australia were more concerned still by the threat of white contact, believing that the very survival of the Aboriginal population was at stake. Even so, Elkin saw no alternative but further development. In the paper he drafted for the minister, which was released in early 1939 as a 'New Deal for Aborigines', assimilation became government policy. The official objective was now 'raising of their status' to 'the ordinary rights of citizenship', but this in turn was to be achieved by extending the practice of forcible removal of Aboriginal children from their families. By a twisted logic that now horrifies all Australians as it then tormented its victims, the popular association of Aboriginality with dirt, disease and neglect allowed whites to deny the civic rights of the stolen generations and deprive them of their culture.

Australia entered a second world war as it had entered the first, automatically. As soon as he was informed that Britain had declared war on Germany, Menzies declared it his melancholy duty to advise his fellow Australians that their country 'is also at war'. This time, however, there was no rush to enlistment; just 20,000 volunteered for the Second Australian Imperial Force in the three months after the outbreak of war in September 1939. Neither the United Australia Party nor the Labor Party welcomed the hostilities. The prime minister, who used the unfortunate phrase 'business as usual', had to be pressured by London to despatch an army division in November.

Again in contrast to the previous war, none of the Allies was keen to fight. Britain and France went to war because, after unsuccessfully appeasing the fascist dictators in repeated acts of belligerence, they felt bound to honour their guarantee to Poland when Germany invaded it. But, as Menzies observed, 'nobody really cares a damn about Poland', and it was already lost. Italy stayed out; so did the Soviet Union, which had cynically entered an agreement with Germany to divide up Poland. As the combatants faced each other on the Western Front during the 'phony war', Menzies still hoped that full hostilities might be avoided. Apart from his lingering preference for appeasement, he had a particular concern for Australia's safety. In 1914 Japan had been an ally, in 1939 it was a potential enemy. Between the wars Australia had run down its defence capacity in the belief that the Royal Navy was the key to its security. The British naval base at Singapore was thus vital, and Menzies insisted on assurances that it would be reinforced before he allowed Australian troops to depart along with naval forces and aircrews.

In the northern spring of 1940 the Germans launched their western offensive and quickly overran France. By the middle of the year Britain was alone and under air attack from an enemy-occupied Europe. Australian enlistments increased rapidly, and two additional divisions went to north Africa, where the Anzacs were once again defending Egypt and the Suez Canal, this time from Italian forces in the Western Desert. They were successful, but the weakness of the Italians in Africa and Greece brought German reinforcement. The British decision in early 1941 to send Anzac forces to Greece proved disastrous; they were quickly driven out and suffered further losses in the subsequent defence of Crete. By the middle of 1941 the German advance across the Western Desert forced a desperate defence of Tobruk. Meanwhile Hitler launched an attack on the Soviet Union and advanced rapidly east.

The entry of Japan into the war with the raid on Pearl Harbor at the end of 1941 realised Australia's worst fears. The British undertaking to protect Singapore with a fleet could not be fulfilled: just an aircraft carrier and a cruiser were sent, and were quickly destroyed. Without air support, the defence of Singapore crumbled and in February 1942 its British commander surrendered. Among those captured were 16,000 Australian infantry. By this time the Japanese were advancing rapidly down the chain of islands to Australia's north, and bombing Darwin.

Australians then and now interpret their initial experience of the Second World War as a betrayal. The valour of the 'rats of Tobruk' (as they were dubbed by an enemy propagandist) joined the heroism on the heights of Gallipoli; but whereas the first sacrifice in the service of Empire was glorious, the second was ignominious.

> Say Crete, and there is little more to tell
>   Of muddle tall as treachery, despair
> And black defeat resounding like a bell:

wrote the disenchanted son of a pastoral dynasty in remembrance of a friend who died there. Mary Gilmore, whose self-appointed role as the conscience of her nation found expression in the inspirational 'No Foe Shall Gather Our Harvest', expressed the outrage at the fall of Singapore in the principal women's magazine:

> And black was the wrath in each hot heart
>   And savage oaths they swore
> As they thought of how they had all been ditched
>   By 'Impregnable' Singapore.

Fifty years later an Australian prime minister used the same sentiment as an argument for republican independence.

The bitterness was all the greater for Australian self-deception. It had provided for its external security with an imperial insurance policy in which the premium was paid in lives rather than military expenditure – a lethal form of defence on the cheap – and now found the coverage had expired. There was an acerbity in relations between Australian and British leaders during the early years of the Second World War unprecedented in the First. The Anglophile Menzies was openly critical of Churchill's lack of consultation, while the head of the British Foreign Office was contemptuous of Dominion concerns: 'what irresponsible rubbish these Antipodeans talk'. If the Australians had known that by the end of 1941 the British agreed with the Americans that it was necessary to beat Hitler first and then worry about the Pacific, their anger would have been even greater. The backbiting affected the armed forces, with constant feuding among the commanders, and the domestic population. The government declared the Communist Party illegal for its opposition to the war and denounced the coalminers for striking in 1940, but failed to curtail the usual round of domestic pleasures. Menzies came under increasing criticism. He 'couldn't lead a flock of homing pigeons', declared the ageing warhorse, Billy Hughes. The government fell in August 1941.

A month later the Labor Party took office under John Curtin. When Japan commenced hostilities in December, the Curtin government made its own declaration of war. At the end of the year the prime minister published a message that 'Australia looks to America, free of any pangs as to our traditional links or kinship with the United Kingdom'. In early 1942 he informed Britain that a failure to defend Singapore would be regarded as an 'inexcusable betrayal' and insisted that Australian troops return to defend Australia rather than join in the defence of Burma. Following the fall of Singapore, which he described as 'Australia's Dunkirk', he proclaimed the 'Battle for Australia' and placed Australian forces under the command of the United States. With the adoption of the Statute of Westminster later in 1942, Australia consummated its constitutional independence. The Australian Broadcasting Commission stopped playing 'The British Grenadiers' before its news bulletin in favour of 'Advance Australia Fair'.

These moves, under dire emergency, to sever the subordination to Britain and perhaps create a new dependence on the United States, constitute a powerful national legend. Japanese air raids on Darwin, naval losses in Australian waters and even an attack on Sydney Harbour reinforced the fear of invasion. That was not intended. The main Japanese thrust was in the north; it sought to occupy the islands of the South-West Pacific and isolate but not invade Australia. The Americans fell back on Australia as a regional base, but neither they nor the British regarded Australia as vital to the war strategy. In their conduct of operations in the region, the Americans consulted Australia no more than the British had done. There was no special relationship. Even the adoption of the Statute of Westminster was prompted by the need to safeguard certain government powers rather than any impulse for independence.

Curtin surrendered military control to Douglas MacArthur, the United States commander. MacArthur in turn ensured that Australian troops did not detract from his glory, or impede his country's post-war plans to impose military and economic control of the region. Even though the 1942 naval engagements between the

7.4 Douglas MacArthur, the United States general and commander of the Allied forces in the Pacific, confers with the Australian prime minister, John Curtin. (National Archives of Australia)

7.5 The Kokoda Track was a route of strategic importance as Australian troops defended the capital of New Guinea against Japanese forces advancing from the north. (Australian War Memorial)

United States and Japan in the Coral Sea and at Midway ensured that there would be no enemy landing in Australia, there was cause for Australian alarm. The Japanese army thrust south across Papua New Guinea until by September 1942 it was only 50 kilometres from the southern capital, Port Moresby. Along a rough track that traversed precipitous ranges and in appalling conditions that spread malaria and dysentery, Australian infantry fought with Papuan support and turned the Japanese advance. This battle along the Kokoda Track cost 12,000 Japanese, 2000 Australian and perhaps 500 Papuan lives. It was here that Australians first fought in jungle green uniforms rather than khaki.

The jungle was at first a strange and menacing environment, recalled by another descendant of a pastoral dynasty from the dry grasslands to the south:

> And I think still of men in green
>   On the Soputa track,
> With fifteen spitting tommy-guns
>   To keep the jungle back.

A communist infantryman who became the most successful of the war novelists wrote of the tropical undergrowth as a malign presence, no less alien and menacing than the fascist enemy: 'a poisonous, material thing, heavy with foul scents; a huge, infested womb, swallowing us, mingling us in its corruption'. In retrospect, a strange metamorphosis allowed Australians to claim the Kokoda Track as their own, so that the Australian prime minister who condemned the British betrayal at Singapore commemorated the fiftieth anniversary of the defence of Port Moresby with the assertion that 'The Australians who served here in Papua New Guinea fought and died not in defence of the old world, but the new world ... They died in defence of Australia, and the civilisation and values which had grown up there.'

After leading the defence of Papua New Guinea, the Australians were relegated to an auxiliary role in the Pacific war effort. The Americans led the advance on Japan, the Australians mopped up. They played no part in the meetings of the three principal Allies, the United States, the Soviet Union and Britain, which thrashed out the allocation of responsibilities and spoils. They were not consulted on the terms of the Japanese surrender and were effectively excluded as the Americans incorporated the beaten enemy into their orbit.

Australian losses in the Second World War were less than in the First, 37,000 deaths out of a population of seven million, and a total enlistment of one million of whom 560,000 served overseas. Improved medical treatment allowed more casualties to survive, though the 10,000 aircrew who mostly died in Europe emphasised the lethal nature of the war in the skies. Perhaps the most disturbing losses were the prisoners of war – 30,000 of them altogether, and of the 22,000 captured by the Japanese only 14,000 lived to return to Australia in 1945. Some were executed, but most died of malnutrition and disease. Those men put to work on the construction of a railway from Burma to Thailand were treated appallingly, while women army nurses suffered equal brutality.

A ship evacuating army nurses from Singapore was sunk in February 1942. Of fifty-three who made it to land, twenty-one were executed and eight more died in captivity.

The stories the survivors told were shocking. Hatred of Japanese brutality was kept alive after the war in memoirs and fiction, notably Nevil Shute's unforgiving novel, *A Town Like Alice* (1950), which became a film. Eventually the hatred softened into an affirmation of human endurance and even a partial reconciliation, especially through the efforts of Edward 'Weary' Dunlop, an army surgeon who showed extraordinary courage and ingenuity in defending his men and improvising treatment for cholera, malaria, typhoid and tropical ulcers. The publication in 1986 of his war diaries, which record the daily struggle with disease, cruelty and hopelessness, consolidated his status as a national hero. Dunlop, a sporting champion and a man's man, represented the older military qualities of loyalty, endurance, egalitarianism and valour with the newer values of healing, compassion and forgiveness.

The Australians held their own prisoners of war, some Japanese and many Italians. The latter were put to work as there was a shortage of labour in a war economy that grew rapidly: by 1943 output was 40 per cent greater than in the last year of peace. Under Curtin the government assumed far-reaching controls of industry and employment. Wages, prices and rents were fixed, essential items rationed, labour directed into essential industries. In early 1943 Curtin overcame his party's opposition to military conscription to allow the deployment of servicemen beyond Australian territory, but in the final years there was a reduction in the armed forces so that the country could produce the food, munitions and other war materials to sustain the war effort in the Pacific. The Labor government largely financed the war from taxation, holding down consumption and running down investment to maximise war production.

While the Americans brought with them a cornucopia of equipment, and provided Australia with lend-lease assistance, the Australians were primarily responsible for feeding and provisioning their guests. Almost a million United States servicemen passed through the cities on their way to the front, and even though the numbers in Australia at any one time were seldom more than

100,000, this was a foreign presence of unprecedented significance. One in ten of the GIs was African-American, in contrast to the restriction on Aboriginal enlistment to those with a European parent (there were probably 3000 Aboriginal soldiers, with a further 3000 working as labourers in the north), and forced Australians to confront their own segregationist practices. The Australian soldiers envied the Americans' higher pay, superior conditions and access to luxury goods. There was particular resentment of their attractiveness to local women, and the image of rampant sexuality was explicit in wartime fiction and art. In occupied Australia the fickle female was the fifth columnist; the war brides who left for the United States were regarded as defectors. Brawls between American and Australian soldiers attested to local sensitivity to the friendly invasion.

That Australia accepted the sacrifice of this second war without the deep divisions of the first was assisted by the quality of its leadership. Hughes, the firebrand, had polarised the country. John Curtin, an austere and self-doubting man, unified it. As the leader during the 1930s of a weak and discordant party, he had learned conciliation. As an idealist gaoled for opposition to conscription in 1916, he persuaded his party to accept it in 1943. As a patriot who customarily began his wartime broadcasts with the vocative 'Men and women of Australia', he accepted the geopolitical realities that made his country co-operate with more powerful allies. Curtin was often criticised for deferring to MacArthur, but behind the scenes the Australian government struggled to assert its interests. A 1944 agreement with New Zealand and attempts to revive the role of the British Commonwealth in the Pacific were intended to provide a counterweight to American dominance. It was now apparent that Australia could not isolate itself from international relations or depend on the fidelity of a protector. The minister for external affairs, H. V. Evatt, therefore pushed for an enhanced authority for the post-war United Nations to check the hegemony of the superpowers.

In return for the hardship and danger of the war, the Labor government undertook far-reaching reform. As early as December 1942 it established a Department of Post-War Reconstruction to plan the new order. The enhanced powers of the wartime

Commonwealth would carry over to peacetime, with regulation of the economy for industrial expansion, immigration, maintenance of full employment, housing, health, education and social welfare. Post-war reconstruction was in fact anticipated during the war as post-Depression reconstruction in a series of measures that mobilised the country's neglected resources. Statutory authorities brought unions into the conduct of strategic industries, and replaced the inefficiencies of the casual labour market with stable employment. Women were drawn into the armed forces and also worked in essential industries, with a special tribunal created to increase their pay. Graduates were recruited for an expanded and far more active bureaucracy. Pensions were improved, unemployment and sickness benefits introduced.

There were setbacks. After winning a sweeping victory in the 1943 national election, the government failed to carry a 1944 referendum to enshrine its wartime powers after the war. Powerful business interests chafed against controls, newspaper magnates challenged censorship. 'Nothing would come to the men and women of the working class as a gift from the gods', Curtin warned. 'Everything they gained had to be fought for.' This fight for national survival succeeded as a people's war, a war to abolish the injustice and insecurity that had weakened democracy and nurtured fascism, a war that would finally end the thirty-year crisis. From the tragic sacrifice of the First World War, and the rancorous discontent that followed, a sufficient unity was created in the Second World War to make the sacrifice seem worthwhile.

8

Golden age, 1946–1974

The third quarter of the twentieth century was an era of growth unmatched since the second half of the nineteenth century. The population almost doubled; economic activity increased more than threefold. There were jobs for all men who wanted them. People lived longer, in greater comfort. They expended less effort to earn a living, had more money for discretionary expenditure, greater choice and increased leisure. Sustained growth brought plenty to Australians and habituated them to further improvement: a belief in the capacity of science to change scarcity to abundance was matched by the institutional confidence to resolve problems and ameliorate social life. The facilities of intellectual life and the possibilities for artistic practice expanded. The country became less isolated from the rest of the world and less beleaguered in its domestic arrangements.

Coming after the sacrifice of the preceding decades and the return to uncertainty that followed in the 1970s, it was a golden age. But as the ancients discerned a cyclical pattern of history, which saw the purposeful vigour of an ascendant civilisation soften into indulgence, disunity and eventual collapse, so post-war Australia followed a worrying trajectory. The iron age of austerity occupied the 1940s; the 1950s were the silver years of growing confidence and conformity; by the golden 1960s atrophy and decay had set in, and the regime could not withstand the dissident forces it had released. This might be too parochial a perspective. The long boom of the 1950s and 1960s was a global phenomenon, the fruits of prosperity shared by all advanced economics. As a trading country, Australia benefited from the revival of world trade and investment, shared in the new technologies, followed the same techniques of management and administration. As a junior partner of the Western Alliance it was also caught up in the Cold War with the communist bloc and drawn into military commitments that ended by the 1970s in overextension and humiliation just as the golden age of plenty ran out. Decision-makers would never again enjoy such luxury of choice or feel the same confidence. Some looked back on the post-war era as a golden age of strong leadership and responsive endeavour; others lamented the lost opportunities and timorous complacency.

The iron age spanned the forging of weapons of war and the beating of swords into ploughshares. By the end of 1942 the wartime Labor government had assumed unprecedented controls over investment, employment, consumption, the media, and practically every aspect of national life. Planning for peace began even then with the establishment of a Department of Post-war Reconstruction under the direction of a young economist, H. C. ('Nugget') Coombs. A railwayman's son with a strong social conscience and a doctorate from the London School of Economics, Coombs was emblematic of the enhanced role of the planner.

His minister was Ben Chifley, who became prime minister when Curtin died in 1945. An engine-driver who had been victimised for his part in a strike during the First World War, Chifley was one of an older generation of stalwarts determined that after this war there would be no return to deprivation and indignity. An austere man of simple dignity with a voice damaged by too many open-air addresses, and possibly his pipe, he did not often venture on flights of rhetoric. Speaking to a Labor Party conference in 1949, however, he conjured a phrase for the goal that sustained him through half a century of service in the cause. It was not simply a matter of putting an extra sixpence in workers' pockets, or elevating individuals to high office. Labor strove to bring 'something better to the people, better standards of living, greater happiness to the mass of the people'. Without that larger purpose, that 'light on the hill', then 'the labour movement would not be worth fighting for'.

His government's plans for post-war reconstruction required the demobilisation of the armed forces and the return of workers in defence support to peacetime employment. The munitions industries were to revert to domestic manufacture behind the traditional tariff wall but with an enhanced capacity. The government therefore provided the American General Motors corporation with generous concessions to establish a local car industry, and the first Holden sedans rolled off the assembly line in 1948. The rural industries, badly run down after the pre-war decade of low prices and then the sudden demand for increased output, were to be modernised. Tractors replaced horses, science guided effort, and 9000 new soldier settlers were placed on the land. The shortage of skills was to be met by retraining ex-servicemen in technical schools and universities: the lecture theatres were packed and an Australian National University was established as a centre of research. The backlog of demand for housing was to be filled with federal funding for State authorities: 200,000 homes were constructed between 1945 and 1949.

This new spurt of state-sponsored development had a social as well as an economic aspect. Planning extended beyond the demobilisation of wartime Australia, for the war had augmented the call to 'populate or perish' and the Labor government embarked on the first major migration programme for two decades. In 1945 Arthur Calwell became Australia's first minister for immigration. He set a target of 2 per cent annual population increase, half of which was to be contributed by new arrivals. The minister sought them in Britain, but the British government was no longer encouraging emigration, so Calwell turned of necessity to continental Europe where millions of refugees had been uprooted by the abrupt shifts of national and political boundaries. In 1947 he toured the refugee camps and confirmed that they offered 'splendid human material', which moreover could be shipped to Australia at international expense and indentured to work for two years under government direction. In the following years 170,000 of these 'displaced persons' were brought to Australia, chiefly from the nations that were transferred from German to Soviet control in the corridor of eastern Europe that ran from the Baltic down to the Aegean Sea.

The ministry also negotiated agreements with western European governments to recruit additional migrants, initially from the north, subsequently from Italy, Greece and other southern countries. In the following decade Australia received a million permanent settlers. Two-thirds of them were non-British, a decisive break with previous practice and one confirmed by the creation of a separate Australian citizenship in 1948 with new provisions for those who were not British subjects to acquire citizenship.

The post-war migration programme, while continued and expanded by the non-Labor government that took office at the end of 1949, was created by Labor. Calwell, a former trade union official deeply embedded in Labor lore, shared the national prejudices and occupational concerns of many Australian workers. 'Two "Wongs" do not make a White', he declared in defence of his decision to deport Chinese refugees in 1947. Yet it was Calwell who coined the

8.1 The magnitude of the post-war migration programme required special accommodation for new arrivals, and the government sought to promote acceptance of non-English-speaking migrants with favourable publicity. Happy families are shown here at the Bonegilla Reception Centre in rural Victoria, 1949. (Department of Immigration and Multicultural Affairs)

term 'new Australian' to encourage the assimilation of polyglot immigrants. The pressure on them to give up their ethnic identities in order to conform to 'the Australian Way of Life', another new locution, was insistent; equally striking was the assumption that so many people from such diverse origins could do so. The acceptance of new Australians was also premised on reassuring the host population that they would not swamp the labour market and threaten local living standards. By winning the co-operation of the unions with its emphasis on full employment, Labor laid the foundations of this large-scale migration.

Full employment was the centrepiece of Labor's post-war planning, the indispensable condition of the light on the hill. In the negotiations at Bretton Woods in 1944 that brought the International Monetary Fund and the World Bank as instruments of trade liberalisation for the post-war economic order, Australia's most distinctive contribution was the demand that there be a guarantee to maintain full employment. In its landmark 1945 White Paper on Full Employment, the government outlined a Keynesian approach to management of the economy by control of aggregate demand. Fatalist reliance on market forces yielded to a close and continuous intervention to ensure that the national interest was served. For good measure, the government prepared a raft of public works schemes to soak up any labour surplus that might emerge once the pent-up demand from the war was satisfied. The widely anticipated slump did not occur – rather, the post-war boom continued and gathered force – but the Commonwealth did proceed with the most ambitious of these schemes, a diversion of the Snowy River into the inland river system with major hydro-electric generation plants and irrigation works. Accompanying full employment was an expanded social security system, in which cash benefits for the unemployed accompanied increased public provision of housing, health and education.

In all this the Chifley government had to juggle with formidable constraints. A shortage of basic materials meant that rationing continued. A reluctance to increase external debt, coupled with support for the British currency and trading bloc, restricted foreign exchange. The government won national elections in 1943 and 1946 but had failed in the 1944 referendum to persuade the

8.2 With pipe in hand, Ben Chifley, the Australian prime
minister, converses with his British counterpart, Clement
Attlee. On his left, the assertive minister for external affairs,
H. V. Evatt, is temporarily silent. (National Library of
Australia)

electorate to extend its wartime powers into peace. In a series of
decisions the High Court struck down some of its more innovative
measures. As wartime consensus faded, the omnipresent hand of
public regulation became irksome. The frank explanation of a
federal minister for the penalties he imposed on State authorities
that sold public housing indicated a growing line of division: 'The
Commonwealth Government is concerned to provide adequate and
good houses for the workers; it is not concerned with making the
workers into little capitalists.' Yet it was the workers who were
expected to show the greatest restraint.

The principal fear of the government as it grappled with shortages in the novel circumstances of full employment was inflation.
Instinctively frugal, Chifley was determined to hold down wages.
His delay in allowing the Arbitration Court to consider the unions'
case for a forty-hour week, which was finally introduced in 1948,
and his even greater reluctance to allow wage increases, imposed a
heavy strain on the loyalty of moderate officials of the Australian
Council of Trade Unions. Communists were prominent in a wave of

strikes in the transport, metal and mining industries, but they were by no means alone in their impatience. Chifley nevertheless interpreted a national stoppage by the coalminers in 1949 as a direct communist challenge, and responded with confiscation of the union's assets, imprisonment of its leaders, raids on the Communist Party and the introduction of soldiers into the pits. Three months after the defeated miners returned to work as victims of the iron discipline of Labor austerity, the government was defeated at the polls.

The silver age, then, began with the election of a Liberal and Country Party coalition under the leadership of the revitalised Robert Menzies. His recovery from humiliating rejection in 1941 involved the formation of a new and more broadly based political movement, the Liberal Party, and the construction of a new political constituency that Menzies characterised as 'the forgotten people' – those salaried and self-employed Australians who identified neither with the company boardrooms nor the tribal solidarity of the manual workers. In extolling the value of his forgotten people, Menzies laid primary emphasis on their 'stake in the country' through 'responsibility for homes – homes material, homes human, homes spiritual'. He solicited the support of wives and mothers whose domestic wellbeing was threatened by the impersonal regimen of bureaucracy and the militant masculinity of striking unionists; yet he also tapped the youthful vigour of the returned servicemen impatient with the regulatory stolidity of Labor politicians still exorcising the memory of the Depression.

The new government came to power with an anti-socialist crusade aimed at an electorate weary of controls and shortages. It undertook to reduce taxation, cut red tape. Restrictions on foreign investment were lifted, private enterprise encouraged, wage increases allowed. Yet the continued emphasis on migration and national development ensured the maintenance of economic management. During the election the new treasurer had singled out H. C. Coombs as a meddling socialist; on the day after the poll he phoned Coombs and said: 'That you, Nugget? You don't want to take any notice of all that bullshit I was talking during the election. We'll be needing you, you know.' As governor of the Commonwealth Bank and then the Reserve Bank, Coombs continued to hold the financial levers.

Exporters benefited from the outbreak of war in Korea in 1950, which caused leading industrial countries to stockpile essential commodities. The price of wool increased sevenfold during 1951 to reach record levels, and other primary producers also prospered as new markets emerged. A trade treaty with Japan in 1957 signalled a shift in orientation from Europe to East Asia as that region began to recover and industrialise. Domestic industry expanded rapidly with the advantage of tariffs and import quotas. The service sector grew even faster as mechanisation released blue-collar workers to join the white-collar salariat and office blocks rose up over the city streetscape. An annual growth rate of over 4 per cent was maintained throughout the 1950s and into the 1960s. There was full employment, higher productivity, improved earnings, a pattern of sustained improvement that no-one could recall. The chief problem that exercised the economic managers was not insufficient but excessive demand: outbreaks of inflation required credit squeezes in the early 1950s and again in 1960. It was a measure of the new mood that when unemployment rose to almost 3 per cent, it almost cost the Menzies government the 1961 election.

This was the era in which an economist could characterise Australia as a 'small, rich, industrial country', the point at which the ambitions of a settler society to outgrow the confines of dependence reached their zenith. When he opened a new stage of the Snowy Mountains project in 1958, Robert Menzies declared that 'this scheme is teaching us and everybody in Australia to think in a big way, to be thankful for big things, to be proud of big enterprises'. A committee of economic inquiry took economic success as the essential dynamic of national life: 'growth endows the community with a sense of vigour and social purpose'. For all its homage to private enterprise, the Menzies government was firmly committed to a strong public sector. Each year the revenue of the Commonwealth increased. The federal government provided grants to the States, which retained primary responsibility for health, education, public transport and other services. It continued to fund development projects, and through taxation and expenditure it encouraged its constituents to help themselves. There was assistance to home buyers, a tax rebate for dependent spouses, subsidies for private medical insurance. Old-age pensions were maintained, other forms of social security neglected. The maxim of the silver age was self-reliance.

The transition from the iron age to the silver age occurred under the shadow of the Cold War. An intense bipolar contest between communism and capitalism dominated world politics from the late 1940s and forced Australia to align itself more closely with the Western Alliance. The inability of the Labor government to preserve an independent distance from the demands of the international Cold War contributed to its fall in 1949. At home the Cold War gripped the country and divided the labour movement. The failure of Labor to withstand the effects of the domestic Cold War kept it out of national office through the 1950s and 1960s. A fear of communism permeated almost every aspect of public life, at once impelling the government to improve the welfare of citizens and inhibiting the opportunities for critical dissent and creative innovation.

At the end of the Second World War the Labor government was both grateful to the United States for its leadership of the war in the Pacific and wary of its ally's plans for the post-war settlement. In 1919, when the victors of the First World War met in Paris, the Australian prime minister had objected obstreperously to President Wilson's schemes of liberal internationalism. In 1945, when the victors of the Second World War converged on San Francisco to establish the United Nations, his successor was conscious that the crucial decisions had already been taken by meetings of the three principal powers, the United States, the Soviet Union and Britain. At Yalta earlier in that year they had allocated the territorial spoils, and the United States was already proceeding with plans that would give it unrestricted economic access to the non-communist sphere. Liberal internationalism through the United Nations now seemed the best chance for lesser countries such as Australia to safeguard their interests. Revival of the British Commonwealth as an economic and military alliance provided the best chance of a counterweight to American dominance.

Britain was clinging to the white Commonwealth while it grappled with the contraction of its capacity. The loss of India, Pakistan, Sri Lanka and Burma, intractable conflict in Palestine and a communist uprising in Malaya brought home the need to reduce the imperial role. After communists won power in China and Indonesian nationalists overthrew Dutch rule in 1949, the independence movement in East Asia was irresistible. In Africa the same impulses forced a less speedy, more contested decolonisation, while the island peoples in what the British high commissioner described as the 'peaceful backwater' of the Pacific proceeded subsequently along the same path to self-government. Britain, France, Holland, Belgium and Portugal either accepted the loss of empire or fought costly rearguard actions to delay the inevitable transfer of sovereignty to their former subject nations. Formal empires based on direct rule and displayed in colour-coded maps returned to an informal pattern of empire based on trade and investment, aid and armaments, these devices creating shifting spheres of influence and a far less stable world order. Under Labor, Australia accepted claims for national independence (and Australian unions assisted the Indonesian uprising) while holding fast to its own colonial regime in Papua New Guinea.

The mercurial minister for external affairs, H. V. Evatt, made this a period of intense busyness in Australian foreign policy. In both international forums and direct dealings with Britain and the United States, Evatt sought to play a prominent role, capped by his presidency of the General Assembly of the United Nations in 1948. But what role could a remote and thinly populated outpost of the white diaspora play? The Americans had no intention of altering their global strategy to accommodate this abrasive representative of a socialist government; they would not share military technology and in 1948 excluded Australia from intelligence information. The British Labour government was also relegated to second-rank status by the United States, and Australia provided important support for its residual economic and strategic interests in the region. The two countries thus embarked on a plan to develop their own atomic weapons with test sites in Australia and forward defence air bases to the north. It was this strategy that brought the Cold War security regime to Australia as British intelligence supervised the formation of the Australian Security and Intelligence Organisation in early 1949 to safeguard defence secrets and the leader of the Australian Communist Party was gaoled.

Labor had sought to avert such harsh dictates of the Cold War. While opposed to communist expansion and solicitous of a defence pact with the unresponsive United States, it could see that the polarisation of world politics into two armed camps would sub-ordinate it to United States foreign policy and impose an extreme anti-communism inimical to its own foreign and domestic aspir-ations. By 1949, however, the Cold War divisions had hardened. Stalinist regimes were installed in eastern Europe, Germany was divided, and the American airlift to west Berlin to break a Soviet blockade signalled the heightened confrontation across the Iron Curtain. The Liberals won office at the end of the year on a plat-form of resolute anti-communism, implemented with military assistance to help Britain defeat the communist insurgency in Malaya and despatch of troops to Korea in 1950 when fighting broke out there between communists and American-led forces. The new minister for external relations discerned a global pattern of communist aggression, now projected south from China to threaten the entire South-East Asian region. In 1951 Robert Menzies warned against the 'imminent danger of war'.

'With our vast territory and our small population', he added later, 'we cannot survive a surging Communist challenge from abroad except by the co-operation of powerful friends.' The first and indisputably the most powerful of those friends was the United States, a friendship formalised in 1951 with the negotiation of a security treaty between Australia, New Zealand and the United States (commonly abbreviated to ANZUS). For the Australian government this treaty cemented a special relationship with its protector, but there were many claimants to such a status and in truth the agreement bound the United States to provide only as much assistance to Australia against an external aggressor as it chose to provide. ANZUS was essentially a corollary to its system of alliances in the Asia-Pacific region, which served to reconcile Australia to America's far more important relationship with the former enemy, Japan. Australia was also included in the South-East Asian Treaty Organisation (SEATO) arranged by the United States in 1954 after communist forces defeated France in Vietnam, but that too guaranteed no more than Washington determined.

Britain was a member of SEATO, and Australia continued to encourage Britain by offering test sites for atomic devices and assisting its military presence in Malaya. This was a special relationship of a different kind and in 1956, when Britain defied the United States to join with France in war on Egypt over the administration of the Suez Canal, Menzies unhesitatingly threw his efforts behind the mother country. A romantic monarchist and fervent admirer of an idealised ancestral homeland, Menzies in his own words was 'British to the bootheels'. His gallantry during the Royal Tour of 1954 was attuned to the immense popularity of the young Queen Elizabeth, the first reigning monarch to visit Australia, but his hyperbole during her subsequent visit a decade later when he recited the verse

> I did but see her passing by,
> And yet I love her till I die

made listeners squirm and the Queen blush. His final gesture on the eve of retirement, a suggestion that the country's new unit of decimal currency should be named the 'royal', was mocked into oblivion. If the delayed but inevitable withdrawal of the British military presence was regretted, the reluctant but equally inescapable turn by Britain away from its Commonwealth trading relationships in order to enter Europe dealt a much heavier blow. It left Menzies's regular trips to London for Commonwealth meetings and Test cricket as a nostalgic anachronism; his discomfort with the multiracial composition of the Commonwealth, as former colonies became new members, and his defence of the apartheid regime in South Africa made Australia seem another outpost of an obsolete white man's club.

While Menzies's foreign ministers displayed greater interest in Asia, they regarded it always through the distorting prism of the Cold War. Even the Colombo Plan, a scheme for co-operative economic development among the Commonwealth countries of South and South-East Asia that brought 10,000 Asian students to study in Australia, was justified as a prophylactic against communist infection. It also brought the beneficiaries into direct experience of a still obdurately White Australia. Australians were

8.3 At a state reception in Parliament House, Canberra, on
18 February 1963, Robert Menzies pays fulsome tribute to
Queen Elizabeth. (National Library of Australia)

present in Asia as advisers, technicians, teachers, diplomats and
journalists, but most of all as soldiers. They engaged with their
neighbours through travel, study, art and literature, and yet Asia
remained a zone of contest and danger that required the presence in

force of their powerful friends. That need in turn required the Australian government during the 1950s and 1960s to play up the communist danger, to reduce the complexities of history, culture and nationality to the Cold War choice: are you ours or theirs?

It also meant that Australia had to follow the United States even when it was ahead. Fearful of the communist threat from the north, the Australian government exerted all of its limited influence to interpose American forces between China and the South-East Asian countries. From 1962 it provided military instructors to assist the anti-communist government of South Vietnam prevent unification with the communist North. Even before this country became directly involved in Indochina, it reintroduced military conscription and as soon as President Johnson made the fateful decision to introduce ground troops, in 1965, Australia responded immediately to the request for assistance it had solicited. South Vietnam itself played little part in the decision; it was regarded by the new minister for external affairs simply as 'our present frontier'. Harold Holt, who succeeded Menzies as prime minister in 1966, told his host at the White House that Australia would 'go all the way with LBJ'. By then, all the way fell some distance short of American expectations: in late 1968, when the American force had grown to 500,000, Australia contributed just 8000. As before with Britain, so now with the United States – obeisance to a powerful protector was payment in kind for defence on the cheap.

A preoccupation with the communist threat from without was linked always to the danger within. During the 1949 election campaign Menzies had undertaken to ban the Australian Communist Party. It was not a legitimate political movement but an 'alien and destructive pest' inimical to religion, civilised government and national security. Once elected, he proceeded with the passage of the Communist Party Dissolution Bill, which was enacted in 1950 but immediately challenged by the Communist Party itself as well as ten trade unions. Evatt, the deputy leader of the federal Labor Party and a former High Court judge, appeared before the court on behalf of the Waterside Workers Federation. He persuaded all but one of the current judges that the legislation, which depended upon the Commonwealth's defence powers, was unconstitutional since the country was not at war.

Menzies persisted with an attempt to gain the constitutional power by referendum and Evatt, who by now had become leader of the Labor Party following the death of Chifley in mid-1951, carried his party into opposing the proposal. The campaign was intense and the outcome close. Although the government failed narrowly to obtain the necessary majority of votes and a majority of States, if just 30,000 voters in South Australia or Victoria had voted Yes rather than No, the proposal would have succeeded. Still, it is difficult to imagine that a similar plebiscite in the United States, Britain or elsewhere would have failed to produce a majority in favour of suppressing communism. The affirmation of political freedom for a small and vilified cause in the fevered atmosphere of the early 1950s did the country credit.

This was Evatt's finest hour. He was in no sense a communist sympathiser but alarmed by the sweeping powers the government proposed to employ. Its legislation would shift the burden of proof to require citizens who were declared to be communists to demonstrate that they were not; upon such a declaration the person named could be dismissed from the public service and disqualified from trade union office; failure to cease activity in a banned organisation would be a crime punishable by up to five years imprisonment. The fact that in introducing the bill Menzies had falsely identified some trade union officials as communists, and even warned a Labor critic that he might be caught up in its provisions, seemed to Evatt and others to threaten essential liberties. The Australian Security and Intelligence Organisation had upon the election of the new government increased its surveillance over a wide range of persons – not just communists and radicals but scientists, academics and writers – and was at this time preparing for the internment of 7000 of them should war be declared. For Evatt to forestall the implementation of this repressive plan was a considerable achievement.

The referendum victory brought him no subsequent success, however. Within the labour movement there was a substantial and growing anti-communist element that condemned Evatt's appearance before the High Court and opposed his decision to fight the referendum. It had its origins in a lay religious organisation, the Catholic Social Studies Movement, led by a masterful zealot, B. A. Santamaria, who conducted his crusade against atheistic materialism with the assistance of powerful members of the church's hierarchy. Through the formation of industrial Groups in trade unions, the Movement had weakened communist influence. Since the unions were affiliated to the Labor Party, the Groupers began to capture leading positions in that organisation also. Labor lost the 1951 election called by Menzies to capitalise on the dissension in the Labor ranks over the banning of the Communist Party, and the following election in 1954 that was dominated by allegations of communist espionage. Following this defeat, Evatt denounced the Movement and the federal executive of the party replaced the Victorian branch leadership. A federal conference of the party in 1955 narrowly affirmed the executive's action. The anti-communists broke away to form their own Anti-Communist Labor Party, later renamed the Democratic Labor Party.

The Split destroyed Labor governments in Victoria and Queensland. Through the preferential system of voting, which enabled the 10 per cent of voters who followed the Democratic Labor Party to direct their support to the Liberal and Country Party coalition, it ensured conservative dominance in national politics for more than a decade. At the end of the war there were Labor governments in the Commonwealth and five of the six States; by 1960 just New South Wales and Tasmania, where Labor moderates cared more for power than ideological purity, remained in the Labor fold. The Split divided workmates and neighbours, poisoned the labour movement and left a Labor leadership clinging to past glories with dogmatic policies that were increasingly remote from the interests and sympathies of younger voters. As affluence and education eroded its manual working-class base, one commentator wondered if it was not doomed to Labor in Vain?

The very failure of Menzies to carry his referendum proposal to ban the Communist Party enabled him to take maximum advantage of the red scare. On the eve of the 1954 election he announced the defection of a Soviet diplomat, Vladimir Petrov, and his wife Evdokia. She was rescued at the Darwin airport from two thugs escorting her back to Moscow. Petrov claimed to have received information from a communist spy ring in Australia that included diplomats, journalists, academics and even members of the staff of the leader of the Labor Party. The government established a royal

8.4 Soviet officials escort Evdokia Petrova, the wife of a
Russian diplomat, onto an aircraft at Sydney after her husband
asked for political asylum. Petrova was released from their
custody and taken off the flight at Darwin. (News Limited,
19 April 1954)

commission to investigate these allegations, before which Evatt
appeared until his intemperate response to its partial conduct led to
his being barred from the hearings.

There was in fact an official of the Communist Party who had
recruited informants during the closing years of the Second World
War and passed on their intelligence to the Soviet embassy. For
that matter, American consular officials also gathered their own
intelligence from informants in far more influential vantage-points
from which to invigilate the unions and the unreliable Labor
government. There were no mandarin agents of the KGB here, no
moles burrowing deep into the establishment; just fervent young
men and women recruited when the Soviet Union was an Australian
ally to provide it with their limited knowledge of Cold War plans.
But by the time of Petrov the Soviet Union was no longer an ally, its
gathering of information no longer a product of naive idealism but
a furtive act of treason. In the Cold War atmosphere of the 1950s,

the Petrov inquiry strengthened Menzies's claim that the Labor Party was contaminated by communism, its leader's 'guise of defending justice and civil liberties' merely a cloak for shielding traitors.

The royal commission found no evidence that would justify the laying of charges against any Australian, but it blackened the names of many Australians who were denied any right of reply, their careers blighted, their children bullied at school. The Communist Party itself was a declining force, the revelations made in 1956 by Khrushchev about the Stalinist terror and then the Soviet repression of Hungarian liberalisation destroying its credibility and reducing the membership to fewer than 6000. Nevertheless, the domestic Cold War continued to excoriate dissent. Apart from the Petrov inquiry and an earlier State royal commission into communism, the demand for loyalty had not produced any Australian equivalent to the American system of loyalty oaths, official tribunals and systematic purges. Rather it operated at two levels, the clandestine surveillance of the Australian Security and Intelligence Organisation and the mobilisation of public opinion to secure acceptance of dismissals and bans.

The process was advanced in a national radio broadcast two months after the defeat of the referendum to ban communism. Advised of an announcement of the gravest national importance, listeners heard the chairman of the Australian Broadcasting Commission deliver the warning that 'Australia is in danger ... We are in danger from moral and intellectual apathy, from the mortal enemies of mankind which sap the will and darken the understanding and breed evil dissensions.' This Call to Australia was released by judges and church leaders, headed by the chief justice of the Victorian supreme court, financed by business magnates and organised by a Movement associate of Santamaria. It set the tone for much of the subsequent campaign in its language of chiliasm (Menzies also would talk of the Cold War as a battle between 'Christ and Anti-Christ'). Tactical Cold War initiatives converged with far more apocalyptic tendencies, as in the creation of the Australian arm of the Congress for Cultural Freedom to fight the war against communism among the intellectuals. The editor of its magazine, *Quadrant*, was James McAuley, a poet converted from anarchism to Catholicism of so conservative a temper that he railed against the liberal humanism his organisation was ostensibly defending.

The Cold War was prosecuted in the government's scientific organisation, the universities, literary associations and almost every corner of civic life. The mother of a well-known communist was expelled from her local branch of the Country Women's Association for refusing its loyalty oath; since she could no longer play the piano at its meetings, the members had to endure an inferior rendering of 'God Save the Queen'. Not even sport escaped. During the 1952 season of the Australian rules football competition in Victoria, ministers gave half-time addresses on the Call to Australia. A prominent Methodist preacher found the audience at the Lakeside Oval in South Melbourne unreceptive and appealed to common ground with the claim that 'After all, we are all Christians.' 'What about the bloody umpire?', came a reply from the outer.

The communist threat operated as a powerful inducement for capitalist democracies to inoculate their peoples with generous doses of improvement. The rivalry between the eastern and western blocs was conducted both as an arms race and a competition for economic growth and living standards. Freedom from hardship and insecurity would deprive the agitator of his audience; regular earnings, increased social provision and improved opportunity would attach beneficiaries to their civic duties. But improvement brought its own dangers. In the Call to Australia there was a concern that a prosperous mass society was vulnerable to a loss of vigour and purpose; hence its admonition against moral and intellectual apathy. As classical civilisations advanced to their silver and golden ages, so comfort bred luxury and vice that softened their iron rigour. Even in 1951 Menzies warned that 'If material prosperity is to induce in us greed or laziness, then we will lose our prosperity.' Prosperity was sustained, but the transformation of social life it effected was accompanied by a cluster of moral anxieties.

In the course of the long boom the mainland cities spread rapidly beyond their earlier limits. The population of Sydney passed two million in the late 1950s, Melbourne in the early 1960s, when Adelaide and Brisbane were approaching one million and Perth had grown to more than half a million. The city centres were rebuilt in concrete and glass to provide for their expanded administrative and commercial activities, but the most significant movement was out of the inner suburbs to new ones on the peripheries. At the end of the war there was an acute housing shortage, forcing families to share dilapidated terraces. By the beginning of the 1960s a modern, detached home on a quarter-acre block had become the norm.

Some of the new housing was publicly constructed; most of it was built either by private developers or the occupiers themselves. The first object of most married couples was to purchase a lot, then save till they could build. A 1957 'portrait of a new community' on the outskirts of Sydney described 'nights and weekends ... alive with the constant beat of the hammer, the whirr of the saw, the odorous skid of the plane'. After this initial occupation came the erection of fences, the making of gardens and the weekend whine of the motor mower; then the working-bee on the church hall and the school playground. The rate of home ownership increased from 53 per cent in 1947, which was the historic norm, to an unprecedented 70 per cent by 1961, among the highest in the world. Along with the residences went the factories. The older workshops and ware-houses that threaded the inner-city streets were abandoned for new purpose-built plants on industrial estates. The sound of the hooter, the bustle of movement, the discharge of waste and the din of industry yielded to the hum of the generator and the orderly motion of the assembly line.

Joining home to work was the motor car. In 1949 one Australian in eight owned a car, by the early 1960s one in five. Cars and trucks freed industry from the older patterns of central location based on rail and coal. They enabled the cities to sprawl; they filled the wedges of country between the rail lines with commuter suburbs. Public transport languished, and except in Melbourne the trams were removed to make way for the rush-hour stream of motor traffic. Cars created new forms of leisure, such as the drive-in theatre; new ways of holidaying with caravan and motel; new forms of shopping at suburban supermarkets; new rituals such as the Sunday drive, customs in common performed separately.

8.5 The convenience and abundance of the supermarket proclaimed the triumph of modernity. This early example combines the technology of the space age with national and imperial flags. (Coles–Myer Archives)

Both the move to the suburbs and the accumulation of posses-sions within the suburban home redefined the role of the housewife. Her contribution as a domestic provider was shrinking, her role as a consumer growing. She did less of the sewing, mending, pro-cessing and improvising, or taking in boarders, on which a family's comfort had once relied. She purchased more goods and services, and her family's standard of living was now more dependent on the washing machine, refrigerator, television and other consumer durables that could not be made at home. Visitors to Australia were struck by the segregation of the sexes; local experts took it as an amenity of the growing affluence. 'Whenever they can, Australian women mostly revert to their favoured roles of full-time wives and mothers', one wrote in 1957. Whether through choice or need, an increasing proportion did not. Between 1947 and 1961 the number of married women in the workforce increased fourfold, and in 1950 the Arbitration Court increased women's pay to 75 per cent of the male basic wage. The basic wage was all many of them received. Women's employment remained subsidiary to their responsibilities in the home. The new commuter suburbs on the edges of the cities were places where men commuted and women stayed.

The cities themselves became far more conscious of their images. When Melbourne won the right to stage the 1956 Olympic Games, its image-makers worried that the licensing restrictions, the lackadaisical taxi drivers and even the bare linoleum on hotel floors might hold it up to ridicule. Friendliness became the motif, the dominant theme a mix of graceful parks and gardens with 'rising tiers and spreading flats of steel and concrete, bronze and glass, in great buildings, modern in conception, at once functional and imaginative in execution'. The year 1956 also brought television, a potent medium to extend familiarity with the plenitude of idealised American family shows and to enlist viewers of the commercial channels in the drama of consumer desire. Advertising became a major business, divining and shaping those desires.

The first television consoles took pride of place in the family living room. Along with the advertising industry, electronic entertainment distinguished the man of the home from the housewife and the children, but took longer to disaggregate its audience into separate markets with distinct styles and tastes. The post-war family was widely regarded as the basic unit of society, undifferentiated in structure and function if not in circumstance. It was a 'nuclear family', that term denoting the absence of additional members in the isolated suburban setting, but also suggesting that this primary element was the essential source of energy. The post-war demographic bulge, with marriages deferred until after the war and then several children coming in rapid succession, encouraged the belief. A higher marriage rate at younger ages increased the birthrate. The 'baby-boomers' swamped the maternity hospitals and infant welfare centres after the war, then during the 1950s burst the capacity of primary schools. By the 1960s they forced a crash programme to build and staff secondary schools for the increasing numbers that stayed on beyond the school-leaving age and even continued to university.

Government welcomed the trend as an investment in social capital and an enhancement of national capacity. The school of physics for nuclear research was the most ambitious and expensive section of the institute of advanced studies at the post-war Australian National University; a nuclear physicist conducted the second major inquiry in 1964 that guided expansion of the universities;

the boost to science education following the success of the Soviet Sputnik led to the first Commonwealth support for private schools in 1963 with funding for their science laboratories. Never before had the custodians of scientific knowledge commanded such authority or flaunted it so confidently. The chairman of the country's Atomic Energy Commission explained that 'technological civilisation' presented a stream of complex problems that 'only a small proportion of the population is capable of understanding'. To submit such issues to the voter or the politician could 'only lead to trouble and possible disaster': 'the experts must in the end be trusted'.

Yet the nuclear family was beset by dangers. It was menaced by sexual irregularity, the repression of homosexuality gathering force from its Cold War associations with disloyalty. It was vulnerable to breakdown, the sharp increase in divorce after the war of intense concern to churches that seemed to be losing their moral authority to materialism and secularism. It was preoccupied with youth, the discovery by psychologists of the adolescent and the cultivation by consumer industries of the teenager helping to mark out a disturbing additional figure, the juvenile delinquent. Two contrary tendencies operated here. On the one hand young people were readily able to find work, had greater disposable income and were presented with an array of products – clothes, records, concerts, comics, dances, cinema, even motorbikes and cars – on which to spend it. On the other, the demands of suburban domesticity and the extended dependence associated with further education enclosed teenagers within heightened expectations. The moral panic generated by the 'bodgie' and 'widgie' in the rock-and-roll era of the 1950s, and variant identities associated with later musical styles, each with its distinctive dress, dialect and ritual, was also a class phenomenon. The teenager from a working-class home was least likely to defer entry to the workforce, most likely to become the 'social misfit' who resisted the suburban dream.

At the same time as conservatives denounced this juvenile delinquent, however, radicals lamented the disappearance of the working-class rebel. Cold War inroads into the trade unions, coupled with new powers of the Menzies government to penalise strikes, reduced industrial conflict. The decline of the older

8.6 Sydney teenagers gather to see the film *Rock Around the Clock* in 1956. The presence of the photographer encourages their self-display. (Sydney *Daily Telegraph*, 16 September 1956)

occupational neighbourhoods, with their dense overlay of work and leisure, family and friendship, seemed to such critics to weaken class solidarity. They saw the increased social and geographical mobility, the new patterns of consumption and recreation, as attaching suburban Australians to the pleasures of the home and family at the expense of work-based loyalties.

As before, when confronted with the failure of millennial expectations, the left retreated into a nostalgic idealisation of national traditions. Its writers, artists and historians turned from the stultifying conformity of the suburban wilderness to the memories of an older Australia that was less affluent and more generous, less gullible and more vigilant of its liberties, less timorous and more independent. In works such as *The Australian Tradition* (1958), *The Australian Legend* (1958) and *The Legend of the Nineties* (1954), the radical nationalists reworked the past (they passed quickly over the militarism and xenophobia in the national experience) to assist them in their present struggles. Try as they might to revive these traditions, the elegiac note was clear. The radical nationalists codified the legend of laconic, egalitarian, stoical mateship just as modernising forces of change were erasing the circumstances that had given rise to that legend.

While the radical romance faded, the conservative courtship of national sentiment prospered. It was embedded in government policies designed to assimilate a population of increasing ethnic diversity into the customs and values of their adopted country. In the two decades after 1947 more than two million migrants settled here, the majority from non-English-speaking countries. With their children they contributed more than half of the population increase to more than twelve million by the end of the 1960s. 'Our aim', Arthur Calwell had laid down in 1949, 'is to Australianise all our migrants ... in as short a time as possible.' While his Liberal successors relaxed the opposition to ethnic societies and foreign-language newspapers, that aim continued. 'I am quite determined', the minister for immigration affirmed twenty years later, 'we should have a monoculture, with everyone living in the same way, understanding each other, and sharing the same aspirations.'

On the ships, in the holding centres and migrant hostels, in language classes and naturalisation ceremonies, through 'Good Neighbour' committees and other voluntary organisations, they were taught the Australian Way of Life. That term allowed a shift from the restrictions of ancestry or the traditions of national legend to the cultivation of life-style. Its depiction of Australia as a sophisticated, urban, industrialised consumer society had clear Cold War implications. An article on 'The Australian Way of Life', written by a refugee for the celebration of the fiftieth anniversary of the Commonwealth, spelt them out: 'What the Australian cherishes most is a home of his own, a garden where he can potter and a motor car ... A person who owns a house, a garden, a car and has a fair job is rarely an extremist or a revolutionary.'

More modest expectations governed Aboriginal policy. In 1951 the Commonwealth minister for territories confirmed the official objective of assimilation: 'Assimilation means, in practical terms, that, in the course of time, it is expected that all persons of Aboriginal blood or mixed blood in Australia will live like White Australians do.' That would require 'many years of slow, patient endeavour'; in the meantime there remained the restrictive regime of protection, the exclusion from white society and pervasive discrimination. Migrant Australians responded to broken promises with protest but their ultimate recourse was to return home. Indigenous Australians had no such opportunity, though they too sought their homelands.

In the Pilbara region of Western Australia, Aboriginal pastoral workers went on strike for better pay in 1946 and despite official harassment they secured improvements; but not all of them returned to work, for they had established their own co-operative settlement. Again in 1966, 200 Gurindji walked off a pastoral station in northern Australia and a claim for equal pay turned into a demand for their own land. Between these two most celebrated actions were numerous lesser ones, fiercely resisted by pastoralists and governments and commonly blamed on communist agitators. There were communists involved on both occasions, and communist-led unions were most active in their support. In Darwin the communist officials of the North Australian Workers Union backed post-war Aboriginal claims for equal pay, while their successors abandoned the campaign. The Federal Council for the Advancement of Aborigines, formed in 1957 as a left initiative, assisted a new generation of Aboriginal activists.

There was growing unrest on the reserves. Palm Island, an Aboriginal settlement off the coast of Queensland used for the confinement of recalcitrants on similar lines to the convict settlements more than a century earlier, saw an uprising against a tyrannical superintendent in 1957. The victimisation of the Aboriginal artist Albert Namatjira, denied permission to build a house in Alice Springs a year after he was presented to Queen Elizabeth, and gaoled for six months in 1958 for supplying alcohol to a relative who was not a citizen, drew attention to the absence of assimilation. That policy was proclaimed in government publications showing Aboriginal children in the classroom, the boys in shorts and white socks, the girls in cotton tunics, novitiates to the Australian Way of Life. It was practised in the removal of children from their families so that they could better be trained in white ways, an activity that continued through the 1950s and 1960s. Not until the early 1980s was there a belated government recognition of

8.7 Aboriginal children form up in military ranks at the Bungalow, Northern Territory, during the Second World War. They were subsequently removed from the Territory for the duration of the war. (Australian War Memorial)

the trauma of separation with the establishment of the first Link-Up agencies. Not until 1992 did an Australian prime minister acknow-ledge the damage it caused and apologise to its victims, in a speech to Aborigines assembled at Redfern Park in inner Sydney to launch the Year of the World's Indigenous People. His successor resolutely refused to do the same. The first cases for compensation are now before the courts.

The casualties of the Australian Way of Life were seldom acknowledged in the celebration of post-war achievement. It was a

8.8 Surf life-saving clubs patrolled Australian beaches to rescue swimmers from being swept out to sea. A formal march was a feature of their competitive carnivals. Here a stylised flag-bearer leads the way. (*History of Bondi Surf Bathers Life Saving Club, 1956*, Bondi, NSW: Bondi Surf Bathers Life Saving Club, 1956)

golden age of sport, with Australian triumphs on the cricket field against England after the war heralding an era of success in athletics, swimming, tennis and golf. The 'golden girls' dominated the track at the Melbourne Olympics, when Australia won thirty-five medals, and both men and women continued supremacy in the pool. In the post-war decades Australian men won half of the major tennis titles and achieved fifteen Davis Cup victories in twenty years. These keenly followed contests with the United States became a surrogate for the relationship between the two countries, mediating dependence as Test cricket had done for the imperial relationship.

Australians liked to think that their egalitarian ethos, favourable climate and broad participation (there were more tennis courts in relation to population than any other country in the 1950s) prevailed over the grim professionalism of the Yanks. In truth tennis in America was restricted to the wealthy amateur, whereas the Australians bent the rules with sponsorship, coaching and other forms of 'shamateur' assistance. It was an American professional who remarked that the Australians had 'short arms and deep pockets'. The amateur ideal was better expressed at the beach where the surf life-saving clubs flourished to patrol the breakers and rescue over-adventurous swimmers from the treacherous rip. With their combination of voluntarism, masculinity (women were initially excluded) and competition, the life-saving clubs blended the hedonism of the beach with the militarised discipline of belt drill and march past. As one club historian put it, they were 'truly Australian in spirit', their free association in 'humanitarian mate-ship' without barriers of creed, class or colour an example of democracy 'as it was meant' to operate.

The golden age lasted through the 1960s until the early 1970s, but before then Australia was caught up in mounting problems. The retirement of Robert Menzies at the beginning of 1966 might be taken as a turning-point in the government's fortunes. The last prime minister to choose his moment of departure, he was at the age of seventy a man out of sympathy with the times. Yet so complete was his political mastery that the task of succession proved beyond the conservatives. The remaining six years of the 'Ming dynasty'

8.9 In 1966 the prime minister, Harold Holt, visited the
United States to proclaim that Australia would go 'all the
way' with its ally in Vietnam. Four months later President
Johnson returned the visit. He is shown here speaking at the
Canberra airport with Holt in submissive deference.
(David Moore Photography)

brought three inept prime ministers, Harold Holt, John Gorton and
William McMahon. The first one drowned; the second fell to a
palace revolt; and the last was routed in a general election that
drove the Liberal and Country Party coalition from office. Some of
the difficulties the government faced were beyond its control, some
of its own making; such were the expectations after two decades
of success that it was blamed for most of them. A new Labor
government took office in 1972 on a wave of enthusiasm for change
that would make good the years of missed opportunity. At break-
neck speed it set out to do so, only to crash three years later when
the long boom ended and the golden era passed.

The Vietnam War proved the heaviest millstone round the
conservatives' neck. At first it was popular and used by them to
renew the coalition's electoral mandate in 1966 and 1969. Visits
by the United States president as well as the leader of South
Vietnam boosted the government's stocks. 'Run over the bastards',
the Liberal premier of New South Wales instructed a police
superintendent when informed that demonstrators were blocking

the motorcade of President Johnson in 1966. But the Tet offensive of 1968 punctured the illusion of American superiority and drove Johnson out of office. His successor resorted to mass bombing and invasion of Cambodia, then Laos, in a forlorn endeavour to stave off inevitable defeat. Meanwhile the Australian casualties mounted. Of 50,000 who served in Vietnam by 1972, 500 were lost and they included nearly 200 conscripts.

Conscription for an unjust war was the primary issue for a peace movement that began with the lonely vigils of the women's group Save Our Sons, and swelled into noisy protest by radical students, until by 1970 it filled city streets with a Moratorium demonstration. Horrifying images of children with napalm burns, random street executions and reports of massacres combined with the bizarre ritual whereby young Australian men were required to register for national service and then be selected by drawing birthdates from a barrel in a 'lottery of death'. A generational divide widened between ministers who sought to justify the war and those they sent to fight it.

> We are the young they drafted out
> To wars their folly brought about.
> Go tell those old men, safe in bed,
> We took their orders and are dead.

By 1970 the government began withdrawing Australian forces and scarcely bothered to pursue the growing numbers of draft resisters.

The war came to an end with the fall of Saigon in 1975, but the Australian involvement ceased in 1972 when it was clear that its strategy of forward defence lay in tatters. President Nixon had signalled the withdrawal of the United States from the Cold War alliance in South-East Asia; his visit to China in 1972, exploiting the breach between that country and the Soviet Union, undermined the insistent logic of Australian foreign policy since 1950 which was built on the assumption of a monolithic communist threat. Australia had eagerly followed its powerful friend into Indochina, only to discover 'how military decisions are being made for political ends', as one minister lamented. More than this, he was astonished to discover 'that public opinion can be mobilised to interfere with public policy', an intrusion he likened to the actions of the London mob on the eighteenth-century British parliament. An egregious colleague attempted a more modern comparison when he described the Moratorium demonstrators as 'political bikies who pack-rape democracy'. This was a government badly out of touch.

The Korean War had stimulated the world economy; the Vietnam War strained it. The United States met its huge cost by printing dollars, which as the reserve currency for international trade washed into the financial system and increased inflationary pressures. By the end of the 1960s there were signs of strain in the Australian economy. Farmers continued to increase production but faced a steady decline in returns; caught in a cost–price squeeze, they had to form larger holdings. By 1971 there was an absolute drop in the rural population to less than two million, just 14 per cent of the national total. It was fortunate that new mining discoveries in Western Australia allowed the export of bauxite and iron ore to Asian markets, and the discovery of a major oilfield in Bass Strait in 1966 brought Australia closer to self-sufficiency in fossil fuels. While the mineral boom excited a speculative flurry on the stock exchanges, the national economy remained heavily dependent on foreign capital and imported technology. Large companies dominated major industries, with tariff protection restricting competition, and a high level of foreign ownership in key sectors such as the car industry. Unions became more aggressive in demands for wage increases. Twenty years of industrialisation and urban growth had created new dissatisfactions. The inner suburbs were pocked with decay and pollution. The outer suburbs lacked basic services. Provision of health and education lagged behind demand. There was a rediscovery that full employment did not bring prosperity for all, and that the piecemeal welfare system failed to assist those in greatest need. A pattern of private affluence and public neglect was clear.

The very beneficiaries of affluence began to reject their inheritance. As the Australian Way of Life was established in the new suburbs, its chief critics were modernist intellectuals who used the weapons of irony and parody. In his stringent condemnation of *Australia's Home* (1952), the architect Robin Boyd condemned the 'aesthetic calamity' of a suburbia that carried bad taste to the 'blind end of the road'. He inveighed against the 'wild scramble of outrageous featurism' that disfigured the wealthier neighbourhoods just as another architect deprecated the 'sterile little boxes tinged with an anaemic echo of wrought iron and a carport' in the mortgage belt. In satirical monologues first developed for a revue in 1955, the entertainer Barry Humphries, who had grown up in the heart of Melbourne's middle-class suburbia in a house designed by his father, created a range of characters addicted to mediocrity: the upwardly mobile Edna Everage and her henpecked husband Norm, the invincibly platitudinous Sandy Stone. 'I always wanted more', Humphries begins his memoirs.

He and other tertiary-educated contemporaries such as Germaine Greer and Clive James would abandon Australia to achieve international success. Unable to reconcile themselves to the dullness, the conformity and the philistinism of their youthful homeland, as 'expats' they would remain trapped in the role of gadflies. Other malcontents fled suburbia for the refuge of the inner-city surrounds, where European migrants were beginning to create a more metropolitan ambience with wine, food and street life – only to assist in the gentrification of their sanctuary. The modernists found the orderly life in the suburbs stultifying and oppressive; freedom and fulfilment were to be found at the extremes, in bohemian irregularity. It took an unusually perceptive historian, Hugh Stretton, to recognise the satisfactions of house and garden on a quarter-acre block in his reformist exploration of *Ideas for Australian Cities* (1970). Only much later, when the suburban dream was finally broken, did younger historians return to the suburbs as a postmodern place of deviance and danger, the habitat of *The Beasts of Suburbia* (1994).

With the baby-boomers' rejection of their parents' way of life, the conservative order crumbled. In the self-styled New Left that came to international prominence on campuses in 1968, the year of the barricades, the Vietnam War was just part of a broader movement to emancipate the Third World from Cold War imperialism that had its domestic counterpart in the struggle to liberate advanced industrial societies from their own excesses. The New Left combined a rejection of consumerism, with its destructive effects on the environment; careerism, with its denial of individuality; and conventional morality, with its inhibition of self-fulfilment. This new radicalism was iconoclastic in its rejection of respectability; theatrical in its use of language, gesture, clothing and personal appearance; ambitious in its attempt to mark out a counter-culture that extended to all aspects of personal relationships; romantic in its expectation that the removal of all barriers to intimacy would create harmony.

The New Left was also oppositional, yet the absorption of its ideas and attitudes gave it a pervasive cultural influence: by the end of the 'sixties an uncomfortable prime minister posed uncomfortably alongside popular singers in an effort to appear attuned to the new mood. It had novel significance in its break from the hierarchical discipline of the Old Left for more informal, participatory and expressive practices, and the associated shift from the organised working class to the progressive intelligentsia. A similar break marked the emergence of women's liberation, gay liberation and similar emancipatory projects. They foreshadowed the emergence of the new social movements as distinctive forms of issue-based politics based on fluid yet compelling identities – the nomads of the present.

The new politics rejected the conformity of mass society and disputed its mechanism of control. Campaigns against censorship, capital punishment and racial discrimination gathered force. An Immigration Reform Group campaigned for the abolition of the White Australia Policy, which was in any case a growing embarrassment to the government – the dictation test was quietly dropped in 1958, naturalisation was facilitated in 1966, and by the end of the decade some 10,000 non-whites were entering annually. Other migrant groups were increasingly assertive of their cultural identity. By far the most dramatic challenge came from the Aboriginal movement, and at the very moment when government belatedly began to give effect to its policy of assimilation. In 1959 the Commonwealth extended welfare benefits to all but 'nomadic or primitive' Aborigines, and in 1962 it provided the right to vote. In 1965 the Arbitration Court awarded equal pay for Aboriginal pastoral workers. In 1967 a national referendum, supported by all major political parties and carried by an overwhelming majority, gave the Commonwealth power to legislate for Aborigines.

The last of these measures marked a watershed. The earlier changes were designed to remove the formal disadvantages that prevented Aborigines from becoming free and equal citizens of Australia; this one, while commonly regarded then and now as conferring citizenship, singled them out as a special category of people for whom the Commonwealth could legislate over the discriminatory arrangements of more conservative States. The coalition government failed to do so. Rather, it resisted the growing demands of Aborigines for recognition of their claims for self-determination. Just as the Commonwealth had rejected the land claim of the Gurindji in northern Australia in 1967, so it dismissed a 1963 bark petition by the Yolngu people of Arnhem Land who opposed a mining project on their land and opposed the unsuccessful court action brought in 1968 for legal recognition of their land rights.

These disappointments in areas of traditional occupation were accompanied by an upsurge of Aboriginal protest in the towns and cities of the south. Young activists no longer worked through white organisations for equality; rather, they celebrated their distinctiveness, their 'black pride' and their 'black power'. 'Black is more than a colour, it is also a state of mind', said Bobbi Sykes. These ideas drew on overseas precedents. Just as a Freedom Ride by student radicals through rural New South Wales in 1965 echoed a tactic of the civil rights movement in the United States, so the more forceful assertion of a separate identity followed a similar turn there. The most spectacular display of black power in Australia was the Aboriginal tent embassy on the lawns in front of Parliament House in Canberra. Erected on Australia Day 1972, it symbolised the changed objective: no longer acceptance but separation. For months it remained until a rattled prime minister created a new ordinance to have it removed. Television screens showed the ensuing struggle between the police and its custodians. 'Everybody knows', the leader of the Labor Party proclaimed, 'that if it were not the young and the black involved in this matter the Government would not have dared to proceed.' He was in fact performing the obsequies for a government that was voted out of office a few weeks later.

The Labor leader was Gough Whitlam, elected to that position in 1967 after a long struggle with the old guard led by its gnarled centurion, Arthur Calwell. Whitlam, a large man of magisterial self-regard, was a moderniser who directed his initial energies into modernising his own party. He sought to discard its socialist shibboleths, its preoccupation with trade union concerns and Cold War arguments, so that it could appeal to the suburban middle class. Accordingly he developed policies designed to make good the failures of twenty years of coalition rule. In modern conditions, he argued, the capacity to exercise citizenship was determined not by an individual's income 'but the availability and accessibility of the services which the community alone can provide and ensure'.

Through an enlargement of government activity, he would apply the national wealth to projects of urban renewal, improved education and health, and an expanded range of public amenities. He would sweep away the accretion of restrictions and special interests to augment the nation's capacity and enlarge the life of its citizens. Whitlam was the first 'silvertail' to lead the federal Labor Party (in South Australia another defector from the establishment, Don Dunstan, anticipated his success with similar policies at the State level) and the first to abandon labourism for social democracy. Tellingly, when asked to give an example of how he understood equality, he replied that 'I want every kid to have a desk, with a lamp, and his own room to study.' The light on the desk replaced the light on the hill.

The renovated Labor Party came into office in 1972 with the election slogan 'It's Time', and commenced to implement its programme at an impetuous tempo. In the first month the government withdrew the last troops from Vietnam, ended military conscription, established diplomatic relations with China, announced independence for Papua New Guinea and the ratification of international conventions on nuclear weapons, labour and racism, and abandoned imperial honours. Here and afterwards Whitlam cultivated a nationalism that allowed for internationalism. Expansion of support for the arts, increased Australian content requirements for television and preservation of historic sites were among the initiatives designed to promote greater national awareness. With the revival of local publishing, theatre and film, they contributed to a cultural renaissance that made it possible to see life in this country as possessing a depth of meaning and richness of possibility. The completion in 1973 of the Sydney Opera House and the acquisition by the new National Gallery of 'Blue Poles', the large, dribbling creation of Jackson Pollock, caught the mood of expansive engagement. For Manning Clark, whose vast and prophetic *History of Australia* also caught the new mood (the third volume, with its emphasis on the struggle for and against an independent Australia, appeared in 1973), this was the end of the ice age.

The Whitlam government recast nationhood to remove official discrimination against non-British migrants and prohibit all forms of discriminatory treatment on the basis of race and ethnicity. Assimilation was abandoned as incompatible with an increasing diversity that was now celebrated for its enrichment of national life. As monoculture yielded to multiculture, so the recognition of difference became an aid to the removal of disadvantage. Ethnic groups were to be accorded their own services to ensure that their particular needs were met. Women finally achieved the full adult minimum wage as the result of an Arbitration Court decision in 1974, and more was promised to give practical effect to that formal equality: maternity leave and child-care centres for working women, along with women's health centres and refuges. The prime minister's appointment of an adviser on women's issues, Elizabeth Reid, brought a new conjunction of feminism and public policy, and soon a new Australianism, 'femocrat', to capture the novel role of those who sought to reconcile their duties as public servants with their loyalties to the women's movement in regulatory affirmative action. Similar strains were apparent in the new Department of Aboriginal Affairs where Aboriginal administrators answered to white superiors as they introduced a range of activities, including a medical service and a legal service, tailored to the particular needs of their people. The simultaneous creation of an elected national council to represent Aboriginal interests did not defuse the tension because it was restricted to an advisory role.

The government introduced its social programme through major national inquiries and implemented it by the creation of new national authorities with national funding for their activities. A Schools Commission provided the charter for Commonwealth support of private as well as government schools, increased university funding and the abolition of tuition fees. A health inquiry created a scheme of universal medical insurance. A commission of inquiry into poverty expanded the welfare system. Another commissioner prepared recommendations for the legal recognition of Aboriginal land rights in the federal territories, though the government fell before they could be implemented. A new Department of Urban and Regional Development assisted State and local government to improve urban amenities, and funded the acquisition and development of land for housing. Whitlam extended the ambit of national government further than any peacetime leader before or since – he even discarded the term 'Commonwealth of Australia' as an anachronism – and encountered growing opposition from the State governments.

His catchphrase, 'crash through or crash', indicated the government's way of dealing with constitutional and political obstacles. He was less attentive to the economic constraints, even though his government doubled public expenditure in its three years of office. In keeping with its modernising ambitions, the government made a 25-per-cent across-the-board cut in the tariff in 1973. With upward revaluation of the currency, many local manufacturers went to the wall. At the same time prices and wages were both rising, at an annual rate of more than 10 per cent by the end of 1973. Then came the oil embargo imposed on the West by the Arab states in retaliation for the Yom Kippur war, and then a fourfold increase in the cost of oil. The direct effect on Australia was limited, for it was able to meet most of its energy needs. The indirect effects were catastrophic. The inflationary effects of the oil crisis sent a shock-wave across the world economy that fractured the networks of trade and investment. In the years following 1974 the advanced industrial nations experienced the novel malaise of 'stagflation' – stagnant production with high inflation. The Keynesian techniques of economic management that had guided the post-war long boom provided no remedy for such a combination because one was meant to be the obverse of the other. For a brief period the Whitlam government ignored Treasury advice and the inflation to keep the throttle open, but unemployment still rose to levels not seen since the 1930s. In 1975 it tackled inflation with a contractionary budget and unemployment passed 250,000. The golden age was over.

By this time the government was beset by crisis. Several senior ministers had resigned or been sacked following scandals. One of them had been negotiating with shady international financiers for an unauthorised $4 billion loan to keep national control over Australian oil, gas and uranium processing. The Opposition, which controlled the Senate, used the 'loans affair' as a reason to refuse supply; by starving the government of funds, it hoped to force it to an election. In this strategy it had many allies. Business leaders had lost confidence in the government, the press was baying for blood. Sir John Kerr, the governor-general, resented his prime minister's imperious manner. Sir Garfield Barwick, a former conservative minister turned chief justice, was advising the governor-general that he had the power as head of state to dismiss the government, and encouraging him to do his duty. Both the United States ambassador and officers of its Central Intelligence Agency were highly critical of the Labor government, especially its desire to exercise some control over the American military communications facilities that had been built at the North-West Cape and Pine Gap during the 1960s.

The government had its loyal defenders – it was remarkable how many libertarians of the New Left accommodated themselves to Whitlam's expansion of state activity – but doubted they would prevail in an election. It therefore determined to hold out in the expectation that some coalition members of the Senate would lose their nerve. Some were close to allowing supply after a deadlock of twenty-seven days, but the governor-general acted first. In the early afternoon of 11 November 1975 he dismissed the government and commissioned the Liberal leader, Malcolm Fraser, as a caretaker prime minister to obtain supply and call an election. Fraser did so and won the election by a record majority.

The Dismissal was the most serious constitutional crisis in Australian history. As news of the governor-general's actions spread, a crowd gathered at the national parliament in Canberra. When the governor-general's secretary stood on the steps of the parliament to read the proclamation that dissolved both its chambers, a minatory Gough Whitlam glared over his shoulder to denounce Fraser as 'Kerr's cur' and exhort the assembly to 'maintain your rage'. In the nation's principal cities work stopped for impromptu demonstrations that canvassed direct action. Yet Whitlam acceded to his dismissal and the leader of the Australian Council of Trade Unions quelled all talk of a strike. The events of 1975 certainly strained the system of government. The heated atmosphere fomented a conspiratorial interpretation of political activity; the willingness of men in high office to bend the rules inflicted severe damage on constitutional propriety. Whitlam himself remains a highly controversial figure. For some he is a hero, cut down in his prime; for others he was a dangerous incompetent. The last national leader to follow his convictions regardless of consequence, he rose and fell as the possibilities for a confident and expansive national government ended.

9

Reinventing Australia, 1975–1999

After the chronic political instability that marked the conservative collapse and then the feverish pace of life under Whitlam, the years afterwards present an outward appearance of equilibrium. Between 1975 and 1991 there was just one change of government, and two prime ministers held office for roughly equal terms. Both in their own ways were striving for the security the electorate desired, and both held to the middle ground. Yet in the circumstances that now prevailed there could be no security without upsetting the ingrained habits of the past. One preferred confrontation and the other consensus as the way to achieve change, but the change they forced was never sufficient. There was always a need to go further, to abandon yet another outmoded practice and take on additional innovation. Both leaders employed their considerable personal authority to advance the process. Both were quickly reviled by their supporters as soon as they lost office for excessive timidity and insufficient leadership. In the pursuit of a constantly receding goal of competitive efficiency, Australians were subjected to an unending process of national reinvention.

The first of these leaders was Malcolm Fraser, who headed a Liberal–National Party coalition from 1975 to 1983. The tall, lean scion of a pastoral dynasty from the Liberal heartland of Victoria, he was educated at private schools and Oxford University. A shy, awkward manner was commonly interpreted as patrician aloofness. The grim determination with which Fraser had pursued power carried over into his exercise of it: he was constantly driving his

9.1 During the constitutional crisis that culminated with the Dismissal of the Labor government in 1975, the caretaker government organised mass rallies. Malcolm Fraser, the leader of the Liberal Party, acknowledges a throng of supporters in Melbourne. (Melbourne *Age*, 1975)

colleagues, involved in every aspect of policy, impulsive yet deliberate. 'Life is not meant to be easy' was a provocative pronouncement from one who seemingly inherited the privileges of a ruling class, but it was the genuine credo of a man who drove himself to the limit. It signified his rejection of the expectations Whitlam had encouraged. Fraser believed that Australians had been coddled into softness and complacency, that they needed to be weaned from dependence on public provision for the stern rigours of competition. Try as he might to reduce government, however, he habitually intervened to ensure strong leadership. A rugged individualism warred with instinctive Tory paternalism.

Fraser won elections in 1977 and 1980 over a discredited Labor Party. In 1983 the voters rejected him for a new Labor leader, Bob Hawke. Apart from also studying at Oxford, as a Rhodes scholar, he differed from Fraser in almost every respect. One was tall, the other short; one was clipped in speech, the other cultivated a stridently vernacular accent. Fraser was angular, Hawke a conciliator; Fraser prim, Hawke a reformed drinker and womaniser; Fraser exercised power as a duty, Hawke wooed popularity with an almost biblical conviction of personal destiny. The new prime minister was a child of a Congregational manse who worked for the Australian Council of Trade Unions and in 1970 became its first president to have bypassed the shopfloor. There would be others but none as skilful in interposing himself between his members and their employers to conjure a settlement of differences. After he entered parliament and laid siege to the leadership, Hawke gave up most of his indulgences. A garish larrikin now appeared in power dress,

9.2 Bob Hawke basked in the success of Alan Bond's yacht, which won the America's Cup in the same year he came to office. (West Australian Newspapers Ltd)

behind an imposing desk and before a fake bookcase, querulously insisting on the need for national reconciliation.

Both leaders endeavoured to find solutions to pressing national problems, for with the end of the golden age governments encountered challenges rather than opportunities. There were strategic difficulties abroad, and symptoms of domestic strain such as environmental degradation, family breakdown, homelessness and crime. In the absence of older certainties, governments sought to restore national cohesion and purpose. Most of all, they wrestled with the task of repairing an economy that no longer provided reliable growth and regular employment. With the end of the long boom the world economy was dogged by weak, unreliable rates of growth, high and persistent unemployment. Australia confronted particular problems: its reliance on commodity exports made it increasingly uncompetitive in a global economy dominated by advanced manufactures and service industries.

The rapid growth of finance markets, the increased mobility of capital and the shift from labour-intensive factory production to high-technology information industries created a new economic order sometimes characterised as post-industrial. Post-industrialism in turn was associated with changed patterns of work, no longer by handling material objects on an assembly line but rather by manipulating symbols on a computer screen, and with corresponding ways of living and thinking in what its prophets heralded as a post-material age. Yet the striking feature of Australian life in the last quarter of the twentieth century was the pervasive influence of the economy. The needs of business came to dominate public life as never before, and those trained in the certainties of neoclassical economics came to dominate the public service. Reports of stock exchange indices and currency movements became the staple fare of daily news. The vocabulary of the market served as the language of public policy and entered into almost every aspect of social life, so that no art gallery or university was complete without its business plan and marketing strategy, the customers for its product determining the bottom line by which it was judged. A new theology arose, neoliberalism, and a distinctive Australian term for it – economic rationalism. It was remarkable not so much for devotees' capacity to incorporate almost every form of human behaviour into its syllogisms as for the assumption that there could be no other form of reason than the logic of the market.

The Fraser government sought a remedy to the country's economic difficulties by tackling the problem of inflation. If prices and wage costs could be reduced and profits restored, then a resumption of activity would occur. Cuts in government expenditure would close the public deficit, reduce the public sector's demands on savings, and ease interest rates to allow increased private investment. For thirty years public revenue and expenditure had grown incrementally with the national product; now Australians were introduced to the activities of razor gangs, taking an axe to government programmes and paring back outlays. Inflation did decline, but by 1978 the number of unemployed passed 400,000. At the same time restrictions on foreign investment were lifted to finance an expansion of export industries. Wool gave way to meat and wheat as the chief farm exports, but the largest foreign earnings came from energy and minerals. The rapid increase in the price of oil allowed Australia to become the principal supplier of coal, along with increased sales of oil, gas and uranium. New mines were developed in Western Australia and Queensland for the export of minerals to Asian markets.

The promotion of Australia as a quarry was a risky strategy. Commodities made up a declining share of world trade and their prices continued to fall. The new mining projects created relatively few jobs: indeed, the effect of the mineral boom on the exchange rate placed increased pressure on other industries. As the mineral boom collapsed in 1982 and drought ravaged the agricultural sector, the government relaxed its tight control over public spending and the monetary supply. Renewed inflation, a breakout of wages and a further jump in unemployment ensured its defeat in the 1983 election.

Labor came to power under Hawke with an alternative strategy based on its special relationship with the unions. Under the terms of a Prices and Incomes Accord negotiated with the Australian Council of Trade Unions, workers would forgo wage increases in return for job creation. Co-operation would replace conflict for a concerted endeavour to put Australia back to work. A National Economic Summit held in Canberra within a month of the election legitimated the arrangements in a theatrical break from normal political practice. The country's elected representatives were banished from Parliament House to make room for business and union leaders to pledge their agreement; the unions would accept wage restraint, the employers a return to the system of centralised wage fixation. There were offsets to compensate wage-earners for their forbearance – restoration of public medical insurance and other improvements in the social wage – and there were government programmes to ensure that key industries such as steel and car production remained viable. The corporatist approach secured the co-operation of business and labour, and at least initially it gave the unions an unprecedented influence.

As an employment strategy, the Accord worked. One and a half million new jobs were created during the remainder of the decade and the jobless rate fell back from over 10 per cent in 1983 to just over 6 per cent in 1989. But in the search for greater competitiveness the Labor government made other changes. At the end of 1983 it abandoned the defence of the currency and allowed the value of the dollar to be set by the market. Foreign exchange controls were lifted, controls on domestic banks reduced and foreign banks allowed to compete with them. If the Accord was the carrot that secured the co-operation of industry in the reconstruction of the Australian economy, financial deregulation was the stick that impelled it forward under the blows of increased competition. Paul Keating, who as treasurer drove these changes, boasted that 'We are the first generation of post-war Australian politicians and economic managers to foster a genuinely open market economy.'

With financial deregulation, Australia's economic performance was subjected to the fickle judgement of international currency traders. The rapid increase of overseas borrowing and a persistent trade deficit placed the dollar at the mercy of speculators. In 1985 and the first half of 1986 the dollar lost 40 per cent of its value as it plumbed new depths. By this time the foreign debt, about half of it public borrowing and half private, represented 30 per cent of the national product, and every new fall in the exchange rate increased its cost. In May 1986 Keating declared that 'We must let Australians know truthfully, honestly, earnestly, just what sort of international hole Australia is in.' Without a reduction of costs and an improvement of trade performance, he warned, 'we will just end up being a third-rate economy ... a banana republic'.

The epithet sent shock waves through the country, for it seemed that Australia was in danger of following other white settler societies on the path to ruin. Like them it had built its amenities and advanced living standards on the prosperity of export staples for which there was no longer a reliable demand. Like them it imitated European civilisation but two economic historians now judged that 'The modern Australian economy is not really very "European".' They saw it rather as a less-efficient Canada, importing most of its advanced technology to support a small population that depended for its comfort on the exploitation of natural resources. 'Of the three classical factors of production, the land was stolen, the capital is borrowed, the labour productivity is low.'

Keating's banana republic speech prepared his audience for shock therapy: cuts in public spending, further wage restraint, further exposure of Australian business to international competition. After the earlier financial deregulation came plans for the progressive reduction of tariff protection of local industry and the first talk of relaxing the centralised system of wage fixation. With these further instalments of deregulation, the essential features that had sustained the Commonwealth since its inception would disappear. The central principle of the Australian Settlement, a strong state to protect living standards, would yield to the operation of the free market – and this at the hand of Labor.

The campaign to dismantle the regulatory edifice of the Australian Settlement drew heavily on overseas precedents. After the end of the long boom and the failure of Keynesian techniques of economic management to restore prosperity, there was a general movement to the right. The election of a Conservative government in Britain and a Republican president in the United States at the end of the 1970s heralded an assault on unions, social welfare and the mixed economy. Fraser himself followed a similar policy at this time as he too sought to weaken labour in order to restore profits, but stopped short of the programmatic zeal of Margaret Thatcher and Ronald Reagan. They aimed at a complete break with the Keynesian legacy. Keynes had sought to rescue capitalism from itself, to correct the dispersed and imperfect decisions of buyers and sellers in the market with the superior intelligence of decision-makers and planners at the centre. His critics, once dismissed as cranks and now awarded Nobel prizes, took the initiative. These apostles of the New Right spoke not of market failure but government failure, not of freedom from insecurity but the freedom of the market as the very foundation of liberty. Their supporters used that designation, the New Right, to distinguish themselves from the older, more pragmatic conservatives, though the familiar distinctions between left and right were beginning to blur. As champions of market freedom and unrelenting enemies of socialism in all its guises, they reinvigorated right-wing politics but they emphatically repudiated conservatism. They regarded themselves as the true radicals, the agents of change.

The ideas of the New Right were taken up in Australia by policy institutes and thinktanks. They appealed to export producers and other enemies of protectionism: a newly formed National Farmers Federation, along with prominent mining magnates, demanded that the crippling burden of tariffs and guaranteed wages be swept away. They were embraced by opponents of public welfare, who suggested that it merely kept recipients in a state of dependence while sustaining an unproductive bureaucracy. They were used by lawyers, who alleged that an unhealthily incestuous 'industrial relations club' shared a vested interest in the state system of arbitration and wage determination. Large employer organisations were at first resistant to the call for its abolition but, as Australian business felt the chill wind of international competition, they too embraced labour market deregulation.

Conservative politicians were more wary of the electoral implications of New Right policies: outflanked by Labor's financial deregulation, they lost an early election in 1984; in 1987 a populist crusade led by the authoritarian premier of Queensland ruined their chances. The legacy of Menzies's paternal liberalism, the whole weight of Australian tradition, made a turn to the radical right a dangerous gamble. Individualism here was made possible by the protection of a powerful state. Individualism as the New Right redefined it, an individualism which allowed unlimited choice so long as the user paid, seemed a recipe for political suicide. The reluctance of the Liberal Party to champion the economic policies of the New Right enabled the Labor Party to appropriate them.

Financial deregulation, together with the volatility of global capital movements, brought a succession of surges and descents on the stockmarket during the 1980s. The resources that might have gone into research, development and improved productivity went instead into the war-chests of a new generation of buccaneers who used debt finance to board successful companies and appropriate their assets. The corporate adventurers created paper empires and built grandiose mansions, acquired private jets and works of art, entertained lavishly and were generous with political donations. The golden age had become a gilded age of rampant excess. Labor politicians found the free-wheeling tycoons far more congenial than the older establishment of the corporate boardrooms. They admired their entrepreneurial zest, welcomed their acquisition of overseas assets at absurdly overvalued prices as evidence of a more outward-looking Australian business. After the inflow of borrowed capital pushed up the national debt, the dollar and therefore the trade deficit, the government finally jammed on the brakes. Having removed the instruments to steer the economy, it could only bring it to a halt by repeated increases of the interest rate, which approached 20 per cent by 1989. The ensuing collapse brought down the high-flying entrepreneurs along with thousands of small businesses. 'This', the defiant treasurer insisted, 'is a recession that Australia had to have.'

By the end of the 1980s unemployment was again on the rise. The effort to realign the Australian economy to new patterns of trade and investment had brought improvements in productivity but a persistent trade deficit and a large external debt. Australia remained dependent on foreign investment, and vulnerable to cycles of boom and bust. The reliance on market forces yielded not higher but lower growth rates than were achieved during the post-war era when governments regulated the economy, together with greater inequality and greater vulnerability – as was the case in other countries that adopted the New Right programme during the 1980s. Australia's experience of deregulation, however, was moderated by its introduction under a Labor government. Labor combined neoliberal economic policies with corporatist methods of government in an attempt to preserve a social dimension in the operation of the market. The Accord maintained some protection from the consequences experienced in Britain and the United States: there was lower unemployment, a floor under wages, greater assistance to those in need. By conceding the economic arguments of the New Right, Labor still hoped to escape its ruthless repudiation of responsibility for the weak and vulnerable.

Like Margaret Thatcher, Paul Keating insisted that there was no alternative. In 1990 he affirmed the necessity 'of removing the meddling hands of bureaucracy from the operation of markets'. The choice he offered was stark: Australia could continue 'to confront the realities of world markets' or it could 'retreat to the failed policies of the past'. Globalisation, the catchword for these realities, served both as diagnosis and remedy for the rapid changes that transformed Australia. They were anticipated by the Australian polymath, Barry Jones, in his book *Sleepers Wake!* (1982), which canvassed the country's future in a post-industrial world with his own prisoner's dilemma. Australia could adapt to the challenges and opportunities of the information age or it could face a future without work. Jones became the minister for science in the Hawke government; he popularised the appellation the 'Clever Country' for the inventive, alert and adaptable Australia he wished to see. But in 1990 Jones was dropped from the ministry.

By this time, his dystopian alternative seemed uncomfortably plausible. The occupations that had once provided secure employment were disappearing. The manufacturers of clothing and footwear could no longer compete with cheap imports; whitegoods were shipped in from low-cost factories in South-East Asia; the city offices that had once been full of typists and clerical workers were now refitted with personal computers, designed in Silicon Valley, assembled offshore. Yet the growth of the new high-tech industries that would supposedly take up the slack remained disappointingly fitful. The jobs most securely anchored here were in service industries such as tourism, commerce and personal services, but they were casual and transient. Employers were no longer prepared to maintain a large permanent workforce. The expectation of a career, of committing oneself to a lifelong vocation that valued experience and allowed workers to retire with dignity, now seemed antediluvian. Among managers and professionals, to remain in the same position for more than a few years was a confession of failure.

The chief burden of these changes fell on those least able to carry it. The loss of process work particularly affected middle-aged migrant men and women who had settled close to the factories in the principal cities. The decline of heavy industry struck industrial centres such as Newcastle and Wollongong in New South Wales, Whyalla and Elizabeth in South Australia. The closure of manufacturing plants in smaller towns placed further strain on rural dwellers who saw schools, hospitals, shops and banks close as farming populations declined. The reconfiguration of staffing practices that combed out the less skilled and replaced permanent full-time employees with part-time and casual ones bore particularly on the young. With fewer jobs for school-leavers, the rate of youth unemployment was persistently high. During the 1980s the rate of workforce participation also increased: a movement of women into paid employment, which had gathered force in the 1960s and 1970s, was assisted by the growth of part-time employment. The discriminatory practices associated with the protection of the male breadwinner were disappearing, and yet many families now found that two incomes were needed to make ends meet. Single-parent families with dependent children, which doubled between 1974 and 1987 to comprise one in six of all families, were particularly vulnerable to poverty.

The Hawke government was uncomfortable with its inability to restore full employment or stem the clear signs of distress; the prime minister's rash election promise in 1987 that 'by 1990 no Australian child will be living in poverty' came back to haunt him. Labor maintained a commitment to social welfare but directed assistance far more closely to those in need with stringent asset and income tests on most benefits. The primary emphasis was on job creation and training, which brought a rapid increase of school retention rates and corresponding expansion of post-secondary education. This in turn was aligned more closely with vocational outcomes through changes in the school curriculum that redefined education as skills acquisition, and the application of the market principle of 'user pays' to universities through the reintroduction of fees. The capitulation of the universities to Canberra's directives, and their ready embrace of hucksterism, was a striking example of how quickly commercial calculations had replaced other measures of value.

The chief casualty of the new public policy was the pursuit of equality. For thirty years after 1945 social-democratic governments had sought to reduce the inequalities of wealth, income, opportunity and outcome generated by the capitalist market. That crusade was abandoned and throughout the world the 1980s brought increased polarisation of the rich and poor. Australia, with its residual system of public welfare and low level of provision in comparison to other countries with universal systems, did ease the plight of the poor. Although it spent less, more of what it spent went to the needy. But this limited redistribution to the poor merely abated their loss of earnings and failed utterly to curb the growing inequality at the other end of the income scale. With wages pegged, the profit share increased. The rich became richer. They paid themselves increased executive salaries, and realised windfall gains on property and financial markets. They became less willing to share their bounty, using tax shelters to minimise their contribution to public revenue, and more ostentatious in flaunting it. Deregulation removed not just the institutional framework that bound individuals into relations of mutual obligation but the sentiments that sustained social solidarity. A meanness of spirit was apparent in the periodic vilification of the victims of unemployment as work-shy 'dole-bludgers'. The weakening of mutuality, the rampant individuality that spurned the virtues of love, duty and sacrifice, allowed a cult of selfishness to flourish.

During the 1980s, then, Australia dismantled most of the institutions that had provided a small, trading economy with a measure of protection from vulnerability to external shocks. Few lamented the demise of the Australian Settlement. Critics blamed it for entrenching sectional interests, sheltering inefficiency and stifling initiative. Most of all, they argued that it was simply unsustainable because globalisation was sweeping away the capacity of national governments to insulate themselves from market forces. Reconstruction was undoubtedly necessary, but the headlong rush into economic deregulation was a reckless gamble. Some in the Labor government wanted to graft a reform process onto egalitarian traditions and maintain a capacity to protect living standards; they liked to think of Australia as an antipodean Sweden that was charting a middle course to renovate the national ethos. That aspiration weakened as deregulation proceeded and the capacity to control its effects diminished. By the end of the decade Australia had cut itself loose from the past and was drifting on the choppy waters of the global market, more exposed, more vulnerable.

The turn to the right in economic and social policy coincided with a revival of the international Cold War. After the American defeat in Vietnam, partial détente with the Soviet Union and reduction of military expenditure, a series of humiliating reversals in the late 1970s brought a new president, Ronald Reagan, and a fresh determination to confront the communist Evil Empire. With the encouragement of Margaret Thatcher, the United States resumed the arms race. Australia was an early and vociferous supporter of the second Cold War. Malcolm Fraser warned repeatedly against the Soviet naval presence in the Indian Ocean; he encouraged the expansion of American communication facilities in Australia and responded to the Soviet intervention in Afghanistan with an attempt to prevent Australian participation in the 1980 Moscow Olympics. Fraser therefore welcomed the advent of Reagan and fully supported his reassertion of American strength. On the other hand, Fraser's relations with Thatcher were much cooler, partly because of arguments within Commonwealth forums over the white-supremacist regimes of Africa. Fraser was a courageous critic of apartheid, and human rights became an important element of his foreign policy. There was also a strong regional element. Fraser saw China as an ally against the Soviet Union. He visited Beijing before Washington; he supported China's 1979 invasion of Vietnam and encouraged a loose coalition of China and Japan with the Association of South-East Asian Nations (ASEAN) to contain the Soviet threat. This in turn guided Australia's closer relations with ASEAN as the principal regional forum, and highlighted the problematic relationship with Indonesia.

Australia's nearest and most populous neighbour, this sprawling new republic had emerged in the second half of the twentieth century as its most proximate threat. Under the presidency of the aggressively anti-imperial Achmad Sukarno, Indonesia's incorporation of the western half of New Guinea in 1962 and then the confrontation with the Malaysian confederation in 1963 aroused fears of further anti-Western belligerence. The suppression by General Suharto in 1965 of the Indonesian Communist Party in an action that slaughtered hundreds of thousands eased that anxiety, but Suharto's corrupt and authoritarian regime proved no less belligerent. In 1975 it invaded the former Portuguese colony of East Timor, and in the following years brutally repressed local resistance both there and in its province of New Guinea. The Whitlam and Fraser governments acceded abjectly to these acts of aggression. The Hawke government continued to extenuate them as it negotiated with Indonesia for a division of the rich oil deposits that lay under the bed of the Timor Sea.

The primacy of the economy reshaped foreign as well as domestic policy: in 1987 the Departments of Foreign Affairs and Trade were amalgamated. Trade patterns increased the regional orientation as the balance of world economic power shifted towards the Pacific: by 1984 the volume of trans-Pacific trade exceeded that of trans-atlantic trade. While European economies stagnated in the 1980s, those of Japan and the 'four tigers' – South Korea, Taiwan, Hong Kong and Singapore – achieved rapid growth. Indonesia and Malaysia followed on the same path of industrial development, and China cast off the shackles of its command economy to rumble into motion. Australia increased trade with Asia (which took half of Australia's exports and provided half of its imports by the end of the 1980s) but the Australian market share was falling. With European and North American trading blocs pressing for greater access to Asian markets, there was a grave danger that Australia would be excluded. Shut out of Asia, it would see the newly industrialised countries of the region surpass its living standards, leaving Australians as the 'poor white trash' of the South Pacific. A flurry of inquiries suggested the need for integration and how it might be achieved.

The desire to fashion an independent role saw Australian initiatives both in the region and beyond it. The foreign minister after 1987, Gareth Evans, was as active in international forums as Evatt,

his predecessor forty years earlier. He promoted a settlement in
Cambodia, contributed peace-keeping forces there and in other
local conflicts, pushed for nuclear disarmament, and generally
played the reforming role of an international good citizen. These
endeavours were always constrained by the Hawke government's
absolute commitment to the Western Alliance, which in the last
phase of the Cold War meant uncritical support of the United States
as it exerted its augmented dominance. The American communication bases in Australia, more important than ever for a new
generation of strategic weapons, were therefore sacred. The right of
American warships to enter local ports, regardless of whether they
were carrying nuclear weapons, was inviolable. When the New
Zealand Labour government refused to allow such visits in 1986
and the Reagan administration suspended its obligations under
ANZUS to the impudent outpost, Australia stuck firmly with its
more powerful ally. ANZUS remained vital, not as a guarantee of
Australian security (for it had been made clear during the Timor
crisis that Indonesia was more important to the United States than
Australia) but because it provided membership of the Western
Alliance and thus afforded access to American technology and
intelligence. Such were the burdens of a medium-size power.

Then, at the end of the 1980s, the second Cold War ended in
communist collapse. The Soviet economy, with its emphasis on
heavy industry, was unable to adapt to the needs of the new
information industries. The need to divert increasing resources from
an ailing economy to match the increased military expenditure of
the United States squeezed the living standards of its people, who
were no longer sustained by belief nor even cowed into submission.
The rigid system of centralised control, the imposition of conformity to a bankrupt ideology, the endemic corruption and
cynicism ended in a chain-reaction of peaceful revolutions in eastern
Europe and the overthrow of Gorbachev by Yeltsin in Russia. The
great twentieth-century contest between capitalism and socialism
was over. Socialism was vanquished, and not just the dead-end
command socialism of the communist countries but the more
moderate collectivism pursued by labour movements in the West.
They had already been driven from the commanding heights of the
economy; now the free market was supreme.

With that triumph and the vindication of the political freedom of
the West came renewed declarations of the end of ideology, even the
end of history. Those pronouncements coincided, paradoxically,
with a sharpening of ideological differences in Australian politics.
The coalition parties, which lost a further election in 1990, turned
to a bone-dry economist, John Hewson, who quickly developed a
thoroughgoing New Right policy that included a regressive tax
system, further reduction of the public sector, speedier removal of
tariff protection, and labour market deregulation. The Labor prime
minister, Hawke, had lost interest in pursuing further change; the
very occupation of office exhausted his energies and he was
overthrown in 1991 by Keating. The former treasurer, who had
forced his party to accept deregulation during the 1980s, pressed
ahead with further instalments: restriction of public expenditure,
the sale or partial sale of major government enterprises, renewed
pressure for industry reform, relaxation of central wage determination for enterprise bargaining. Under the provisions of a
national competition policy these changes were also forced down
onto State and local government, where privatisation and competitive tendering for provision of services rapidly transformed
public activity.

At the same time Keating used the opportunities of his prime
ministerial office, and the spectre of Hewson's more doctrinaire
embrace of the New Right, to reinvent himself. He was no longer
the combative economic rationalist dismantling the obstacles to
efficiency and competitiveness; now he was the competent manager
who appreciated that government had a larger responsibility. 'When
Australia opted for an open economy', his government maintained,
'the nation committed itself to succeed in an endless race', but the
capacity to endure relentless change depended on the resilience of
what Keating now recognised as the 'social fabric'. Those countries
that would prosper were 'social democracies where government is
involved in making the societies tick, where there is a happy mix
between efficient economics and a comprehensive social policy in
this post-monetarist, post-communist era'. In marking these dis-
continuities, Keating increasingly cast back to national traditions of
fortitude and achievement; he invoked the instinctive loyalty of the
labour movement to vouchsafe his concern for the underdog. 'This

was a victory for the true believers', he proclaimed when he defeated Hewson in the 1993 election.

He cast back in order to look forward. As the collapse of old industries ate into Labor's working-class constituency, as the membership and the capacity of the unions declined, the Labor Party was increasingly dependent on the support of a coalition of social movements. The women's movement, the environmentalists, ethnic associations and the Aboriginal movement became vital to the electoral survival of the government. During the 1980s they had been drawn into the corporatist constellation. Through the encouragement of peak bodies that were provided with funding and bound into the determination of public policy, erstwhile critics learned to speak the corporate argot of vision statements, targets and key performance indicators. Keating, a product of the brutally pragmatic school of right-wing Labor politics in New South Wales, who had once derided the left as standing for 'wider nature strips, more trees and let's go back to making wicker baskets in Balmain', emerged as an unlikely champion of these causes.

He took them up in statements of unusual eloquence by the standards of Australian public life – assisted by his speechwriter, Don Watson, a historian with the gift of whimsy to complement the prime minister's earthy vernacular – which renewed national legends by enlarging them. His 1992 address to an Aboriginal audience at Redfern Park opened with the conventional earnest of good intentions, and those of his listeners who had too often heard such pieties interjected their scepticism. Then came the frank recognition – 'We took the traditional lands and smashed the traditional way of life. We brought the diseases. The alcohol. We committed the murders. We took the children from their mothers ...' – and the dissident voices fell away, replaced by growing applause as the litany continued. Keating's frequent evocations of sacrifice in overseas wars were more controversial; they affirmed national heroism at the expense of imperial folly to serve his call for a final break with Britain and an Australian republic. The republican cause, in turn, served to differentiate the forward-looking Labor Party from the backward-looking Liberals, to engage the creative energies of the cultural sector, and to use the diversity of a multicultural society as a national strength.

Keating's nationalism looked outwards to equip Australians with the confidence to operate in the globalised economy and attach them to their Asian destiny – he even suggested that the traditional mateship could be understood as an Asian value. Some Asian leaders were not so sure. Indonesia's rulers found criticism by the Australian press a sign of disrespect, the preoccupation with human rights an indication that the white outpost was still wedded to Western values. Australia was denied membership of ASEAN, and thwarted by Malaysia's prime minister Mahathir in its attempt to promote an Asia-Pacific Economic Cooperation forum as a broader regional bloc. Keating's frustrated description of his counterpart as 'recalcitrant' did not assist his cause.

After the electoral triumph in 1993 Keating became more preoccupied with his 'big picture', more petulant with commentators who suggested that he was no longer attentive to economic reform. The Liberal Party, meanwhile, had returned to a former leader, John Howard. A cautious political veteran, he avoided the forthright naivety of Hewson who had helpfully laid out a comprehensive New Right programme for Keating to demonstrate its unpalatable implications. Capitalising on the growing dissatisfaction of electors with a tired government, Howard offered as small a target as possible. He took advantage also of the cumulative results of more than a decade of progressive deregulation, and especially its differential effects on incomes. Between 1982 and 1994 the top 10 per cent of income-earners had gained a real increase of $100 a week, and the bottom 10 per cent (assisted by Labor's direction of welfare spending) had gained $11 a week, but the 80 per cent in between suffered an actual decline. It was to this amorphous statistical construct that the coalition parties had appealed with the equally fuzzy appellation of 'Middle Australia'. It was a far cry from Menzies's forgotten people: he had divined that expressive term in a reflective renovation of the conservative tradition; the geographically implausible middle Australia was a product of research consultants. Howard hit upon a more potent designation: these were the 'battlers'. Juxtaposing their practical concerns to the indulgences of Labor's corporatist 'elites', he made major inroads into the Labor heartland to gain a decisive majority in the 1996 election.

The Howard government embarked on a further round of economic reform: more trade liberalisation, relaxation of environmental safeguards, increased deregulation of the financial sector, along with a determined assault on the labour market through the replacement of industrial awards with workplace agreements and individual contracts. The new treasurer's discovery of a 'black hole' in the public accounts enabled the government to abandon many of its commitments, make further cuts in public expenditure, sell off more public assets, and retrench the public service. The collapse of stock exchanges in Bangkok, Seoul, Hong Kong, Singapore, Kuala Lumpur and Jakarta at the end of 1997, and the deep recession that followed in South-East Asia, provided further justification for these policies as well as for changing the tax system with a flat charge on all forms of consumption. By 1998 the government could point to increased output, reduced unemployment and negligible inflation, and was returned to office in the election at the end of that year.

The prime minister declared on his assumption of office that he wanted Australians to feel 'relaxed and comfortable'. They should certainly not agonise over antique injustices: Howard adopted a phrase of the historian Geoffrey Blainey to repudiate the 'black-armband' view of the national past and condemn those engaged in 'endless and agonised navel-gazing' who had made Australian history 'a basis for obsessive and consuming national guilt and shame'. He refused to renew his predecessor's apology for past wrongs, despite the plea of a national assembly that sought to reconcile Aboriginal and non-Aboriginal Australians. His government curtailed the Aboriginal land rights that had recently been recognised by the High Court – on the grounds that such rights were discriminatory and divisive. Even the term multiculturalism was shunned in official usage.

'One Nation' had been the title of the Keating government's 1992 programme to foster greater inclusiveness. After the 1996 election it acquired a quite different meaning when a small businesswoman ignited a new populist bushfire with racially inflammatory statements. Pauline Hanson's One Nation Party expressed an exclusive and insular nationalism that was antagonistic to all forms of separatism except its own: multiculturalism, 'Asianisation' and 'the

Aboriginal industry' were among its grievances, along with gun laws and economic rationalism. Tough times created hard hearts. One Nation's prejudices found a substantial response among Australians buffeted by globalisation. Its founder's credentials as a battler were far more impressive than the prime minister's and he studiously refrained from condemning her utterances. Howard set himself against political correctness in all of its progressive guises; protection from 'fashion' was inscribed in the new preamble for the country's constitution he drafted in 1999.

This left one fashion sacrosanct, the cult of market forces. As globalisation in both its economic and cultural forms worked upon the Australian nation-state in the closing years of the twentieth century, governments of both political persuasions were hard-pressed to maintain effective control of the national destiny. Like a long-forgotten European philosopher, they defined freedom as the recognition of necessity. Both major parties bowed to the regimen of the market. The Labor government of Hawke sought to ease its introduction with consensual co-operation, that of Keating by attaching globalisation to the values of diversity and inclusiveness. The Liberal–National government of Howard intensified its rigour in a more populist mode. His battlers were stern individualists who preferred tax cuts to public provision. They were weary, resentful of the constant uprooting of the fixtures of national life, but resigned to further change in the cause of greater efficiency and international competitiveness. They were cynical but gullible: they mistrusted politicians, yet they hungered for certainty and firm leadership.

The difficulties Australia encountered slowed the increase of population. There were 13.5 million inhabitants when the long boom ended, nearly 19 million by the end of the century. Economic change uprooted many. Supposedly the new technologies dissolved space but, far from weakening constraints of location, the information and service industries increased them. Children from the rural hinterland had long been forced to shift to the nearest city to pursue their ambitions, but now a move to Sydney, Los Angeles or Hong Kong was a condition of a managerial or professional career.

Tasmania and South Australia stagnated, Queensland and Western
Australia grew more rapidly, but the concentration of population in
the south-eastern corner of the continent remained the dominant
feature. Sydney approached 4 million by the late 1990s and
Melbourne 3.5 million.

Sydney and Melbourne were also the destinations of most
migrants – the overwhelmingly European composition of lesser
centres contrasted with the heterogeneity and cosmopolitan ambience of the two great entrepots. By 1996 one in five of Australia's
inhabitants was born elsewhere and, because of the recasting of
boundaries, 'elsewhere' now comprised nearly 200 countries. This
proliferation of new states accelerated with the conclusion of the
Cold War and not simply in the former communist countries, for
after its victory in the great ideological contest the Western model of
the liberal, secular nation-state could not withstand the revival
of ethnic, cultural and religious divisions. Nor could the post-
communist international order prevent the lethal convulsions that
accompanied such divisions and the consequent displacement of
victims from their homelands. The humanitarian crisis became
commonplace, the refugee a familiar figure. During the 1970s Australia gave sanctuary to refugees from Chile and Central America. It
accepted responsibility for those who fled from Timor and more
reluctantly took in Vietnamese boat people, though their unauthorised arrival created new problems of immigration control. By the
1980s there were clear signs of compassion fatigue, and the Labor
government treated further voyagers as illegal immigrants to be
confined in isolated detention centres and repatriated. By the 1990s,
as the result of cost-cutting, the government was hard-pressed to
detect such entrants.

When Australians debated their responsibilities for refugees, the
government distinguished those fleeing from tyranny from those
who merely aspired to escape from destitution. It was a rare
instance where the economic motive was the less commendable,
and in any case such comparisons rested on a fine distinction for
those buffeted by the dictates of the global market. Globalisation
created unprecedented movements of labour as well as capital. The
advanced industrial economies of Europe brought in factory
workers, the oil-rich states of the Middle East imported labourers

from South Asia, the prosperous centres of South-East Asia brought their domestic servants from the impoverished backwaters. Australia avoided the increasingly common recourse to short-term visas for unskilled wage-earners: its preference was for families who would be admitted to citizenship as permanent settlers. But with persistent unemployment came increasing argument over the costs and benefits of immigration. Annual targets were trimmed and greater preference given to those who brought capital and business expertise.

Migration has always contained an element of economic choice. Just as the decision of the migrant to relocate carried an expectation of material improvement, so the willingness of the host country to accept newcomers was conditional on the need for additional human resources. But relocation is a traumatic experience that calls for readjustment to new ways, and Australia has always chosen settlers who would conform to national practices. The application of market principles to immigration policy relegated such considerations of compatibility to secondary significance. In contrast to other countries that retained a strong attachment to ethnic definitions of national citizenship, Australia no longer discriminated. It made the acquisition of citizenship easy and the privileges of citizenship slight. As a settler society, it exchanged the outworn emphasis on British descent for the postcolonial model of multiculturalism.

Multiculturalism, as an official policy, extended during the 1970s and 1980s from immigration to the provision of all kinds of services to the very principles of nationhood. Multiculturalism, as a word and an idea, remained fluid and contested. Its supporters celebrated the richness and diversity of cultural practices, the tolerance and pluralism of the reconstituted nation. Traditional nationalists decried the emphasis on separate identities and entrenchment of difference. Muffled by the bipartisan support for multiculturalism as practised by the Fraser and Hawke governments, these arguments erupted periodically in heated controversy. In 1984 the historian Geoffrey Blainey challenged the non-discriminatory principle when he claimed that the level of Asian immigration was straining public acceptance. Stung by accusations of racism, he responded with his own allegations that the government was following a 'surrender Australia' policy, that the 'multicultural lobby'

was distorting the national interest, and that the immigration programme was designed in a 'secret room' and concealed from the
public. At the end of the 1980s John Howard again suggested that
the level of Asian immigration was too high, and also took issue
with the champions of multiculturalism. Public outcry forced a
retreat.

Neither of these episodes clarified the meaning of multiculturalism. On the contrary, they suggested that culture was little
more than a euphemism for race: the protagonists concentrated on
'Asianisation' and their critics foreclosed any further discussion by
accusing them of wanting to return to the White Australia Policy
and warning of the damage to the national reputation – both
episodes received extensive coverage in the neighbouring countries
of South-East Asia. This left the demagogues of talkback radio and
the One Nation Party to exploit the lode of raw bigotry. But the
champions of multiculturalism hardly assisted with their own
claims. They presented old Australia as an island of prejudice
redeemed only by the post-war new Australians who overthrew its
oppressive monoculture. In their insistence on a multicultural
national identity which took diversity as the defining characteristic,
they reduced that nebulous concept to vacuity. In their arraignment
of the host culture, they failed to explain how it had accommodated
the transformation. In failing to acknowledge that it occurred
peacefully, and that Australia had escaped the revival of ethnic
hatreds that erupted in other parts of the world, they reproduced
the insularity they decried.

The history that has been narrated here provides plentiful
evidence of discrimination and conflict, but also of containment and
resolution. The first and most persistent conflict with the original
inhabitants began with the European invasion, yet among the
invaders there were divisions of nationality, religion and civic status.
The remarkable feature of colonial history was how quickly these
divisions were reconciled. Incorporation of newcomers is the logic
of a settler society but in Australia it was particularly strong
because the demands of loyalty were weak. Australians could not
invoke binding national foundations since self-government and
individual autonomy preceded nationhood. They could hardly
appeal to a sacred link between blood and soil in a land they had

only recently appropriated. There was sectarian prejudice and religious toleration, ancestral sentiment and an absence of ethnic enclaves. Exclusion served as a prophylactic against domestic separatism, economic growth as a guarantor of assimilation, so that when immigration ceased to be discriminatory the country was committed to incorporation. The novel conjunction of inclusive immigration and blockage of opportunity has strained, but so far not broken, this rough-and-ready acceptance.

After two hundred years of overseas recruitment to build the population of Australia, a new voice called for immigration control, that of environmentalists. Throughout the European occupation of the country there had been efforts to conserve its resources and protect fauna and flora, water and forest, from wanton destruction, but the developmental impulse usually prevailed. The end of the long boom coincided with an enhanced appreciation of the costs of development. The great triumphs of the post-war period turned out to be illusory. The Snowy Mountains Authority had turned back the rivers from the south-east coast to water the Riverina plains, and poisoned the soil with salt; the Ord River on the north-west coast had been dammed, but infestations of insects killed most of the crops; the government's scientific organisation waged biological warfare against the rabbit, but the survivors returned to compete for pasture. A loss of confidence in the capacity to direct economic growth was accompanied by similar doubts about the ability of science to control nature.

The environmental movement emerged in a series of actions during the 1970s. In Sydney the builders' labourers union pioneered Green Bans against the developers' wanton destruction of urban amenity. Campaigners in Queensland prevented the mining of mineral sands on Fraser Island and the bulldozing of rainforest on the mainland coast. In Tasmania the Wilderness Society blockaded the construction of a hydro-electric project on the Franklin River. In forests across the country activists fought to prevent the clear-felling of native timber for wood-chip exports. The membership of environmental groups grew from 100,000 in 1974 to 700,000 in 1991. They spawned a new political party, the Greens, new forms of public engagement and a new consciousness that put natural values before human uses. The earlier concern for heritage and national

9.3 The campaign in the early 1980s to save the Franklin
River from damming by the Tasmanian Hydro-Electric
Commission marked the triumph of environmental over
developmental values. Photographic images of pristine
wilderness catalysed Green sentiment. (Peter Dombrovskis,
West Wind Press)

estate yielded to an identification with wilderness and reverence for
the organic foundations of life; hence the ecological argument to
rescue nature from human depredation, to restrict immigration and
even reduce the population.

Government and industry resisted these pressures by incorpor-
ating them into procedures of environmental management. A
repertoire of sustainable development allayed the popular concern
for the environment. The consequent modification of practices was
assisted by the dwindling fortunes of primary producers and the
rapid growth of the tourist industry. The burden of adjustment fell
on rural dwellers who were encumbered with debt, deprived of
services, and locked into occupations that seemed to have no future
– the gulf between the city and the country had never been wider.
Populists exploited it: 'Thousands of country jobs have been sacrificed to satisfy the trendies and basket weavers, the greenies and
the opulent armchair environmentalists.' It found expression in
farmers' protest marches on parliament and defiance of restrictions
on gun ownership. It increased the animosity between Aboriginal

and non-Aboriginal residents of country towns; as employment declined and disorder increased, shopfronts were boarded up after dark.

In the closing years of the twentieth century the Aboriginal presence became inescapable. The census revealed a dramatic increase of numbers, from 156,000 in 1976 to 352,000 by the late 1990s. The rebuilding of population was apparent throughout the country, in towns and cities as well as the bush. Tasmania, where the original inhabitants were long thought to have disappeared, now found that it had 14,000 of them. Aboriginal natives of Australia had only been included in the census from the 1960s, and on every occasion since then more Australians ticked the indigenous box. Some of them were reclaiming an identity that had been discouraged, while others were discovering a hidden indigenous ancestry. Sally Morgan, an artist and writer who had grown up in suburban Perth, related a journey from childhood silence and evasion to recovery of family links that culminated in a return to *My Place* (1987). Her book became a best-seller that reworked a stigma into a celebration: 'What had begun as a tentative search for knowledge had grown into a spiritual and emotional pilgrimage. We had an Aboriginal consciousness now, and were proud of it.' Here, as well as in the census, Aboriginality was becoming more fluid, less a product of biology than a cultural and emotional affinity. Aboriginal communities were understandably suspicious of the change; they insisted on both descent and connection, and challenged the authenticity of several prominent Aboriginal figures during the 1990s.

There were few advantages in being Aboriginal. Those who identified themselves in the census had a higher rate of unemployment and lower income levels than the rest of the population. More of them were arrested and imprisoned. Their life expectancy was fifteen years below the national average, and this despite a quarter-century of government programmes that were meant to overcome their disadvantages. Under its policy of self-determination, the Commonwealth created Aboriginal organisations to administer these programmes and then subjected them to close bureaucratic surveillance. The older reserves and missions in the remote areas of the north were replaced by land councils, rations by cash payments;

but much of the cash went on alcohol and cars, not enough on food. The white administrators in the cities and towns of the south gave way to self-managed agencies that were then blamed for the disappointing results. The contradictions in these arrangements, whereby the state was an integral part of the problem it was meant to be solving, have been characterised as 'welfare colonialism'; in practice the policy of self-determination seemed to mean the assimilation of Aborigines to the material practices of other Australians through forms of welfare that would secure their consent to dependence.

Self-determination had another side. Throughout this period there was an upsurge in Aboriginal culture, both the traditional culture that was assisted by the recovery of control over land and new cultural forms that reached a wider, commercial audience in music, theatre, dance, art and literature. Among the most powerful voices were those of Jack Davis, the playwright; Jimmy Chi, the composer of *Bran Nue Day* (1990); and Ruby Langford, who wrote *Don't Take Your Love to Town* (1988). All explored dispossession and affirmed survival. Yothu Yindi, an Aboriginal band from Arnhem Land, found an international audience for songs both in English and their own language. After two centuries of loss that had reduced some five hundred Aboriginal languages to perhaps a score in common use, there was a revival. At the tail-end of the assimilation era the poet and activist, Kath Walker, had returned her imperial honour and assumed her traditional name, Oodgeroo Noonuccal. Others, including Ruby Langford Ginibi and Lowitja O'Donoghue (the former head of the Aboriginal and Torres Strait Islander Commission) now followed her example.

This Aboriginal renaissance intensified the unease of the latecomers. The striking simplicity of the Aboriginal flag, black, gold and ochre, made the presence of the Union Jack on the Australian flag increasingly anomalous. There was a growing recognition of prior occupation, symbolised by new protocols and ceremonies. From the 1980s it was increasingly likely that organisers of a conference who were sensitive to proprieties would begin with a welcoming ceremony conducted by a local elder. Correct usage required acknowledgement of regional identities such as the Koori in south-east Australia, the Nyungar and Murri in Queensland, the Nyoongah in southern Western Australia. The generic term Aboriginal became more problematic, the more specific cognate 'Indigenous Australians' increasingly common. These changes were not peculiar to Australia: in Canada, the United States and New Zealand there was a similar move towards recognition of 'first nation' peoples. Australians, however, were discomfited by the realisation that they had no equivalent terminology for the majority of the population except for the negative 'non-Aboriginal' or 'non-indigenous'. The descriptors 'white' and 'European' no longer accurately described them; 'settler' and 'colonial' seemed anachronistic, 'invader' too embarrassing.

Some of these Australians sought to attach themselves to their country through identification with indigenous culture. Aboriginal heritage was treasured for its exotic otherness and enriching presence. Aboriginal ecology and spirituality gave new meaning to the land; Aboriginal design and fashion provided distinctive motifs so that Qantas, the international airline, applied it to the decoration of its aircraft as a uniquely Australian marketing feature. Participation in this culture often took the form of appropriation. Commercialisation, both in the mass market for tourism and the connoisseur's market for Papunya dot paintings, raised the stakes. Ultimately the arguments over intellectual property turned back to a renewed contest over real property. In 1992 the High Court determined that Eddie Mabo, a Torres Strait Islander, had common law rights to native title in his land on Mer Island. The decision overturned the longstanding belief that British settlement had extinguished any indigenous property in land, and in doing so it recast the basis of nationhood. As two of the judges declared, 'Dispossession is the darkest aspect of the history of this nation. The nation as a whole must remain diminished unless and until there is an acknowledgement of, and retreat from, those past injustices.'

Not all members of the nation were prepared to make such an accommodation. Mining companies and farmers' organisations denounced the High Court. Conservative State premiers incited alarm with wild allegations that even homeowners were at risk. The Keating government resisted the scare campaign, clarified the basis on which native title operated, and created a tribunal to determine further claims. The High Court, in a further case concerning the

9.4 The adoption of Aboriginal decoration by Qantas, the Australian airline, attested to popular acceptance of indigeneity as a distinctive national marker. (Qantas Airways Limited)

Wik people's traditional lands on Cape York Peninsula, decided in 1996 that native title could coexist with pastoral leases. This redoubled the efforts of the opponents of Aboriginal land rights. Insisting that no Australians should possess special rights, the new Howard government re-established the special rights of the pastoralists in new legislation that reduced the scope for acknowledgement of native title to a remnant. Groups that seek to have a disadvantage removed are often accused of seeking to obtain an advantage – a strategy that was here turned against an expropriated people. For a time it appeared that the government's legislation might be blocked by the Senate, but an independent Senator who held the casting vote allowed it to pass because he feared the destructive effects of an election fought on the issue. The Mabo decision had suggested a new moral foundation for the nation; instead it intensified division.

There was an edginess, an unease in public life that easily turned to rancour. As they engendered doubt during their campaign against the Mabo decision, the conservative State premiers demanded certainty. Certainty was a luxury Australians could no longer afford once they embarked on the process of national reinvention. The States themselves had turned to gambling as a source of revenue, and in one of them the principal financial department was restyled – without trace of irony – the Department of Gaming and Finance. Deregulation swept away the fixtures of economic life, smaller government removed the mechanisms of public support, the maxim of user pays eroded the ethos of the fair go. The churches emerged in the late twentieth century to care for many of the casualties the state had abandoned, and to help articulate the residual social conscience. Having accepted their complicity in the separation and confinement of earlier Aboriginal generations, church leaders supported the call for restitution. But the principal denominations were themselves losing moral authority.

Along with the disappearance of stable employment, there was a weakening of the social structures that gave direction to the lifecourse. The journey from infancy to old age had once occurred as a familiar sequence of transitions: childhood within the domestic household, education, employment, then marriage and acquisition of your own home and your own children, culminating in retirement after they achieved independence. Each stage in this cycle was now under strain: many children had only one parent; schools were expected to cope with a host of special needs, employment was insecure, home ownership less accessible; fewer adults married, more lived in same-sex relationships, and the birthrate reached an all-time low; compulsory retirement might come long before it was expected; intergenerational transfers of money stretched further as longevity increased. That basic social unit of the 1950s, the nuclear family, was becoming the exception. By the late 1990s fewer than one in five households consisted of mum, dad and the kids.

Many abandoned it without regret. When women achieved greater economic independence as income-earners, they were less prepared to remain trapped in unhappy marriages. The Family Law Act of 1975 made divorce easier and more common, though remarriage also increased. Many more heterosexual couples lived together, with or without children, and same-sex couples also reared children – the family had become more diverse, less constrictive. Greater freedom did not necessarily bring greater happiness, however, since desertion of a partner and abandonment of children created poverty and distress. The baby-boomers had rebelled against parental expectations and rejected their suburban inheritance for personal fulfilment. Their own children no longer had the satisfaction of rebellion, for the familiar sequence of life-stages no longer operated. There was no necessary connection between education, employment, independence, partnership and reproduction. A young person might leave home and return, finish school but resume training years later, be in or out of work, form a relationship or end one. Such freedom was a painful necessity.

The closing years of the twentieth century presented a sequence of unnatural and unnerving events. In the winter of 1980 a baby named Azaria disappeared from a tent pitched at the base of Ayers Rock in Central Australia; the parents said a dingo must have carried her off but rumour associated the mother, Lindy Chamberlain, with a satanic cult. She was convicted of murder, then exonerated. The original coronial inquest heard of Aboriginal beliefs that if children wandered near Uluru, 'The Dingo Spirit will get them', and some years later the Commonwealth government established a national inquiry that revealed how thousands of Aboriginal children had been taken from their families.

Meanwhile the British parliament was investigating the fate of thousands of children from that country who had been sent to Australia and subjected to 'quite exceptional depravity'. A television series, 'The Leaving of Liverpool', showed the despatch of orphan children from post-war Britain to an alien destination. Its story of exile revived echoes of convict transportation, except that Britain and Australia were now seen as wholly different countries and the sending of children from one to the other as utterly inexcusable. While such 'orphans of the Empire' came forward with stories of maltreatment by the Catholic order to which they were entrusted, so local parish priests were convicted of sexual molestation of young boys. Paedophilia became a lightning rod for the anxieties of family breakdown.

Another public inquiry, into British nuclear tests in Central Australia during the 1950s, accused the governments of both countries of reckless disregard for the Aboriginal inhabitants of the test site. Through such investigations of the past, events that once signified national and imperial endeavour crumbled into disfavour, though other scandals shook contemporary orthodoxies. In 1994 a young Brisbane woman published a novel, *The Hand that Signed the Paper*, under the name Helen Demidenko. The novel dealt with the complicity of Ukrainians with the Nazis during the Second World War, and drew on multicultural conventions to relieve their Australian descendants from the burden of guilt. It won several literary prizes before the author was revealed as a fraud and a plagiarist.

In 1997 another baby disappeared, Jaidyn Leskie, and his father, mother and her partner exchanged allegations of guilt. The story that emerged in media reportage was one of unemployment, alcohol, violence and irresponsibility in a country town that had lost its chief industry. The town itself became the victim and the culprit, a place of cheap housing and cheap taste, a ghetto of the abandoned. Yet the young Tasmanian man who opened fire on tourists at Port Arthur in 1996, killing thirty-five, was not impoverished; he was, rather, a wealthy and seriously disturbed loner left to live out his fantasies.

The media turned these and other events into stories about national anxieties. The visual intimacy of television made news more personal and dramatic. Newspapers redefined their role from reportage to commentary and interpretation, from the breaking of news to the creation of issues and anticipation of response. Talkback radio drew listeners to the prejudices of the 'shock jocks'. Critics condemned the lack of restraint and blurring of fact and prejudice, though tabloid sensationalism was hardly new and its intrusiveness often voluntarily accepted. From baby Azaria to baby Jaidyn, those caught up in real-life soap dramas sold their exclusive stories to media organisations; indeed, it was the popular media that provided some of the most troubled figures with the scripts for their fleeting celebrity.

The media swallowed up those activities that were unscripted, turning pastime into spectacle. In 1977 a television network bought the services of the country's leading cricketers, put them into coloured clothing and reworked a leisurely game into a frenetic performance. Other sporting codes soon succumbed to the same commercial pressures. Clubs became corporations, local supporters were brushed aside for national markets, sporting heroes were turned into media celebrities. The distinction between the amateur and the professional had once affirmed a preference for the voluntary participant over the mercenary, enjoyment over reward; professionalism was now synonymous with success. Victory in international sporting competitions became an index of the country's wellbeing – after increasingly disappointing results at the Olympic Games following the golden haul at Melbourne in 1956, the government established an Institute of Sport that outlaid millions of dollars for every medal. The most celebrated sporting triumph in the 1980s came when a leading entrepreneur captured the America's Cup, a trophy reserved for those rich enough to race multi-million dollar yachts. Such was the euphoria of the new prime minister, Bob Hawke, that he appeared on television to urge bosses to give their employees the day off.

The winner of the America's Cup was Alan Bond, perhaps the most audacious of the corporate buccaneers who flourished in the 1980s. He was an English migrant who began working life as a signwriter in Perth, moved into property development and assembled a multinational corporate empire with interests in property, mining, brewing and the media. The stockmarket crash of 1987 left him overexposed, and by 1990 receivers were picking over the wreckage in an effort to track down shareholders' assets. Bond himself was gaoled, in contrast to other entrepreneurs who fled overseas or escaped conviction. He was a more popular figure, given to more ostentatious display of his riches, and more anxious for public acceptance. In 1989, as the financial journalists who had puffed Bond's business acumen began to question his solvency, he spoke at the National Gallery where part of his art collection was on display and compared his treatment to that of the impressionist painters. Like him, these bold and creative men had been subjected to 'criticism and mockery'. They too were victims of that peculiarly Australian tendency to cut down tall poppies.

The original Australian tall poppies were senior public servants, criticised in the early twentieth century for enjoying excessive salaries at the public expense. In the course of the century the egalitarian epithet was extended to other forms of privilege and unwarranted eminence. Such healthy irreverence was celebrated as a national virtue, along with the habit of 'knocking' those who got above themselves. Then, in the last year of the Whitlam government when the impulse for greater equality was faltering, a senior Liberal sounded a new note: 'tall poppies, more and more tall poppies, are what this country needs'. By the 1980s the term had lost all pejorative connotations. Tall poppies were now national treasures, celebrated in lavish encomiums across almost every field of endeavour – a tribute to successful Australian women appeared in 1984 as *Tall Poppies*. As inequalities of prestige, wealth and power were a necessary correlate of enterprise and achievement, so Australians were urged to cast off their unseemly modesty in order to achieve. Knocking had become a national vice in a country which had forgotten that achieve is a transitive verb.

One of Alan Bond's less successful deals was the acquisition of a television network from its owner, Kerry Packer – Packer bought it back later at a much reduced price. His family began in newspapers and expanded into magazines and television; he took up the new electronic media, acquiring cricket and later rugby league along the way as fodder for the mass entertainment industry. His chief rival was Rupert Murdoch, who had inherited an Adelaide newspaper and built an international media conglomerate that published the majority of Australian newspapers. By the end of the 1980s Packer and Murdoch were the two richest Australians (though Murdoch had become a United States citizen as a condition of his expansion there). It was a rash politician who defied them. When the Hawke government was dismantling the limits on concentration of media ownership, a member of the cabinet asked the prime minister, 'Why don't you just tell us what your mates want?' The rivalry of the media mates provided some temporary leeway, since cross-media ownership laws restricted the one to television and the other to newspapers, but the growing convergence of media technologies put even that restriction in doubt. The role of the media was supposedly to invigilate the actions of government so that voters could hold their elected representatives to account. Now media tycoons had a direct interest in government policy across the full range of their business interests.

There was a discernible loss of public confidence in government. While Australians had never held high expectations of their politicians and public servants, few were prepared for the revelations of the 1980s. The Fraser government was rocked by allegations that it had allowed the wealthy to profit from loopholes in the tax laws; an inquiry revealed the involvement of prominent members of the Liberal Party. In Queensland, where the conservatives had governed since the 1950s, a pattern of systematic graft and corruption was uncovered. In Western Australia, where Labor won office in 1983 and established close links with Alan Bond and his associates, similar favours were exchanged. In New South Wales special deals for mates were a way of life and embroiled even a High Court judge. By the end of the decade a flurry of royal commissions sent some of the culprits to trial. Police commissioners, cabinet members and a premier all served prison sentences.

Politics itself fell into greater disrepute as politicians became more skilful in their manipulation of electors. Paul Keating presented the electorate with tax cuts in 1993 and then withheld them. John Howard undertook to preserve government services in 1996 and then, on winning office, drew a distinction between 'core' and 'non-core' promises. Every government, State and federal, that came to office from the 1980s immediately discovered a black hole in the public finances that justified a retreat from its commitments. Since voters wanted lower taxes without giving up the benefits of public provision, they were victims of their own gullibility. Politicians fed their cynicism by accusing each other of malpractice. The unearthing of scandals became a substitute for policy.

The diminution of government accompanied a loss of confidence in social policy. The golden years of the long boom had been the heyday of the public agency as an instrument of progress; town planners and health authorities, educationalists and criminologists applied their specialist expertise through large, centralised instrumentalities to the improvement of conditions and modification of behaviour. Now, that progressive confidence was challenged and with it the administrative machinery. The persistence of social problems belied the doctrines of pastoral care. Large custodial institutions were closed, their inmates 'deinstitutionalised'. Support services were run down, public provision replaced by private. The left hand of the state – the social workers, teachers and health workers – was marginalised by the right hand of the state – the treasury and finance departments – that withdrew their resources.

Even those activities that were not privatised became less public as governments turned to consultants for policy advice and contractors for the provision of services. The drive for greater efficiency was at the expense of public accountability.

The state withdrew from many areas of social policy, and citizens who were abandoned by the state in turn rejected it. Throughout the closing years of the century there were efforts to revive citizenship and make good the apparent deficiencies in the civic capacity. The prime mover was government, and such official initiatives were beset by their inherent contradictions. The state, having hollowed out much of its substance and attenuated the relationship with its sovereign subjects, now sought to restore their attachment. Its notion of active and informed citizens was narrowly functional: the idea of civil society as standing outside government and its purposes was scarcely acknowledged.

The bicentenary of European settlement had come and gone in 1988 with public spectacles that discouraged such reflection. The uncertainty of purpose was apparent in the arguments over the festival's theme. The government's Bicentennial Authority began in 1981 with the propitiatory slogan 'Living Together', but Fraser preferred the more assertive 'Australian Achievement'. The Hawke government initially restored 'Living Together' and then settled on 'Celebration of a Nation'. The official jingle was as vacuous as the public events:

> The celebration of a nation,
>   Give us a hand!
> Celebration of a nation,
>   Let's make it grand!
> Let's make it great in '88,
>   C'mon give us a hand.

The nation's largest and most expensive birthday present was a new Parliament House, buried into the hill above the older one. That modest stucco building used a common entrance giving onto King's Hall, where legislators rubbed shoulders with citizens. The new edifice had separate entrances for ministers, members and the public. The prime minister's suite was larger than either of the legislative chambers. In this huge and sumptuous setting it was clear who ruled.

9.5 For more than a century Australians projected national
and civic aspirations onto the dream of the future republic.
As the republic became an imminent possibility, it dwindled
into arguments over the machinery of government. The prime
minister's anti-republicanism is here likened to the threadbare
traditionalism of the penny-farthing. (Peter Nicholson)

Those Australians who aspired to something more were attracted
to the goal of an Australian republic. The approaching centenary
of the Commonwealth, in 2001, provided them with an opportunity to revise the constitution and make it properly expressive of
the enlarged nationhood. But republicanism, also, succumbed to
the very forces it was meant to overcome. The sponsors of the
republican movement, a self-appointed group of celebrities, bound
themselves to the goal of a minimal republic – a formal replacement
of the monarchical head of state by a president. To do more than
this, to apply the republican principle to the machinery and processes of government, would in their judgement risk scaring the
citizenry. Their chief argument turned out to be no more than
the narrowly national one that the Australian head of state should
be an Australian and, since the monarchical function was in fact
exercised by an Australian governor-general, this seemed a fine

distinction. The monarchist John Howard capitalised on their timidity. After his election as prime minister he convened a half-elected, half-nominated constitutional convention (a less democratic assembly than had met a century earlier). Its delegates resolved in favour of a republic with a president elected by a joint sitting of parliament. A more minimal republic could scarcely be devised, and yet it is still unclear whether the people will accept it. After twenty-five years of change, it seemed that the capacity for reinvention was exhausted.

10

What next?

'Historical events, like mountain ranges, can best be surveyed as a whole by an observer who is placed at a good distance from them.' So wrote an early professor of history (the chair I occupy is named after him) in the closing pages of his concise history of Australia. Ernest Scott wrote those words more than eighty years ago, and the idea of the historian as an observer of events has since fallen into disrepute. The historian is now inside the history, inextricably caught up in a continuous making and remaking of the past. History once served as an authoritative guide to decision-making. The great nineteenth-century literary historians produced compelling accounts of the forces that had shaped their civilisation; through these lessons in statecraft and morality, they provided contemporaries with the capacity and the confidence to anticipate their destiny. That idea of the historian as guide or prophet has also lapsed. Futurology is the province of the economist, the environmental or information scientist; whatever the future holds, it will be utterly different from what has gone before.

Scott applied his caveat to the final fifteen years of his narrative. For him, the first years of the Commonwealth period constituted the 'closer range' of ephemeral change, but then his history of Australia spanned only five centuries. Completed in the year that his compatriots returned on imperial service to scramble up the slopes of Gallipoli, it began 'with a blank space on the map' at the dawn of European discovery and ended 'with a new name on the map, that of Anzac'. Australian history now stretches over many millennia. In this dramatically extended past, the last two hundred years or so of European habitation might well be regarded as too close to discern its essential features. The colonisation and settlement that began in 1788 could be seen, at greater distance, as no more than a temporary interruption in the longer history of Australia.

Two thousand years ago Britain was itself colonised. After voyages of discovery, reconnaissance and trade, a Roman army took possession. Initially the invasion met with little resistance, but as the newcomers extended their presence they put down revolts by the local tribes and sent back the trophies of those they conquered. They built towns, settled ex-soldiers on the land, imposed their law, language and customs, built walls to keep out alien incursions, exploited the natural resources to create export industries, provided troops for imperial service. As new powers arose in the region, the emperor Constantine came to shore up the island's defences, but eventually the imperial capacity declined and the province was left to defend itself. The indigenous people had blended many of the ways of the colonisers with their own traditions, but waves of new arrivals quickly eroded the Roman civilisation. It lasted for more than four hundred years and its traces are still apparent in historic sites and place-names, a thin slice of the island's multi-layered past. Will the British colonisation of Australia be sustained so long? Will it too be overlaid by the languages and practices of other peoples?

The relationship between the settlers and the Indigenous peoples remains uncertain. From the beginning it caused unease. The proclamation of sovereignty, the seizure of land and the violent confrontations this caused always troubled some colonists. All attempts to ease their conscience, whether by protection, reservation, conversion or assimilation of the Aborigines, failed. The relationship is more important than ever because its terms have changed. It used to be said that whenever the English thought they had found an answer to the Irish question, the Irish would alter the question. Eventually it became apparent that the problem had to be turned around: for the Irish, it was the English question.

In Australia the altered relationship between coloniser and colonised became apparent in Aboriginal demands for self-determination. The Commonwealth's land rights legislation in 1976 appeared to meet that call, but in fact the transfer of land to Aboriginal ownership during the later 1970s and 1980s was hampered by State governments and largely confined to the desert and savannah regions of the centre and the north. Land rights in theory and rhetoric broke with the old assumptions by transferring title as a matter of Indigenous entitlement. Land rights in practice were similar to the setting aside of reserves during the nineteenth century – a benevolent act by a sovereign colonist. The work of the land rights tribunals served indeed to ratify that earlier expropriation because they made demonstration of continuing ties to the land a condition of its restoration – in effect, as a belated act of recompense, the claimants were given the land the whites had not taken. In much the same way the pursuit of Reconciliation, made possible by the generosity of Aboriginal participants, depended in the end on the willingness of non-Aboriginal Australians to acknowledge past wrongs that could never be undone. One commentator described the efforts of those involved in the Reconciliation process as providing 'therapy for whites'.

The Mabo judgement of 1992 shattered this humanitarian framework. By their decision the judges of the High Court shifted the basis of Aboriginal policy from the operation of statutory law, where parliament authorised the restitution of Aboriginal land, to the very foundations of the Australian legal system. The court did not overturn the sovereignty of the government that had been established in 1788, but recognised the existence in common law of Aboriginal property rights that preceded the European settlement and continued past it. The subsequent Wik judgement confirmed that these rights could coexist with other property rights. The Commonwealth has since legislated to confine the ambit of the judicial decisions, but their implications have yet to be fully worked out and their import is irrevocable. The colonisers are confronted with the fact that they share the land with the colonised.

Australia, in name and substance, is a product of the European supremacy that began five hunded years ago and ended in the second half of the present century. In Asia and Africa the process of decolonisation saw the expulsion or withdrawal of the imperial powers and the creation of new states. The Europeans departed. In the colonies of settlement where independent nation-states had already emerged there was no departure, but it became necessary to rework the relationship between the settlers and the indigenous people. New Zealand and Canada provide some guidance on how this can be done peacefully. Zimbabwe suggests the consequences of refusal; in South Africa the outcome is still unclear. While the different paths to a postcolonial settlement are influenced by the relative sizes of the indigenous populations, it is clear that the claims of first nation peoples carry a much greater authority than before. That influence is unlikely to diminish.

Visiting Australia for the first time in 1987, the English writer Angela Carter was struck by the signs of a society 'inexhaustibly curious about itself'. Her hosts were constantly pondering the national identity, repeatedly asking and telling themselves what it meant to be Australian. She thought this an effect of the end of empire. The writers with whom she travelled from one literary festival to another were all 'addressing themselves to questions of which the sub-text is post-colonialism', but these discussions took place 'in the context of a society in which the points of reference were no longer British' and the participants were 'still in the act of defining themselves'. Carter's observation of the national preoccupation was keen, her explanation of it perhaps rather too British. The empire had not simply ended, it was in danger of being forgotten. The points of reference had ceased to be British long before she came here; the difficulty was in finding new ones.

Colonies of settlement find it easier to throw off their tutelage than to reconstitute themselves as fully autonomous entities. Australian nationalism emerged in the nineteenth century by asserting its difference from the place of origin. This nationalism emphasised the freedom and opportunity of the New World against the constriction and debility of the Old. It was the product of people set loose in a new place where they could discard their fetters. It constructed the Commonwealth as a young nation starting afresh in a land of unlimited promise. This Australia remained tied to its origins, however, by the silken bonds of trade and investment, the continuing reliance on a powerful protector and, above all, by the emphasis on consanguinity. However much the settlers sought to attach themselves to the new homeland, they could not share it with those who were here first and they would not share it with others of the region. The insistence on exclusive possession operated on almost every aspect of foreign and domestic policy during the first half of the twentieth century, only to perpetuate the condition of insecurity, the feeling of being out of place, alone and exposed. Its legacy is apparent in the recent characterisation by an Indonesian journalist of Australians as the 'white tribe of Asia'.

Such is the power of the past that the appellation retains its force long after it has ceased to be accurate. The attempt to maintain the purity of a transplanted people has given way to the ethnic diversity of contemporary Australia. Forty per cent of present Australians have at least one parent who was born overseas. The insistence on a common culture has yielded to the acceptance, even celebration, of many cultures. Ethnic diversity is greater, more harmonious and better appreciated than in the countries of the region. The denial of the original inhabitants has been replaced by a growing recognition. For all the difficulties in accepting its implications, the Aboriginal renaissance is an indisputable feature of contemporary Australia.

True, this rearrangement has left the dominance of the ethnic majority intact – the descendants of those who claimed exclusive possession continued to define the comfortable limits of pluralism. The gradual, piecemeal manner in which they have done so has in turn allowed for their own reconstitution, so that they now partake of the very characteristics that were once alien and threatening. The transfer of Ayers Rock back to Aboriginal ownership and the restoration of its name, Uluru, has augmented its significance to all Australians. The incorporation of Asian peoples and cultures into the fabric of Australian life is least threatening to those who most directly experience it. The problem with this slow, often grudging, transition is that it provides no clear break that would settle the ghosts of White Australia. Perhaps the Australian republic, which must eventually come, will allow a final settlement.

As a young woman recently arrived in Australia, Catherine Spence worried that new colonies were too easily disrupted by sudden change: hence her observation that the gold rush had unfixed everything. As the 'Grand Old Woman of Australia', she looked back in 1910 on a lifetime of service with the observation that 'Nothing is insignificant in the history of a young community, and – above all – nothing seems impossible.' The history related here is one of rapid change. Colonists applied a familiar repertoire of practices to novel circumstances. The false starts were quickly started anew. The first settlements in New South Wales, Tasmania, Victoria and Queensland all shifted to alternative sites, but Sydney, Hobart, Melbourne and Brisbane, along with the more carefully planned beginnings at Perth and Adelaide, soon established a durable presence. They remain the centres of their States to this day. After early difficulties, the settlers found how to work the land. They learned how to treat it as a greenfield site on which they could employ the most advanced technologies and secure the greatest efficiency in the production of commodities for world markets. They applied their prosperity to schemes of improvement and adapted their institutions with similar ingenuity. This nineteenth-century Australia thrust aside obstacles, confident in its capacity to control destiny.

A hundred years later the confidence has dissipated. The motorist who now travels between the major cities sees abandoned home-steads, relics of a rural industry that was once the basis of the country's prosperity but now can scarcely make ends meet. The foreshortened interval between innovation and obsolescence is nowhere more apparent than in the New World of the south. The greenfield site is now brown and fragile, a young country has become old and weary. In its arrangements, also, there are signs of a premature senility. The capacity for political innovation is apparently spent. At the beginning of the century investigators came here to learn of the Australian achievement; now we take our lead from the nostrums of the New Right and our signals from the credit ratings agencies of New York. Australians are followers rather than leaders, and careless of their earlier achievements – for much is insignificant in the fading memory of a people who no longer learn from the past.

What might be learnt from it? For those who were here first, the modern history of Australia is deeply traumatic and the healing has only begun. For those who came, it is a story of fresh beginnings. A place of exile became a land of choice and a sanctuary for successive waves of new arrivals who have continually reworked it. It has dazzled them with its light, intimidated them with its space, oppressed them with its indifference. It makes no declaration of its virtues. No Statue of Liberty welcomes the newcomer, no proclamation of guiding principles is offered. They are to be found in the way that Australians live and the advantages that they usually take for granted. The majority enjoy a modest comfort; as one newcomer in the 1960s discovered, this is a place where 'you did not need to be wealthy to be warm'. There is a wide measure of freedom; differences are resolved peacefully and a healthy suspicion of extremes protects Australians from despotism. These and other achievements had to be won in the past as they need to be defended today. The history of Australia works backwards and forwards to rework our understanding of how we came to be what we are. Its presence is inescapable. To enter into it provides a capacity to determine what still might be.

SOURCES OF QUOTATIONS

I BEGINNINGS

Barron Field, *First Fruits of Australian Poetry* (Sydney, 1819) p. 5; the naval officer who imagined a second Rome was J. H. Tuckey, *Account of a Voyage to Establish a Colony at Port Phillip* (London: Longman, 1805), pp. 185–90.

Wandjuk Marika tells the Djankawa story in Jennifer Isaacs (ed.), *Australian Dreaming: 40,000 Years of Aboriginal History* (Sydney: Ure Smith, 1980), p. 76; Paddy Japaljarri Stewart, 'Dreamings', in David Horton (ed.), *The Encyclopaedia of Aboriginal Australia* (2 vols, Canberra: Aboriginal Studies Press, 1994), vol. 1, pp. 305–6; James Bonwick, *Daily Life and Origins of the Tasmanians* (London: Sampson, Low, 1870), pp. 1–2; Claude Lévi-Strauss is quoted in Josephine Flood, *Archaeology of the Dreamtime: The Story of Prehistoric Australia and its People*, rev. edn (Sydney: Angus and Robertson, 1994), p. 15.

2 NEWCOMERS, c. 1600–1792

Confusion in C. M. H. Clark, *A History of Australia. Volume I. From the Earliest Times to the Age of Macquarie* (Carlton, Vic.: Melbourne University Press, 1962), p. 77, quoted by Alan Frost, *Botany Bay Mirages: Illusions of Australia's Convict Beginnings* (Carlton, Vic.: Melbourne University Press, 1994), p. 110.

The prime minister was Robert Menzies, quoted in R. G. Neale (ed.), *Documents on Australian Foreign Policy, 1937–49* (vol. 2, Canberra: Australian Government Publishing Service, 1976), p. 96; Spanish and Dutch disappointment quoted in Glyndwr Williams and Alan Frost (eds), *Terra Australis to Australia* (Melbourne: Oxford University Press, 1988), pp. 9, 103; Swift in P. J. Marshall (ed.), *The Oxford History of the British Empire. Vol. II. The Eighteenth Century* (Oxford: Oxford

University Press, 1998), p. 554; Cook and Banks in J. C. Beaglehole, *The Life of Captain James Cook* (London: A. and C. Black, 1974), pp. 148, 251–2, and J. C. Beaglehole (ed.), *The Endeavour Journal of Joseph Banks, 1768–1771* (Sydney: Angus and Robertson, 1962), vol. 2, p. 51.

Colonial surgeon quoted in Frost, *Botany Bay Mirages*, pp. 91–2; Grose in Alan Frost, *Arthur Phillip, 1738–1814: His Voyaging* (Melbourne: Oxford University Press, 1987), p. 192; instructions to Phillip in Russel Ward, *Concise History of Australia* (St Lucia: University of Queensland Press, 1992), p. 55; Tench on Aborigines in *A Complete Account of the Settlement at Port Jackson in New South Wales* (London: G. Nicol and J. Sewell, 1793), p. 135, Collins quoted in David Day, *Claiming a Continent: A History of Australia* (Sydney: Angus and Robertson, 1996), pp. 65–6.

3 COERCION, 1793–1821

Arthur Phillip in *The Voyage of Governor Phillip to Botany Bay* (London: John Stockdale, 1789), p. 47; Elizabeth Macarthur quoted in Hazel King, *Elizabeth Macarthur and Her World* (Sydney: Sydney University Press, 1980), pp. 21–2; Phillip on homosexuality quoted in Gary Wotherspoon, 'A Sodom in the South Pacific: Male Homosexuality in Sydney, 1788–1809', in Graeme Aplin (ed.), *A Difficult Infant: Sydney Before Macquarie* (Kensington, NSW: University of New South Wales Press, 1988), p. 94; descriptions of Aboriginal women in Ann McGrath, 'Aboriginal–Colonial Gender Relations at Port Jackson', *Australian Historical Studies*, vol. 24, no. 95 (October 1990), p. 199.

Sydney Smith quoted in A. G. L. Shaw, *Convicts and the Colonies* (London: Faber, 1966), p. 77; Samuel Marsden quoted in A. T. Yarwood, *Samuel Marsden: The Great Survivor* (Carlton, Vic.: Melbourne University Press, 1977), p. 54; Hunter quoted in Russel Ward, *Concise History of Australia* (St Lucia: University of Queensland Press, 1992), p. 81; Blackstone quoted in David Neal, *The Rule of Law in a Penal Colony: Law and Power in Early New South Wales* (Cambridge: Cambridge University Press, 1991), p. 6.

Macquarie quoted in Shaw, *Convicts and the Colonies*, p. 88, and Brian Fletcher, *Landed Enterprise and Penal Society: A History of Farming and Grazing in New South Wales Before 1821* (Sydney: Sydney University Press, 1976), pp. 128–9; treasury official quoted in Shaw, *Convicts and the Colonies*, p. 93; Spanish priest quoted in K. S. Inglis, *The Australian Colonists: An Exploration of Social History, 1788–1870* (Carlton, Vic.: Melbourne University Press, 1974), p. 74; Marsden on Maoris quoted in Yarwood, *Samuel Marsden*, p. 164; Macquarie on Aborigines quoted in D. J. Mulvaney, *Encounters in Place: Outsiders and Aboriginal Australians, 1606–1985* (St Lucia: University of Queensland Press, 1989), p. 43, and Inglis, *The Australian Colonists*, p. 160; Flinders, *A Voyage to Terra Australis* (London: G. and W. Nicol, 1814), vol. 1, p. iii;

D. W. Meinig, quoted in Tom Griffiths and Libby Robin (eds), *Ecology and Empire: Environmental History of Settler Societies* (Carlton, Vic.: Melbourne University Press, 1997), p. 9; Palmer quoted in Alan Atkinson, *The Europeans in Australia. Volume 1. The Beginning* (Melbourne: Oxford University Press, 1997), p. 295.

4 EMANCIPATION, 1822–1850

Macquarie quoted in *Australian Dictionary of Biography*, vol. 2, p. 194; Bigge in *Australian Dictionary of Biography*, vol. 1, p. 99.

Mitchell quoted in R. H. W. Reece, *Aborigines and Colonists: Aborigines and Colonial Society in New South Wales in the 1830s and 1840s* (Sydney: Sydney University Press, 1974), p. 120; events at Slaughterhouse Creek described and Charles Harpur quoted in Reece, *Aborigines and Colonists*, pp. 33, 60; those at Bells Falls in David Roberts, 'Bells Falls Massacre and Bathurst's History of Violence', *Australian Historical Studies*, vol. 26, no. 105 (October 1995), p. 615; the Rufus River exchange was narrated in J. W. Bull, *Early Experiences of Colonial Life in South Australia* (Adelaide: Advertiser, 1878), pp. 140–1, quoted in J. J. Healy, *Literature and the Aborigine in Australia* (2nd edn, St Lucia: University of Queensland Press, 1989), p. 12; Hobbles Danaiyairi's saga of Captain Cook is presented by Deborah Bird Rose in *Australian Aboriginal Studies*, vol. 2 (1984), pp. 24–39; Henry Reynolds on pantheon of national heroes in *The Other Side of the Frontier: An Interpretation of the Aboriginal Response to the Invasion and Settlement of Australia* (Townsville: James Cook University, 1981), p. 165; fear of Aborigines quoted in Henry Reynolds, *Frontier: Aborigines, Settlers and Land* (North Sydney: Allen and Unwin, 1987), p. 10; Aboriginal rejoinder quoted in L. L. Robson, *A History of Tasmania. Volume I. Van Diemen's Land from the Earliest Times to 1855* (Melbourne: Oxford University Press, 1983), p. 212; spot of blood in Henry Reynolds, *This Whispering in Our Hearts* (St Leonards, NSW: Allen and Unwin, 1998), p. 43; report of select committee quoted in Henry Reynolds, *The Law of the Land* (Ringwood, Vic.: Penguin, 1987), p. 85; the secretary of state and the 'settlement' of Myall Creek quoted in Reece, *Aborigines and Colonists*, pp. 41, 135, who also quotes the minister on the Port Phillip Association agreement, p. 124; Colonial Office on South Australia in Reynolds, *The Law of the Land*, p. 106; Mahroot in J. P. Townsend, *Rambles and Observations in New South Wales* (London, 1849), p. 120, quoted in Reece, *Aborigines and Colonists*, p. 12; the account of Eliza Fraser quoted in Kay Schaffer, *In the Wake of First Contact: The Eliza Fraser Stories* (Cambridge: Cambridge University Press, 1995), p. 5.

Arthur quoted in A. G. L. Shaw, *Sir George Arthur, Bart, 1784–1854* (Carlton, Vic.: Melbourne University Press, 1980), p. 71; 'ferocious severity' quoted in Shirley Hazzard, *Punishment Short of Death:*

A History of the Penal Settlement at Norfolk Island (Melbourne: Hyland House, 1984), p. 223; Mary Sawyer's experience is discussed by Kay Daniels, *Convict Women* (St Leonards, NSW: Allen and Unwin, 1998), p. 195; Robinson quoted in C. M. H. Clark, *A History of Australia. Volume II. New South Wales and Van Diemen's Land, 1822–1838* (Carlton, Vic.: Melbourne University Press, 1968), p. 55; Darling on Wentworth quoted in K. S. Inglis, *The Australian Colonists: An Exploration of Social History, 1788–1870* (Carlton, Vic.: Melbourne University Press, 1974), p. 42; minister on end of transportation quoted in A. G. L. Shaw, *Convicts and the Colonies* (London: Faber, 1966), pp. 288–9; Governor Gipps on the squatters in *Historical Records of Australia*, ser. 3, vol. 21, p. 127.

Description of Thomas Peel in Geoffrey Bolton and Heather Vose (eds), *The Wollaston Journals. Volume 1. 1840–1842* (Nedlands: University of Western Australia Press, 1991), p. 185; Wakefield, *A Letter from Sydney and Other Writings* (1929), (London: J. M. Dent, 1929); Chisholm quoted in Margaret Kiddle, *Caroline Chisholm* (Carlton, Vic.: Melbourne University Press, 1950), p. 83; Frank the Poet, 'Farewell to V.D. Land', quoted in Noel McLachlan, *Waiting for the Revolution: A History of Australian Nationalism* (Ringwood, Vic.: Penguin, 1989), p. 73; Robinson's and Wentworth's verse quoted in Robert Dixon, *The Course of Empire: Neo-Classical Culture in New South Wales 1788–1860* (Melbourne: Oxford University Press, 1986), pp. 43, 135.

5 IN THRALL TO PROGRESS, 1851–1888

Hargraves and Clarke on gold quoted in Geoffrey Blainey, *The Rush that Never Ended* (3rd edn, Carlton, Vic.: Melbourne University Press, 1978), pp. 8, 13; Spence, *Clara Morison*, quoted in David Goodman, *Goldseeking: Victoria and California in the 1850s* (St Leonards, NSW: Allen and Unwin, 1994), p. 37; Kennedy and Eureka oath quoted in Noel McLachlan, *Waiting for the Revolution: A History of Australian Nationalism* (Ringwood, Vic.: Penguin, 1989), pp. 79, 96; the conservative historian was Henry Gyles Turner, *Our Own Little Rebellion* (Melbourne: Whitcombe and Tombs, 1912); Lawson quoted in Goodman, *Goldseeking*, pp. 7–8.

British minister quoted in C. C. Eldridge, *Victorian Imperialism* (Atlantic Highlands, N.J.: Humanities Press, 1978), p. 39; Deniehy in E. A. Martin, *The Life and Speeches of Daniel Henry Deniehy* (Sydney: George Robertson, 1884), pp. 53–4; Higinbotham quoted in Stuart Macintyre, *A Colonial Liberalism: The Lost World of Three Victorian Visionaries* (Melbourne: Oxford University Press, 1991), p. 57.

Land Convention notice quoted in Macintyre, *A Colonial Liberalism*, p. 32; Charles Thatcher, 'Hurrah for Australia', in *Thatcher's Colonial Minstrel* (Melbourne: Charlwood, 1859), quoted in Stuart Macintyre, *Winners and Losers: The Pursuit of Social Justice in Australian History*

(North Sydney: Allen and Unwin, 1985), p. 30; *Argus*, 21 April 1856, quoted in Patricia Grimshaw, Marilyn Lake, Ann McGrath and Marian Quartly, *Creating a Nation* (Ringwood, Vic.: McPhee Gribble, 1994), p. 104; Barcroft Boake, first published in *Bulletin* in 1891, quoted in Geoffrey Blainey, *A Land Half Won* (Melbourne: Macmillan, 1980), p. 188; the anti-Chinese editorial quoted in Andrew Markus, *Australian Race Relations, 1788–1993* (St Leonards, NSW: Allen and Unwin, 1994), p. 68; the phrase 'workin' longa tucker' is a chapter title in Ann McGrath, *'Born in the Cattle': Aborigines in Cattle Country* (North Sydney: Allen and Unwin, 1987); Victorian Board of Aborigines in D. J. Mulvaney, *Encounters in Place: Outsiders and Aboriginal Australians, 1606–1985* (St Lucia: University of Queensland Press, 1989), p. 148; Curr quoted in J. J. Healy, *Literature and the Aborigine in Australia* (2nd edn, St Lucia: University of Queensland Press, 1989), p. 17.

The English Scot was J. M. Barrie, *The Oxford Dictionary of Quotations* (3rd edn, Oxford: Oxford University Press, 1979), p. 34; Marcus Clarke, *The Future Australian Race* (Melbourne: A. H. Massina, 1877), p. 22, quoted in *Australian Dictionary of Quotations*, p. 50; Fergus Hume, quoted in Robert Dixon, *Writing the Colonial Adventure: Race, Gender and Nation in Anglo-Australian Popular Fiction, 1875–1914* (Cambridge: Cambridge University Press, 1995), p. 161; Harpur and Higinbotham quoted in H. R. Jackson, *Churches and People in Australia and New Zealand, 1860–1930* (North Sydney: Allen and Unwin, 1987), p. 126; Higinbotham on education quoted in Denis Grundy, *'Secular, Compulsory and Free': The Education Act of 1872* (Carlton, Vic.: Melbourne University Press, 1972), p. 91; *Age*, 15 February 1908, on Syme, quoted in Macintyre, *A Colonial Liberalism*, p. 83; Parkes and Centennial cantata quoted in Graeme Davison, J. W. McCarty and Ailsa McLeary (eds), *Australians 1888* (Broadway, NSW: Fairfax, Syme and Weldon Associates, 1987), pp. 7, 24; the critic of the national pantheon quoted in K. S. Inglis, *Sacred Places: War Memorials in the Australian Landscape* (Carlton, Vic.: Melbourne University Press, 1998), p. 32.

6 NATIONAL RECONSTRUCTION, 1889–1913

The shearer was Julian Stuart, *Part of the Glory: Reminiscences of the Shearers' Strike, Queensland, 1891* (Sydney: Australasian Book Society, 1967), p. 99, quoted in Jan Walker, *Jondaryan Station: The Relationship Between Pastoral Capital and Pastoral Labour, 1840–1890* (St Lucia: University of Queensland Press, 1988), p. 175; president of Sydney Chamber of Commerce quoted in John Rickard, *Class and Politics: New South Wales, Victoria and the Early Commonwealth, 1890–1910* (Canberra: Australian National University Press, 1976), p. 13; Deakin in *Victorian Parliamentary Debates*, vol. 64, p. 1368 (2 September 1890); the military commander quoted in Stuart Svensen, *The Sinews of War: Hard*

Cash and the 1890 Maritime Strike (Kensington, NSW: University of New South Wales Press, 1995), p. 191; Henry Lawson, *Poems*, with preface by Colin Roderick (Sydney: John Ferguson, 1979), pp. 50–1; Louisa Lawson's motto quoted by John Barnes, 'Louisa Lawson', in Graeme Davison, John Hirst and Stuart Macintyre (eds), *The Oxford Companion to Australian History* (Melbourne: Oxford University Press), p. 382; Lane quoted in Philip Bell and Roger Bell, *Implicated: The United States in Australia* (Melbourne: Oxford University Press, 1993), p. 29; Gilmore in W. H. Wilde, *Courage a Grace: A Biography of Dame Mary Gilmore* (Carlton, Vic.: Melbourne University Press, 1988), p. 91; W. G. Spence, *Australia's Awakening: Thirty Years in the Life of an Australian Agitator* (Sydney: The Workers Trustees, 1909), pp. 78, 220; Ryan quoted in *Dictionary of Australian Quotations*, p. 232; Deakin quoted in J. A. La Nauze, *Alfred Deakin: A Biography* (Carlton, Vic.: Melbourne University Press, 1965), vol. 1, p. 144.

The unique national type is described by Francis Adams, *The Australians: A Social Sketch* (London: Fisher Unwin, 1893), p. 165; Miles Franklin, *My Brilliant Career* (Edinburgh: Blackwood, 1901), p. 2; Joseph Furphy, *Such Is Life* (Sydney: Bulletin, 1903), p. 1; 'The Shearers', in Henry Lawson, *Poems*, p. 178; Lawson to Emma Brooks, 16 January 1893, in Henry Lawson, *Letters, 1890–1922*, ed. Colin Roderick (Sydney: Angus and Robertson, 1970), p. 53; Mary Gilmore's poem is quoted by Jennifer Strauss, 'Stubborn Singers of their Full Song: Mary Gilmore and Lesbia Harford', in Kay Ferres (ed.), *The Time to Write: Australian Women Writers, 1890–1930* (Ringwood, Vic.: Penguin, 1993), p. 114; the Labor leader was George Black, quoted in *Dictionary of Australian Quotations*, p. 18; WCTU quoted in Patricia Grimshaw, Marilyn Lake, Ann McGrath and Marian Quartly, *Creating a Nation* (Ringwood, Vic.: McPhee Gribble, 1994), p. 182.

Parkes quoted in J. A. La Nauze, *The Making of the Australian Commonwealth* (Carlton, Vic.: Melbourne University Press, 1972), p. 11; Deakin in *'And Be One People': Alfred Deakin's Federal Story*, introd. Stuart Macintyre (Carlton, Vic.: Melbourne University Press, 1995), p. 173; Barton in *Australian Dictionary of Biography*, vol. 7, p. 197; the celebrant is John Hirst, *A Republican Manifesto*, Melbourne: Oxford University Press, 1994, p. 35; *Official Report of the Federation Conference held in the Courthouse, Corowa, on Monday 31 July and Tuesday 1 August* (Corowa, NSW: James C. Leslie, 1893), p. 25; Deakin quoted in *Creating a Nation*, p. 192; Charles Pearson and Deakin quoted in Noel McLachlan, *Waiting for the Revolution: A History of Australian Nationalism* (Ringwood, Vic.: Penguin, 1989), pp. 172, 185; Deakin in *Commonwealth Parliamentary Debates*, vol. 4, p. 4807 (12 Sept. 1901); Labor platform in L. F. Crisp, *The Australian Federal Labour Party, 1901–1951* (London: Longmans, 1955), p. 271; Wattle Day League quoted in Richard White, *Inventing Australia: Images and Identity, 1688–1980*

(North Sydney: Allen and Unwin, 1981), p. 118; Deakin's characterisation of 'independent Australian Britons' appears in La Nauze, *Alfred Deakin*, vol. 2, p. 483.

Deakin quoted in Robert Birrell, *A Nation of Our Own: Citizenship and Nation-Building in Federation Australia* (Melbourne: Longman, 1995), p. 172; Deakin on New Protection quoted in Stuart Macintyre, *The Oxford History of Australia. Volume 4, 1901–1942, The Succeeding Age* (Melbourne: Oxford University Press, 1986), pp. 102–3; Higgins quoted in Stuart Macintyre, *Winners and Losers: The Pursuit of Social Justice in Australian History* (North Sydney: Allen and Unwin, 1985), pp. 55, 57; the commentator is Francis Castles, *The Working Class and Welfare: Reflections on the Political Development of the Welfare State in Australia and New Zealand, 1891–1980* (North Sydney: Allen and Unwin, 1985); the critical assessments are from Colin White, *Mastering Risk: Environment, Markets and Politics in Australian Economic History* (Melbourne: Oxford University Press, 1992), pp. 231, 223, and Paul Kelly, *The End of Certainty: The Story of the 1980s* (St Leonards, NSW: Allen and Unwin, 1992), pp. 1, 13; businessman quoted in Ken Buckley and Kris Klugman, *The History of Burns Philp: The Australian Company in the South Pacific* (Sydney: Burns Philp, 1981), p. 198.

7 SACRIFICE, 1914–1945

Cook and Fisher quoted in Neville Meaney (ed.), *Australia and the World: A Documentary History from the 1870s to the 1970s* (Melbourne: Longman Cheshire, 1985), p. 217: instructions to the governor-general quoted in E. M. Andrews, *The Anzac Illusion: Anglo-Australian Relations During World War I* (Cambridge: Cambridge University Press, 1993), p. 130; British war correspondent and C. E. W. Bean quoted in John F. Williams, *Quarantined Culture: Australian Reactions to Modernism, 1913–1939* (Cambridge: Cambridge University Press, 1995), p. 235, and Alastair Thomson, *Anzac Memories: Living with the Legend* (Melbourne: Oxford University Press, 1994), pp. 53, 54; the verse from Western Front is by Frederic Manning, 'The Trenches', in Les Murray (ed.), *The New Oxford Book of Australian Verse* (Melbourne: Oxford University Press, 1986), p. 109; the formula for mandate territories in Meaney (ed.), *Australia and the World*, p. 272; Hughes quoted in L. F. Fitzhardinge, *The Little Digger, 1914–1952: William Morris Hughes, A Political Biography* (Sydney: Angus and Robertson, 1979), p. 396.

Bruce quoted in Stuart Macintyre, *The Oxford History of Australia. Volume 4, 1901–1942: The Succeeding Age* (Melbourne: Oxford University Press, 1986), p. 201; Lillian Wooster Greave, 'British Boys', quoted in J. M. Powell, *Watering the Western Third: Water, Land and Community in Western Australia, 1826–1998* (Perth: Water and Rivers Commission, 1998), p. 23; tribute to Amy Johnson in Adelaide *Advertiser*, quoted by

Julian Thomas, 'Amy Johnson's Triumph, Australia 1930', *Australian Historical Studies*, vol. 23, no. 90 (April 1988), p. 79; Australian artist quoted in Williams, *Quarantined Culture*, p. 175; American State Department official quoted in Meaney (ed.), *Australia and the World*, p. 367.

Unemployed activist quoted in Wendy Lowenstein, *Weevils in the Flour: An Oral Record of the 1930s Depression in Australia* (Newham, Vic.: Scribe Publications, 1981), p. 177; New Guard methods in Eric Campbell, *The Rallying Point: My Story of the New Guard* (Carlton, Vic.: Melbourne University Press, 1965), pp. 70, 107–8; the feminist critic of the family wage was Lena Lynch, quoted in Marilyn Lake, 'A Revolution in the Family: The Challenge and Contradictions of Maternal Citizenship in Australia', in Seth Koven and Sonya Michel (eds), *Mothers of a New World: Maternalist Policies and the Origin of Welfare States* (New York: Routledge, 1993), p. 387; Charles Hawker, the minister who resigned from the government in 1932, quoted in Macintyre, *The Oxford History of Australia. Volume 4*, p. 299; Hughes quoted in *Australian Dictionary of Biography*, vol. 9, p. 399; Menzies quoted in Cameron Hazlehurst, *Menzies Observed* (Hornsby, NSW: Allen and Unwin, 1979), p. 138; Day of Mourning resolution quoted in Bill Gammage and Peter Spearritt (eds), *Australians 1938* (Broadway, NSW: Fairfax, Syme and Weldon Associates, 1987), p. 29; the anthropological advice came from A. P. Elkin, quoted in Russell McGregor, *Imagined Destinies: Aboriginal Australians and the Doomed Race Theory, 1880–1939* (Carlton, Vic.: Melbourne University Press, 1997), p. 196, and Geoffrey Gray, 'From Nomadism to Citizenship: A. P. Elkin and Aboriginal Advancement', in Nicolas Peterson and Will Sanders (eds), *Citizenship and Indigenous Australians: Changing Conceptions and Possibilities* (Cambridge: Cambridge University Press, 1998), p. 59; ministerial statement quoted in John Chesterman and Brian Galligan, *Citizens Without Rights: Aborigines and Australian Citizenship* Cambridge: Cambridge University Press, 1997), p. 148.

Menzies in R. G. Neale (ed.), *Documents on Australian Foreign Policy, 1937–49*, vol. 2 (Canberra: Australian Government Publishing Service, 1976), pp. 221, 256, and A. W. Martin, *Robert Menzies, A Life. Volume 1, 1894–1943* (Carlton, Vic.: Melbourne University Press, 1993), p. 295; John Manifold, 'The Tomb of Lt John Learmonth, AIF', in Chris Wallace-Crabbe and Peter Pierce (eds), *The Clubbing of the Gunfire: 101 Australian War Poems* (Carlton, Vic.: Melbourne University Press, 1984), p. 119; Mary Gilmore quoted in Denis O'Brien, *The Weekly* (Ringwood, Vic.: Penguin, 1982), p. 75; head of Foreign Office quoted in Martin, *Robert Menzies*, p. 332; Hughes quoted in Donald Horne, *The Little Digger: A Biography of Billy Hughes* (Melbourne: Macmillan, 1979), p. 123; Curtin quoted in Meaney (ed.), *Australia and the World*, p. 473, D. M. Horner, *High Command: Australia and Allied Strategy, 1939–1945* (St Leonards, NSW: Allen and Unwin, 1982), p. 152, and Paul Hasluck,

The Government and the People, 1942–1945 (Canberra: Australian War Memorial, 1970), p. 70; David Campbell, 'Men in Green', in Pierce and Wallace-Crabbe (eds), *The Clubbing of the Gunfire*, p. 130; Eric Lambert, *The Veterans* (London: Shakespeare Head, 1954), p. 137, quoted in David Walker, 'The Writers' War', in Joan Beaumont (ed.), *Australia's War, 1939–45* (St Leonards, NSW: Allen and Unwin, 1996), p. 149; the prime minister who returned to Kokoda was Paul Keating, quoted in Hank Nelson, 'Gallipoli, Kokoda and the Making of National Identity', *Journal of Australian Studies*, no. 53 (1997), p. 160; Curtin quoted in *The Oxford Companion to Australian History*, p. 169.

8 GOLDEN AGE, 1946–1974
Chifley in A. W. Stargadt (ed.), *Things Worth Fighting For: Speeches by Joseph Benedict Chifley* (Melbourne: Australian Labor Party, 1952), pp. 61, 65; Calwell quoted in Andrew Markus, 'Labour and Immigration 1946–9: The Displaced Persons Program', *Labour History*, no. 47 (November 1984), p. 78, and in *Australian Dictionary of Quotations*, p. 36; ministerial statement on public housing in Andrew Spaull, *John Dedman: A Most Unexpected Labor Man* (South Melbourne: Hyland House, 1998), p. 97; Menzies quoted in Judith Brett, *Robert Menzies' Forgotten People* (Sydney: Macmillan, 1992), p. 7; the treasurer, Arthur Fadden, quoted in Russel Ward, *A Nation for a Continent: The History of Australia, 1901–1975* (rev. edn, Richmond, Vic.: Heinemann, 1988), p. 300; the economist was Heinz Arndt, quoted with the committee of economic inquiry in Nicholas Brown, *Governing Prosperity: Social Change and Analysis in Australia in the 1950s* (Cambridge: Cambridge University Press, 1995), p. 123; Menzies' eulogy to bigness is quoted in George Seddon, *Landprints: Reflections on Place and Landscape* (Cambridge: Cambridge University Press, 1997), p. 57.

British high commissioner quoted in Roger C. Thompson, 'Winds of Change in the South Pacific', in David Lowe (ed.), *Australia and the End of Empires: The Impact of Decolonisation on Australia's Near North, 1945–65* (Geelong, Vic.: Deakin University Press, 1996), p. 161; Menzies quoted in Neville Meaney (ed.), *Australia and the World: A Documentary History from the 1870s to the 1970s* (Melbourne: Longman Cheshire, 1985), pp. 598, 616, and Ann Curthoys, A. W. Martin and Tim Rowse (eds), *Australians from 1939* (Broadway, NSW: Fairfax, Syme and Weldon Associates, 1987), p. 32; the verse is quoted in Glen St J. Barclay, *Friends in High Places: Australian–American Diplomatic Relations since 1945* (Melbourne: Oxford University Press, 1985), p. 128; the minister for external affairs on Vietnam was Garfield Barwick, quoted in Peter Edwards with Gregory Pemberton, *Crises and Commitments: The Politics and Diplomacy of Australia's Involvement in Southeast Asian Conflicts, 1848–1965* (St Leonards, NSW: Allen and Unwin, 1992), p. 246; Holt quoted in Barclay, *Friends in High Places*, p. 154; Menzies on communism quoted in Frank Cain and Frank Farrell, 'Menzies' War on the Communist Party, 1949–1951', in Ann Curthoys and John Merritt (eds), *Australia's First Cold War, 1945–1953 Volume 1. Society, Communism and Culture* (North Sydney, NSW: Allen and Unwin, 1984), p. 115; the commentator on the predicament of the Labor Party was D. W. Rawson, *Labor in Vain? A Survey of the Australian Labor Party* (Melbourne: Longmans, 1966); Menzies on Evatt in Meaney (ed.), *Australia and the World*, p. 605; Call to Australia quoted in Andrew Moore, *The Right Road: A History of Right-wing Politics in Australia* (Melbourne: Oxford University Press, 1995), p. 60; Menzies's Cold War rhetoric in Meaney (ed.), *Australia and the World*, p. 605; the episode at the Lakeside Oval was recounted to me by Senator Barney Cooney.

Menzies on prosperity quoted in John Murphy, 'Shaping the Cold War Family', *Australian Historical Studies*, vol. 26, no. 105 (October 1995), p. 550; description of house-building in Peter Spearritt, *Sydney Since the Twenties* (Sydney: Hale and Iremonger, 1978), p. 104; the Australian expert on the family is quoted in Stella Lees and June Senyard, *The 1950s* (South Yarra, Vic.: Hyland House, 1987), p. 83; Olympic programme quoted in Graeme Davison, 'Welcoming the World: The 1956 Olympic Games and Re-presentation of Melbourne', *Australian Historical Studies*, vol. 28, no. 109 (October 1997), p. 74; the chairman of the Atomic Energy Commission was Philip Baxter, quoted in Patrick O'Farrell, *UNSW, A Portrait: The University of New South Wales, 1949–1999* (Kensington, NSW: University of New South Wales Press, 1999), p. 76; the radical nationalist works cited are A. A. Phillips, *The Australian Tradition* (Melbourne: Cheshire, 1958), Russel Ward, *The Australian Legend* (Melbourne: Oxford University Press, 1958) and Vance Palmer, *The Legend of the Nineties* (Carlton, Vic.: Melbourne University Press, 1954); Calwell quoted in Gwenda Tavan, '"Good Neighbours": Community Organisations, Migrant Assimilation and Australian Society and Culture, 1950–1961', *Australian Historical Studies*, vol. 28, no. 109 (October 1997), p. 78, and his successor, Billie Snedden, in Geoffrey Sherington, *Australia's Immigrants, 1788–1988* (2nd edn, North Sydney: Allen and Unwin, 1990), p. 160; article on 'The Australian Way of Life' quoted in Richard White, *Inventing Australia: Images and Identity, 1688–1980* (North Sydney, NSW: Allen and Unwin, 1981), p. 163; the minister for territories, Paul Hasluck, quoted in Tim Rowse, 'Assimilation and After', in Ann Curthoys, A. W. Martin and Tim Rowse (eds), *Australians from 1939*, p. 135, and Andrew Markus, *Australian Race Relations, 1788–1993* (St Leonards, NSW: Allen and Unwin, 1994), p. 164; the American tennis player was Jack Kramer, quoted in Kevin Fewster, 'Advantage Australia: Davis Cup Tennis, 1950–1959', *Sporting Traditions*, vol. 2, no. 1 (November 1985), p. 59; surf life-saving club in White, *Inventing Australia*, p. 155.

The Liberal premier was Robin Askin, quoted in *Dictionary of Australian Quotations*, p. 9; the Vietnam poem by A. D. Hope is in Chris Wallace-Crabbe and Peter Pierce (eds), *The Clubbing of the Gunfire: 101 Australian War Poems* (Carlton, Vic.: Melbourne University Press, 1984), p. 197; the minister who drew the comparison with the London mob was Peter Howson, quoted in Greg Pemberton, *All the Way: Australia's Road to Vietnam* (North Sydney, NSW: Allen and Unwin, 1987), p. 326, and recorded in his diaries edited by Don Aitkin as *The Life of Politics* (Ringwood, Vic.: Penguin, 1994), p. 631; his colleague who spoke of 'political bikies' was Billie Snedden, quoted in Peter Edwards, *A Nation at War: Australian Politics, Society and Diplomacy during the Vietnam War, 1965–1975* (St Leonards, NSW: Allen and Unwin, 1997), p. 266; Robin Boyd and J. Freeland quoted in Brown, *Governing Prosperity*, p. 159, and Alastair Greig, *The Stuff Dreams Are Made Of: Housing Provision in Australia, 1945–1960* (Carlton, Vic.: Melbourne University Press, 1995), pp. 149–50; Barry Humphries, *More Please* (Ringwood, Vic.: Penguin, 1992), p. xiii; Bobbi Sykes and Gough Whitlam quoted in Rowse, 'Assimilation and After', pp. 142, 144; Whitlam's explanation of social citizenship was recorded in Gough Whitlam, *The Whitlam Government, 1972–1975* (Ringwood, Vic.: Penguin, 1985), pp. 182–3; his call for a light on every desk is in Graham Freudenberg, *A Certain Grandeur: Gough Whitlam in Politics* (Melbourne: Macmillan, 1977), p. 82, and the response to the Dismissal in *Dictionary of Australian Quotations*, pp. 281–2.

9 REINVENTING AUSTRALIA, 1975–1999

Malcolm Fraser quoted in Frank Crowley, *Tough Times: Australia in the Seventies* (Richmond, Vic.: Heinemann, 1986), p. 309; Keating quoted by Kevin Davis, 'Managing the Economy', in Brian W. Head and Allan Patience (eds), *From Fraser to Hawke* (Melbourne: Longman Cheshire, 1989), p. 67, and in Paul Kelly, *The End of Certainty: The Story of the 1980s* (St Leonards, NSW: Allen and Unwin, 1992), p. 212; the two economic historians were Eric Jones and Geoffrey Raby, 'Establishing a European Economy', in John Hardy and Alan Frost (eds), *Studies from Terra Australis to Australia* (Canberra: Australian Academy of the Humanities, 1989), p. 155; Keating on recession quoted in Kelly, *The End of Certainty*, p. 504, and posing the stark choice in John Wiseman, *Global Nation? Australia and the Politics of Globalisation* (Cambridge: Cambridge University Press), pp. 43–4; Hawke quoted in Kelly, *The End of Certainty*, p. 350.

The endless race was declared in a 1994 government white paper on employment, quoted in Wiseman, *Global Nation?*, p. 40, and Keating's glosses on it appear in Kelly, *The End of Certainty*, p. 664, and Stuart Macintyre, 'Who Are the True Believers?', *Labour History*, no. 68 (May 1995), p. 155; his ridicule of basket-weavers was reported in the *Age*,

7 December 1981; the Redfern Park speech in Mark Ryan (ed.), *Advancing Australia: The Speeches of Paul Keating, Prime Minister* (Sydney: Big Picture Publications, 1995), p. 228; Howard in *Australian*, 19 November 1996.

Geoffrey Blainey quoted in *The Oxford Companion to Australian History*, p. 75; the rural discontent quoted in Rob Linn, *Battling the Land: 200 Years of Rural Australia* (St Leonards, NSW: Allen and Unwin, 1999), p. 167; Sally Morgan, quoted in Bain Attwood, 'Portrait of an Aboriginal as an Artist: Sally Morgan and the Construction of Aboriginality', *Australian Historical Studies*, vol. 25, no. 99 (October 1992), pp. 305–6; 'welfare colonialism' is expounded by Jeremy Beckett, 'Aboriginality, Citizenship and the Nation State', *Social Analysis*, no. 24 (1988), p. 14; Justices Deane and Gaudron quoted in Tim Rowse, *After Mabo: Interpreting Indigenous Traditions* (Carlton, Vic.: Melbourne University Press, 1993), p. 8.

Dingo Spirit and the British inquiry into child migration quoted in Peter Pierce, *The Country of Lost Children: An Australian Anxiety* (Cambridge: Cambridge University Press, 1999), pp. 174, 195; Alan Bond is quoted in Stuart Macintyre, 'Tall Poppies', *Australian Society*, September 1989; their defender was John Gorton, quoted in G. A. Wilkes, *A Dictionary of Australian Colloquialisms* (Sydney: Collins Books, 1980), p. 260; the cabinet minister was John Button, quoted in Paul Barry, *The Rise and Rise of Kerry Packer* (Sydney: Bantam, 1993), p. 322; Bicentennial song quoted in Peter Spearritt, 'Celebration of a Nation: The Triumph of Spectacle', in Susan Janson and Stuart Macintyre (eds), *Making the Bicentenary* (Melbourne: Australian Historical Studies, 1988), p. 3.

10 WHAT NEXT?

Ernest Scott, *A Short History of Australia* (London: Oxford University Press, 1916), pp. 308, v; the commentator on Reconciliation was Nicholas Jose in *London Review of Books*, vol. 21, no. 3 (18 February 1999), and I have drawn on an unpublished paper by Tim Rowse for my discussion of land rights; Angela Carter's 'Constructing an Australia' is reprinted in *Shaking a Leg: Journalism and Writings* (London: Vintage, 1997), pp. 227–30; Ratih Hardjono is the author of *White Tribe of Asia* (Australian translation, Clayton, Vic.: Monash Asia Institute, 1993); Spence's status is noted in Susan Magarey, *Unbridling the Tongues of Women: A Biography of Catherine Helen Spence* (Sydney: Hale and Iremonger, 1985), p. 192, and her own observation is in Helen Thomson (ed.), *Catherine Helen Spence* (St Lucia, University of Queensland Press, 1987), p. 425; the newcomer was Michael Wilding, 'Sydney', *Overland*, no. 151 (Winter 1998), p. 4.

GUIDE TO FURTHER READING

REFERENCE

Frank Crowley and Peter Spearritt (gen. eds), *Australians: A Historical Library*. 5 vols: *A Historical Atlas, A Historical Dictionary, Events and Places, Historical Statistics, A Guide to Sources* (Broadway, NSW: Fairfax, Syme and Weldon Associates, 1987).

John Hirst, Graeme Davison and Stuart Macintyre (eds), *The Oxford Companion to Australian History* (Melbourne: Oxford University Press, 1998).

David Horton (gen. ed.), *The Encyclopaedia of Aboriginal Australia* (2 vols, Canberra: Aboriginal Studies Press, 1994).

James Jupp (gen. ed.), *The Australian People: An Encyclopedia of the Nation, Its People and Their Origins* (Sydney: Angus and Robertson, 1988).

Stephen Murray-Smith (ed.), *The Dictionary of Australian Quotations* (Richmond, Vic.: Heinemann, 1984).

Douglas Pike, Bede Nairn, Geoffrey Serle and John Ritchie (gen. eds), *Australian Dictionary of Biography* (14 vols, Carlton: Melbourne University Press, 1966–90). Twelve volumes cover the period 1788–1939; a further six volumes, of which two have so far appeared, will cover the period 1940–80.

W. S. Ramson, *The Australian National Dictionary: Australian Words and Their Origins* (Melbourne: Oxford University Press, 1988).

GENERAL

Geoffrey Blainey, *A Land Half Won* (Melbourne: Macmillan, 1980).

Geoffrey Bolton (ed.), *The Oxford History of Australia* (Melbourne: Oxford University Press, vol. 2, 1992; vol. 3, 1988; vol. 4, 1986; vol. 5, 1990).

Verity Burgmann and Jenny Lee (eds), *A People's History of Australia
since 1788* (4 vols, Fitzroy, Vic.: McPhee Gribble/Penguin, 1988).
Hilary Carey, *Believing in Australia: A Cultural History of Religions*
(St Leonards, NSW: Allen and Unwin, 1996).
C. M. H. Clark, *A History of Australia* (6 vols, Carlton, Vic.: Melbourne
University Press, 1962–87).
Alan D. Gilbert and K. S. Inglis (gen eds), *Australians: A Historical
Library*. 5 vols: *Australians to 1788, Australians 1838, Australians
1888, Australians 1938, Australians from 1939* (Broadway, NSW:
Fairfax, Syme and Weldon Associates, 1987).
Jeffrey Grey, *A Military History of Australia* (Cambridge: Cambridge
University Press, 1990).
Patricia Grimshaw, Marilyn Lake, Ann McGrath and Marian Quartly,
Creating a Nation (Ringwood, Vic.: McPhee Gribble, 1994).
Ann McGrath (ed.), *Contested Ground: Australian Aborigines Under the
British Crown* (St Leonards, NSW: Allen and Unwin, 1995).
J. M. Powell, *An Historical Geography of Modern Australia: The Restive
Fringe* (Cambridge: Cambridge University Press, 1988).
John Rickard, *Australia: A Cultural History* (Melbourne: Longman
Cheshire, 1988).
Bernard Smith, *Australian Painting, 1788–1970* (2nd edn, Sydney:
Harper and Row, 1985).

I BEGINNINGS

Jim Allen, John Golson and Rhys Jones (eds), *Sunda and Sahul* (London:
Academic Press, 1977).
Geoffrey Blainey, *The Triumph of the Nomads* (Melbourne: Macmillan,
1982).
N. G. Butlin, *Economics and the Dreamtime: A Hypothetical History*
(Cambridge: Cambridge University Press, 1993).
Donald Denoon (ed.), *The Cambridge History of the Pacific Islanders*
(Cambridge: Cambridge University Press, 1997).
Jared Diamond, *Guns, Germs and Steel: A Short History of Everybody
for the Last 13,000 Years* (London: Jonathan Cape, 1997).
Timothy Fridtjot Flannery, *The Future Eaters* (Chatswood, NSW: Reed,
1994).
Josephine Flood, *Archaeology of the Dreamtime: The Story of Prehistoric
Australia and its People* (rev. edn, Sydney: Angus and Robertson,
1994).
Harry Lourandos, *Continent of Hunter-Gatherers: New Perspectives
in Australian Prehistory* (Cambridge: Cambridge University Press,
1997).
D. J. Mulvaney, *The Prehistory of Australia* (Ringwood, Vic.: Penguin,
1975).

D. J. Mulvaney and J. Peter White (eds), *Australians to 1788* (Broadway, NSW: Fairfax, Syme and Weldon Associates, 1987).

D. J. Mulvaney, *Encounters in Place: Outsiders and Aboriginal Australians, 1606–1985* (St Lucia: University of Queensland Press, 1989).

Stephen J. Pyne, *Burning Bush: A Fire History of Australia* (North Sydney, NSW: Allen and Unwin, 1992).

2 NEWCOMERS, C. 1600–1792

Alan Atkinson, *The Europeans in Australia. Volume 1. The Beginning* (Melbourne: Oxford University Press, 1997).

C. A. Bayly, *Imperial Meridian: The British Empire and the World, 1780–1830* (London: Longman, 1989).

J. C. Beaglehole, *The Life of Captain James Cook* (London: A. and C. Black, 1974).

C. M. H. Clark, *A History of Australia. Volume I. From the Earliest Times to the Age of Macquarie* (Carlton, Vic.: Melbourne University Press, 1962).

Alan Frost, *Botany Bay Mirages: Illusions of Australia's Convict Beginnings* (Carlton, Vic.: Melbourne University Press, 1994).

John Hardy and Alan Frost (eds), *Studies from Terra Australis to Australia* (Canberra: Australian Academy of the Humanities, 1989).

Chris Healy, *From the Ruins of Colonialism: History as Social Memory* (Cambridge: Cambridge University Press, 1997).

E. L. Jones, *The European Miracle: Environments, Economies and Geopolitics in the History of Europe and Asia* (2nd edn, Cambridge: Cambridge University Press, 1987).

David Mackay, *A Place of Exile: The European Settlement of New South Wales* (Melbourne: Oxford University Press, 1985).

P. J. Marshall (ed.), *The Oxford History of the British Empire. Vol. II. The Eighteenth Century* (Oxford: Oxford University Press, 1998).

Ged Martin (ed.), *The Founding of Australia: The Argument about Australia's Origins* (Sydney: Hale and Iremonger, 1978).

Anthony Pagden, *Lords of All the World: Ideologies of Empire in Spain, Britain and France, c. 1500 to c. 1800* (New Haven: Yale University Press, 1995).

Henry Reynolds, *Aboriginal Sovereignty: Reflections on Race, State and Nation* (St Leonards, NSW: Allen and Unwin, 1996).

Bernard Smith, *European Vision and the South Pacific* (2nd edn, Sydney: Harper and Row, 1985).

Bernard Smith, *Imagining the Pacific: In the Wake of the Cook Voyages* (Carlton, Vic.: Melbourne University Press, 1992).

O. H. K. Spate, *The Pacific Since Magellan* (3 vols, Canberra: Australian National University Press, 1979–88).

W. E. H. Stanner, *White Man Got No Dreaming: Essays, 1938–1973*
(Canberra: Australian National University Press, 1979).
Glyndwr Williams and Alan Frost (eds), *Terra Australis to Australia*
(Melbourne: Oxford University Press, 1988).

3 COERCION, 1793–1821

Graeme Aplin (ed.), *A Difficult Infant: Sydney Before Macquarie*
(Kensington, NSW: University of New South Wales Press, 1988).
Alan Atkinson, *The Europeans in Australia. Volume 1. The Beginning*
(Melbourne: Oxford University Press, 1997).
Frank Broeze, *Island Nation: A History of Australians and the Sea*
(St Leonards, NSW: Allen and Unwin, 1997).
C. M. H. Clark, *A History of Australia. Volume I. From the Earliest
Times to the Age of Macquarie* (Carlton, Vic.: Melbourne University
Press, 1962).
Joy Damousi, *Depraved and Disorderly: Female Convicts, Sexuality and
Gender in Colonial Australia* (Cambridge: Cambridge University Press,
1997).
Kay Daniels, *Convict Women* (St Leonards, NSW: Allen and Unwin,
1998).
Brian Fletcher, *Landed Enterprise and Penal Society: A History of
Farming and Grazing in New South Wales Before 1821* (Sydney:
Sydney University Press, 1976).
D. R. Hainsworth, *The Sydney Traders: Simeon Lord and his
Contemporaries, 1788–1821* (Carlton, Vic.: Melbourne University
Press, 1981).
J. B. Hirst, *Convict Society and Its Enemies: A History of Early New
South Wales* (North Sydney: Allen and Unwin, 1983).
Robert Hughes, *The Fatal Shore: A History of the Transportation of
Convicts to Australia, 1787–1868* (London: Collins Harvill, 1987).
K. S. Inglis, *The Australian Colonists: An Exploration of Social History,
1788–1870* (Carlton, Vic.: Melbourne University Press, 1974).
Sharon Morgan, *Land Settlement in Early Tasmania: Creating an
Antipodean England* (Cambridge: Cambridge University Press, 1992).
David Neal, *The Rule of Law in a Penal Colony: Law and Power in Early
New South Wales* (Cambridge: Cambridge University Press, 1991).
Stephen Nicholas, *Convict Workers: Reinterpreting Australia's Past*
(Cambridge: Cambridge University Press, 1988).
John Ritchie, *Lachlan Macquarie: A Biography* (Carlton, Vic.: Melbourne
University Press, 1986).
L. L. Robson, *The Convict Settlers of Australia* (Carlton, Vic.: Melbourne
University Press, 1965).
L. L. Robson, *A History of Tasmania. Volume I. Van Diemen's Land from
the Earliest Times to 1855* (Melbourne: Oxford University Press, 1983).

A. G. L. Shaw, *Convicts and the Colonies: A Study of Penal Transportation from Great Britain and Ireland to Australia and Other Parts of the British Empire* (London: Faber, 1966).

Keith Willey, *When the Sky Fell Down: The Destruction of the Tribes of the Sydney Region, 1788–1850s* (Sydney: Collins, 1979).

4 EMANCIPATION, 1822–1850

Alan Atkinson and Marian Aveling (eds), *Australians 1838* (Broadway, NSW: Fairfax, Syme and Weldon Associates, 1987).

C. M. H. Clark, *A History of Australia. Volume II. New South Wales and Van Diemen's Land, 1822–1838* (Carlton, Vic.: Melbourne University Press, 1968).

C. M. H. Clark, *A History of Australia. Volume III. The Beginning of an Australian Civilization, 1824–1851* (Carlton, Vic.: Melbourne University Press, 1973).

Jan Critchett, *A 'distant field of murder': Western District Frontiers, 1834–1848* (Carlton, Vic.: Melbourne University Press, 1990).

F. K. Crowley, *Australia's Western Third: A History of Western Australia from the First Settlement to Modern Times* (Melbourne: Heinemann, 1960).

Joy Damousi, *Depraved and Disorderly: Female Convicts, Sexuality and Gender in Colonial Australia* (Cambridge: Cambridge University Press, 1997).

Kay Daniels, *Convict Women* (North Sydney: Allen and Unwin, 1998).

David Denholm, *The Colonial Australians* (Ringwood, Vic.: Allen Lane, 1979).

Donald Denoon, *Settler Capitalism: The Dynamics of Dependent Development in the Southern Hemisphere* (Oxford: Oxford University Press, 1983).

Robert Dixon, *The Course of Empire: Neo-Classical Culture in New South Wales, 1788–1860* (Melbourne: Oxford University Press, 1986).

Ian Duffield and James Bradley (eds), *Representing Convicts: New Perspectives on Convict Forced Labour Migration* (London: Leicester University Press, 1997).

Chris Healy, *From the Ruins of Colonialism: History as Social Memory* (Cambridge: Cambridge University Press, 1997).

J. B. Hirst, *Convict Society and its Enemies: A History of Early New South Wales* (North Sydney: Allen and Unwin, 1983).

K. S. Inglis, *The Australian Colonists: An Exploration of Social History, 1788–1870* (Carlton, Vic.: Melbourne University Press, 1974).

Grace Karskens, *The Rocks: Life in Early Sydney* (Carlton, Vic.: Melbourne University Press, 1997).

Bruce Kercher, *An Unruly Child: A History of Law in Australia* (St Leonards, NSW: Allen and Unwin, 1995).

Ann McGrath (ed.), *Contested Ground: Australian Aborigines under the British Crown* (St Leonards, NSW: Allen and Unwin, 1995).

Roger Milliss, *Waterloo Creek: The Australia Day Massacre of 1838, George Gipps and the British Conquest of New South Wales* (Ringwood, Vic.: McPhee Gribble, 1992).

Stephen Nicholas, *Convict Workers: Reinterpreting Australia's Past* (Cambridge: Cambridge University Press, 1988).

Douglas Pike, *Paradise of Dissent: South Australia, 1829–1857* (2nd edn, Carlton, Vic.: Melbourne University Press, 1967).

R. H. W. Reece, *Aborigines and Colonists: Aborigines and Colonial Society in New South Wales in the 1830s and 1840s* (Sydney: Sydney University Press, 1974).

Henry Reynolds, *Fate of a Free People* (Ringwood, Vic.: Penguin, 1995).

Henry Reynolds, *Frontier: Aborigines, Settlers and Land* (North Sydney: Allen and Unwin, 1987).

Henry Reynolds, *The Law of the Land* (Ringwood, Vic.: Penguin, 1987).

Henry Reynolds, *This Whispering in Our Hearts* (St Leonards, NSW: Allen and Unwin, 1998).

S. H. Roberts, *History of Australian Land Settlement (1788–1920)* (Melbourne: Macmillan, 1924).

L. L. Robson, *A History of Tasmania. Volume I. Van Diemen's Land from the Earliest Times to 1855* (Melbourne: Oxford University Press, 1983).

Michael Roe, *Quest for Authority in Eastern Australia, 1835–1851* (Carlton, Vic.: Melbourne University Press, 1965).

Lyndall Ryan, *The Aboriginal Tasmanians* (St Lucia, University of Queensland Press, 1981).

Simon Ryan, *The Cartographic Eye: How Explorers Saw Australia* (Cambridge: Cambridge University Press, 1996).

Kay Schaffer, *In the Wake of First Contact: The Eliza Fraser Stories* (Cambridge: Cambridge University Press, 1995).

A. G. L. Shaw, *Convicts and the Colonies: A Study of Penal Transportation from Great Britain and Ireland to Australia and Other Parts of the British Empire* (London: Faber, 1966).

5 IN THRALL TO PROGRESS, 1851–1888

Bain Attwood, *The Making of the Aborigines* (North Sydney: Allen and Unwin, 1988).

Geoffrey Blainey, *The Rush that Never Ended* (3rd edn, Carlton, Vic.: Melbourne University Press, 1978).

Geoffrey Bolton, *A Thousand Miles Away: A History of North Queensland to 1920* (Canberra: Australian National University Press, 1963).

Graeme Davison, *The Rise and Fall of Marvellous Melbourne* (Carlton, Vic.: Melbourne University Press, 1978).

Graeme Davison, J. W. McCarty and Ailsa McLeary (eds), *Australians 1888* (Broadway, NSW: Fairfax, Syme and Weldon Associates, 1987).

Lionel Frost, *The New Urban Frontier: Urbanisation and City Building in Australasia and the American West* (Kensington, NSW: University of New South Wales Press, 1991).

Bill Gammage, *Narrandera Shire* (Narrandera, NSW: Shire Council, 1986).

David Goodman, *Goldseeking: Victoria and California in the 1850s* (St Leonards, NSW: Allen and Unwin, 1994).

Andrew Hassam, *Sailing to Australia: Shipboard Diaries by Nineteenth-Century British Emigrants* (Carlton, Vic.: Melbourne University Press, 1994).

Roslynn D. Haynes, *Seeking the Centre: The Australian Desert in Literature, Art and Film* (Cambridge: Cambridge University Press, 1998).

John Hirst, *Adelaide and the Country, 1870–1917: Their Social and Political Relationship* (Carlton, Vic.: Melbourne University Press, 1973).

John Hirst, *The Strange Birth of Colonial Democracy: New South Wales, 1848–1884* (North Sydney: Allen and Unwin, 1988).

H. R. Jackson, *Churches and People in Australia and New Zealand, 1860–1930* (North Sydney: Allen and Unwin, 1987).

Beverley Kingston, *The Oxford History of Australia. Volume 3, 1860–1900: Glad, Confident Morning* (Melbourne: Oxford University Press, 1988).

Stuart Macintyre, *A Colonial Liberalism: The Lost World of Three Victorian Visionaries* (Melbourne: Oxford University Press, 1991).

Stuart Macintyre, *Winners and Losers: The Pursuit of Social Justice in Australian History* (North Sydney: Allen and Unwin, 1985).

Dawn May, *Aboriginal Labour and the Cattle Industry: Queensland from White Settlement to the Present* (Cambridge: Cambridge University Press, 1994).

Ann McGrath, *'Born in the Cattle': Aborigines in Cattle Country* (North Sydney: Allen and Unwin, 1987).

Clive Moore, *Kanaka: A History of Melanesian Mackay* (Port Moresby: University of Papua New Guinea Press, 1985).

D. J. Mulvaney, *Encounters in Place: Outsiders and Aboriginal Australians, 1606–1985* (St Lucia: University of Queensland Press, 1989).

Alan Powell, *Far Country: A Short History of the Northern Territory* (2nd edn, Carlton, Vic.: Melbourne University Press, 1988).

Henry Reynolds, *With the White People* (Ringwood, Vic.: Penguin, 1990).

Andrew Sayers, *Aboriginal Artists of the Nineteenth Century* (Melbourne: Oxford University Press, 1994).

Geoffrey Serle, *The Golden Age: A History of the Colony of Victoria, 1851–1861* (Carlton, Vic.: Melbourne University Press, 1963).

Duncan Waterson, *Squatter, Selector and Storekeeper: A History of the Darling Downs, 1859–93* (Sydney: Sydney University Press, 1968).

6 NATIONAL RECONSTRUCTION, 1889–1913

Judith Allen, *Rose Scott: Vision and Revision in Feminism* (Melbourne: Oxford University Press, 1994).

Verity Burgmann, *'In Our Time': Socialism and the Rise of Labor, 1885–1905* (North Sydney: Allen and Unwin, 1985).

John Chesterman and Brian Galligan, *Citizens Without Rights: Aborigines and Australian Citizenship* (Cambridge: Cambridge University Press, 1997).

Robin Gollan, *Radical and Working Class Politics: A Study of Eastern Australia, 1850–1910* (Carlton, Vic.: Melbourne University Press, 1960).

Jeffrey Grey, *A Military History of Australia* (Cambridge: Cambridge University Press, 1990).

Helen Irving, *To Constitute a Nation: A Cultural History of Australia's Constitution* (Cambridge: Cambridge University Press, 1997).

Susan Magarey, Sue Rowley and Susan Sheridan (eds), *Debutante Nation: Feminism Contests the 1890s* (St Leonards, NSW: Allen and Unwin, 1993).

Ann McGrath (ed.), *Contested Ground: Australian Aborigines under the British Crown* (St Leonards, NSW: Allen and Unwin, 1995).

Russell McGregor, *Imagined Destinies: Aboriginal Australians and the Doomed Race Theory, 1880–1939* (Carlton, Vic.: Melbourne University Press, 1997).

Ross McMullin, *The Light on the Hill: The Australian Labor Party, 1891–1991* (Melbourne: Oxford University Press, 1991).

John Merritt, *The Making of the AWU* (Melbourne: Oxford University Press, 1986).

John Rickard, *Class and Politics: New South Wales, Victoria and the Early Commonwealth, 1890–1910* (Canberra: Australian National University Press, 1976).

Michael Roe, *Nine Australian Progressives: Vitalism in Bourgeois Social Thought, 1890–1960* (St Lucia: University of Queensland Press, 1984).

Gavin Souter, *Lion and Kangaroo. Australia: 1901–1919, The Rise of a Nation* (Sydney: William Collins, 1976).

Stuart Svensen, *The Shearers' War: The Story of the 1891 Shearers' Strike* (St Lucia: University of Queensland Press, 1989).

Stuart Svensen, *The Sinews of War: Hard Cash and the 1890 Maritime Strike* (Kensington, NSW: University of New South Wales Press, 1995).

Roger Thompson, *Australian Imperialism in the Pacific: The Expansionist Era, 1820–1920* (Carlton, Vic.: Melbourne University Press, 1980).

Jan Todd, *Colonial Technology: Science and the Transfer of Innovation to Australia* (Cambridge: Cambridge University Press, 1995).

Luke Trainor, *British Imperialism and Australian Nationalism: Manipulation, Conflict and Compromise in the Late Nineteenth Century* (Cambridge: Cambridge University Press, 1994).

7 SACRIFICE, 1914–1945

E. M. Andrews, *The Anzac Illusion: Anglo-Australian Relations During World War I* (Cambridge: Cambridge University Press, 1993).

C. E. W. Bean, *Anzac to Amiens* (Canberra: Australian War Memorial, 1946).

Sean Brawley, *The White Peril: Foreign Relations and Asian Immigration to Australasia and North America, 1919–78* (Kensington, NSW: University of New South Wales Press, 1995).

Judith Brett, *Robert Menzies' Forgotten People* (Sydney: Macmillan, 1992).

Joy Damousi and Marilyn Lake (eds), *Gender and War: Australians at War in the Twentieth Century* (Cambridge: Cambridge University Press, 1995).

L. F. Fitzhardinge, *The Little Digger, 1914–1952: William Morris Hughes, A Political Biography* (Sydney: Angus and Robertson, 1979).

Bill Gammage, *The Broken Years: Australian Soldiers in the Great War* (Ringwood, Vic.: Penguin, 1975).

Bill Gammage and Peter Spearritt (eds), *Australians 1938* (Broadway, NSW: Fairfax, Syme and Weldon Associates, 1987).

Stephen Garton, *The Cost of War: Australians Return* (Melbourne: Oxford University Press, 1996).

D. M. Horner, *High Command: Australia and Allied Strategy, 1939–1945* (St Leonards, NSW: Allen and Unwin, 1992).

Lesley Johnson, *The Unseen Voice: A Cultural Study of Early Australian Radio* (London: Routledge, 1988).

K. S. Inglis, *Sacred Places: War Memorials in the Australian Landscape* (Carlton, Vic.: Melbourne University Press, 1998).

Marilyn Lake, *The Limits of Hope: Soldier Settlement in Victoria, 1915–38* (Melbourne: Oxford University Press, 1987).

Stuart Macintyre, *The Oxford History of Australia. Volume 4, 1901–1942: The Succeeding Age* (Melbourne: Oxford University Press, 1986).

Stuart Macintyre, *The Reds: The Communist Party of Australia from Origins to Illegality* (St Leonards, NSW: Allen and Unwin, 1998).

Judy Mackinolty, *The Wasted Years? Australia's Great Depression* (North Sydney: Allen and Unwin, 1981).

A. W. Martin, *Robert Menzies, A Life. Volume 1, 1894–1943* (Carlton, Vic.: Melbourne University Press, 1993).

Janet McCalman, *Struggletown: Public and Private Life in Richmond, 1900–1965* (Carlton, Vic.: Melbourne University Press, 1984).

Janet McCalman, *Journeyings: The Biography of a Middle-Class Generation, 1920–1990* (Carlton, Vic.: Melbourne University Press, 1993).

Russell McGregor, *Imagined Destinies: Aboriginal Australians and the Doomed Race Theory, 1880–1939* (Carlton, Vic.: Melbourne University Press, 1997).

Andrew Moore, *The Secret Army and the Premier* (Kensington, NSW: University of New South Wales Press, 1989).

John Mordike, *An Army for a Nation: A History of Australian Military Developments, 1880–1914* (St Leonards, NSW: Allen and Unwin, 1992).

Hank Nelson, *P.O.W. Prisoners of War: Australians Under Nippon* (Sydney: Australian Broadcasting Commission, 1985).

Avner Offer, *The First World War: An Agrarian Interpretation* (Oxford: Clarendon Press, 1989).

Peter Read, *The Stolen Generations: The Removal of Aboriginal Children in New South Wales from 1883 to 1969* (Sydney: New South Wales Ministry of Aboriginal Affairs, n.d.).

John Robertson, *1939–1945: Australia Goes to War* (Sydney: Doubleday, 1984).

L. L. Robson, *The First A.I.F.: A Study of its Recruitment, 1914–1918* (Carlton, Vic.: Melbourne University Press, 1970).

Michael Roe, *Australia, Britain, and Migration, 1915–1940: A Study of Desperate Hopes* (Cambridge: Cambridge University Press, 1995).

C. B. Schedvin, *Australia and the Great Depression* (Sydney: Sydney University Press, 1970).

Alastair Thomson, *Anzac Memories: Living with the Legend* (Melbourne: Oxford University Press, 1994).

8 GOLDEN AGE, 1946–1974

Geoffrey Bolton, *The Oxford History of Australia. Volume 5, 1942–1988: The Middle Way* (2nd edn, Melbourne: Oxford University Press, 1996).

Judith Brett, *Robert Menzies' Forgotten People* (Sydney: Macmillan, 1992).

Nicholas Brown, *Governing Prosperity: Social Change and Analysis in Australia in the 1950s* (Cambridge: Cambridge University Press, 1995).

L. F. Crisp, *Ben Chifley* (Melbourne: Longmans, 1961).

Ann Curthoys, A. W. Martin and Tim Rowse (eds), *Australians from 1939* (Broadway, NSW: Fairfax, Syme and Weldon Associates, 1987).

Hugh Emy, Owen Hughes and Race Mathews (ed.), *Whitlam Re-visited: Policy Development, Policies and Outcomes* (Leichhardt, NSW: Pluto Press, 1993).

Graham Freudenberg, *A Certain Grandeur: Gough Whitlam in Politics* (Melbourne: Macmillan, 1977).

Robin Gerster and Jan Bassett, *Seizures of Youth: The Sixties and Australia* (Melbourne: Hyland House, 1991).

Donald Horne, *The Lucky Country: Australia in the Sixties* (Ringwood, Vic.: Penguin, 1964).

Lesley Johnson, *The Modern Girl: Girlhood and Growing Up* (St Leonards, NSW: Allen and Unwin, 1993).

John Lack and Jacqueline Templeton, *Bold Experiment: A Documentary History of Australian Immigration since 1945* (Melbourne: Oxford University Press, 1995).

Jill Julius Matthews, *Good and Mad Women: The Historical Construction of Femininity in Twentieth-Century Australia* (North Sydney: Allen and Unwin, 1984).

David McKnight, *Australian Spies and Their Secrets* (St Leonards, NSW: Allen and Unwin, 1994).

John Murphy, *Harvest of Fear: A History of Australia's Vietnam War* (St Leonards, NSW: Allen and Unwin, 1993).

Mark Peel, *Good Times, Hard Times: The Past and the Future in Elizabeth* (Carlton, Vic.: Melbourne University Press, 1995).

Greg Pemberton, *All the Way: Australia's Road to Vietnam* (North Sydney, NSW: Allen and Unwin, 1987).

Scott Prasser, J. R. Nethercote and John Warhurst (eds), *The Menzies Era: A Reappraisal of Government, Politics and Policy* (Sydney: Hale and Iremonger, 1995).

Tim Rowse, *White Flour, White Power: From Rations to Citizenship in Central Australia* (Cambridge: Cambridge University Press, 1998).

Michael Sexton, *Illusions of Power: The Fate of a Reform Government* (North Sydney: Allen and Unwin, 1979).

Tom Sheridan, *Division of Labour: Industrial Relations in the Chifley Years, 1945–1949* (Melbourne: Oxford University Press, 1989).

Peter Spearritt, *Sydney Since the Twenties* (Sydney: Hale and Iremonger, 1978).

Greg Whitwell, *Making the Market: The Rise of Consumer Society* (Fitzroy, Vic.: McPhee Gribble, 1989).

9 REINVENTING AUSTRALIA, 1975–1999

Philip Ayres, *Malcolm Fraser* (Richmond, Vic.: William Heinemann, 1987).

Stephen Bell, *Ungoverning the Economy: The Political Economy of Australian Economic Policy* (Melbourne: Oxford University Press, 1997).

Geoffrey Bolton, *The Oxford History of Australia. Volume 5, 1942–1988: The Middle Way* (2nd edn, Melbourne: Oxford University Press, 1996).

Barry Jones, *Sleepers Wake!* (Melbourne: Oxford University Press, 1982).
James Jupp, *Immigration* (2nd edn, Melbourne: Oxford University Press, 1998).
Paul Kelly, *The End of Certainty: The Story of the 1980s* (St Leonards, NSW: Allen and Unwin, 1992).
Stephen Knight, *The Selling of the Australian Mind: From First Fleet to Third Mercedes* (Melbourne: Mandarin, 1990).
John Langmore and John Quiggin, *Work for All: Full Employment in the Nineties* (Melbourne: Melbourne University Press, 1994).
Robert Manne, *How We Live Now: The Controversies of the Nineties* (Melbourne: Text Publishing, 1998).
Meaghan Morris, *Too Late Too Soon: History in Public Culture* (Bloomington: Indiana University Press, 1998).
Stephen Muecke, *Textual Spaces: Aboriginality and Cultural Studies* (Kensington, NSW: University of New South Wales Press, 1992).
Nicolas Peterson and Will Sanders (eds), *Citizenship and Indigenous Australians: Changing Conceptions and Possibilities* (Cambridge: Cambridge University Press, 1998).
Tim Rowse, *After Mabo: Interpreting Indigenous Traditions* (Carlton, Vic.: Melbourne University Press, 1993).
Peter Saunders, *Welfare and Inequality: National and International Perspectives on the Australian Welfare State* (Cambridge: Cambridge University Press, 1994).
Paul Smyth and Bettina Cass (eds), *Contesting the Australian Way: States, Markets and Civil Society* (Cambridge: Cambridge University Press, 1998).
Hugh Stretton, *Political Essays* (Melbourne: Georgian House, 1987).
Trevor Sykes, *The Bold Riders: Behind Australia's Corporate Collapse* (St Leonards, NSW: Allen and Unwin, 1994).
James Walter, *Tunnel Vision: The Failure of Political Imagination* (St Leonards, NSW: Allen and Unwin, 1996).
John Wiseman, *Global Nation? Australia and the Politics of Globalisation* (Cambridge: Cambridge University Press, 1998).

10 WHAT NEXT?

Miriam Dixson, *The Imaginary Australian: Anglo-Celts and Identity, 1788 to the Present* (Sydney: University of New South Wales Press, 1999).
David Headon, Joy Hooton and Donald Horne (eds), *The Abundant Culture: Meaning and Significance in Everyday Australia* (St Leonards, NSW: Allen and Unwin, 1995).
Wayne Hudson and Geoffrey Bolton (eds), *Creating Australia: Changing Australian History* (St Leonards, NSW: Allen and Unwin, 1997).

Hugh Mackay, *Reinventing Australia: The Mind and Mood of Australia in the 90s* (Sydney: Angus and Robertson, 1993).

David Malouf, *A Spirit of Play: The Making of Australian Consciousness* (Sydney: ABC Books, 1998).

Greg Melleuish, *The Packaging of Australia: Politics and Culture Wars* (Sydney: University of New South Wales Press, 1998).

Paul Sheehan, *Among the Barbarians* (rev. edn, Milsons Point, NSW: Random House, 1998).

INDEX

Page numbers in **bold italic** refer to photographs and illustrations